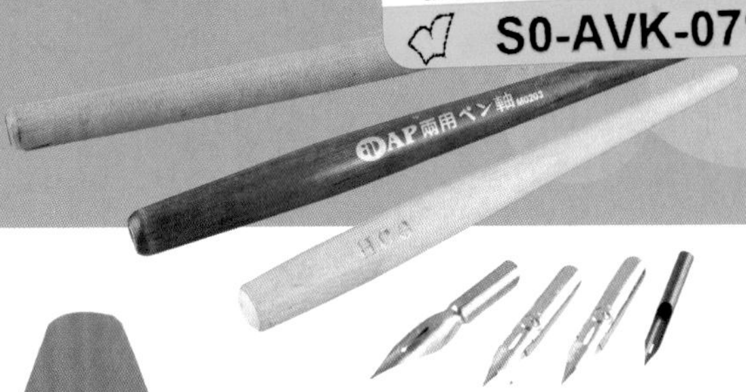

MANGA SCHOOL

WITH SELENA LIN

Draw Your Own Manga

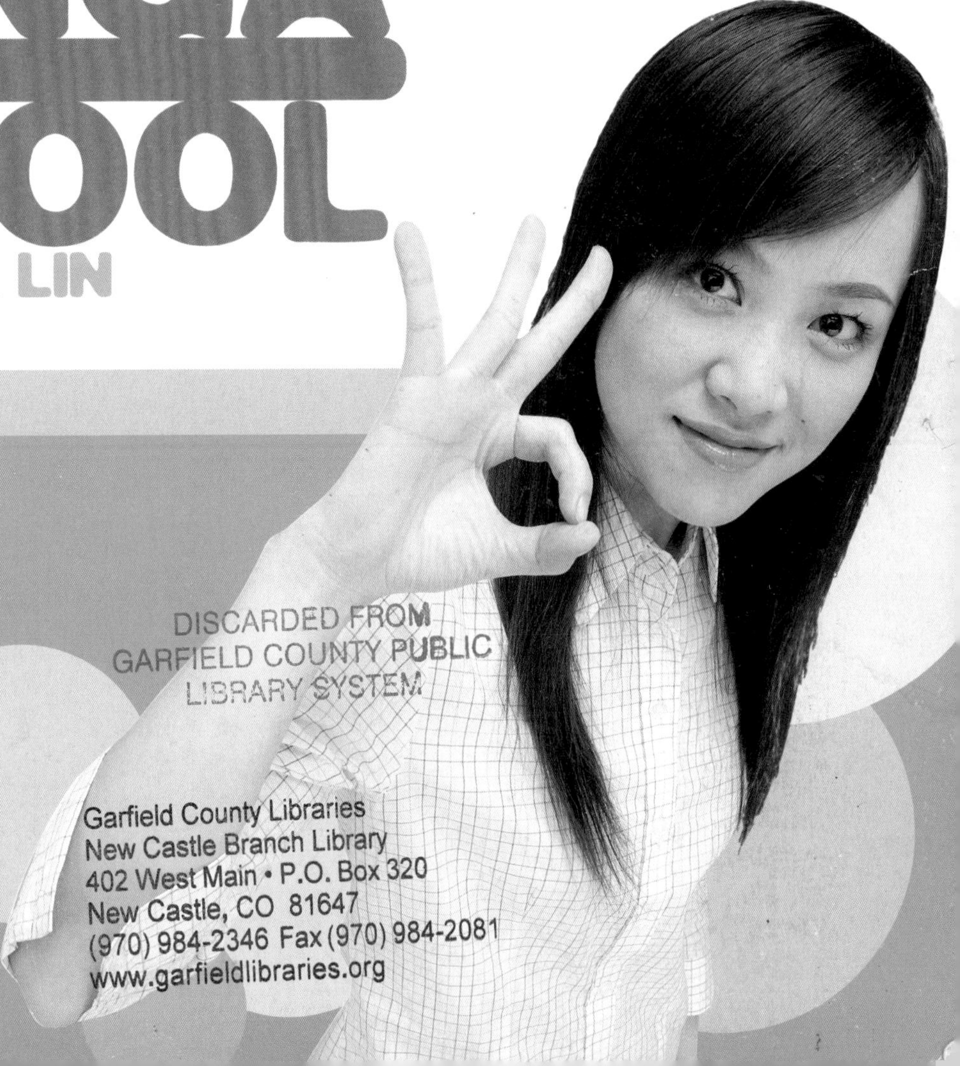

Welcome to Selena's one-on-one manga course!

Always wanted to draw manga, but never knew where to start? Manga artist Selena Lin will tell you what tools and supplies you need, how to plot your story, draft your ideas and complete a finished manga. With detailed panel-by-panel explanations, you'll experience the joy of creating your own manga and become an experienced manga artist in the process!

CONTENTS

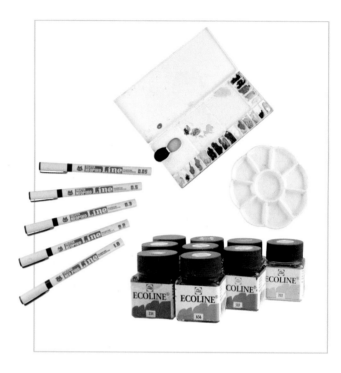

Lesson One
Manga Drawing Tools and Supplies

Lesson Two
Getting Ready to Draw

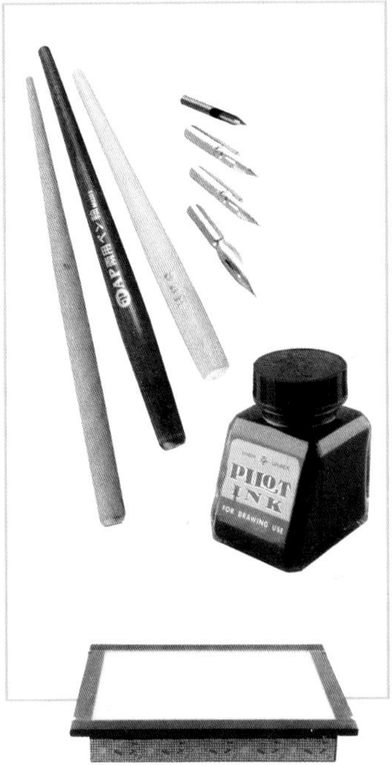

Lesson Three

Creating Finished Work

Lesson Four

Special Techniques for Manga Creators

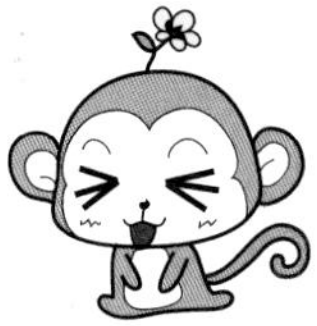

Lesson Five

Coloring

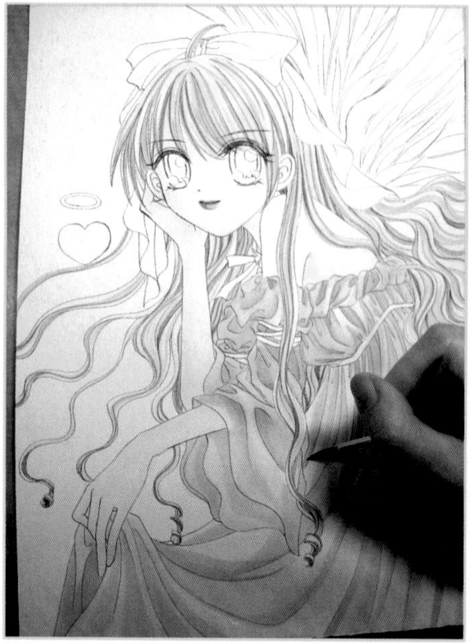

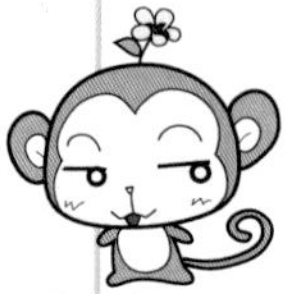

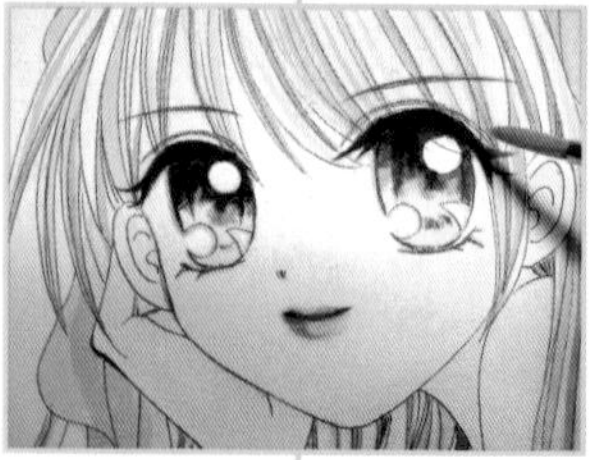

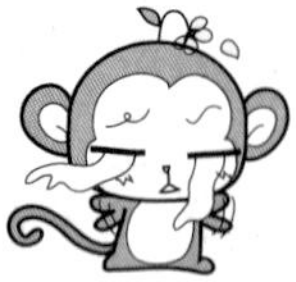

Selena's Gallery

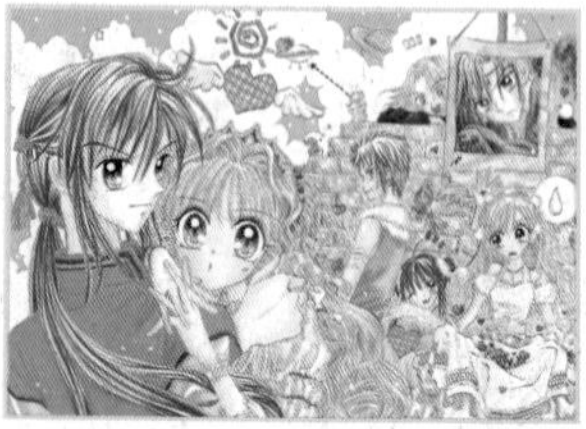

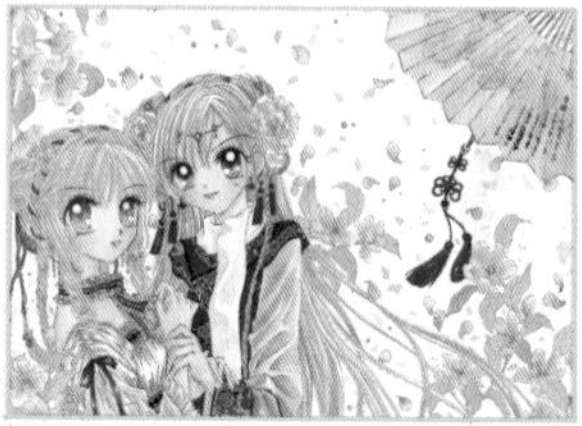

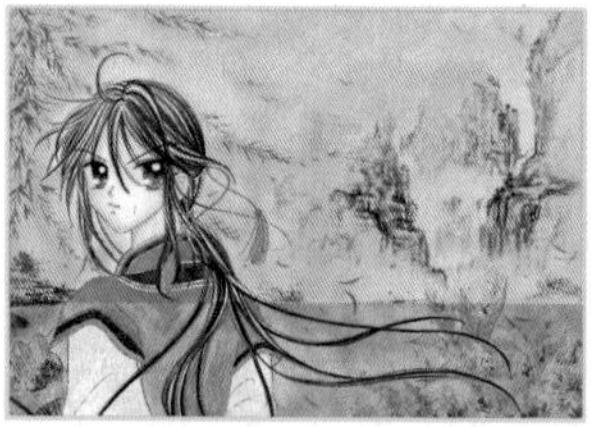

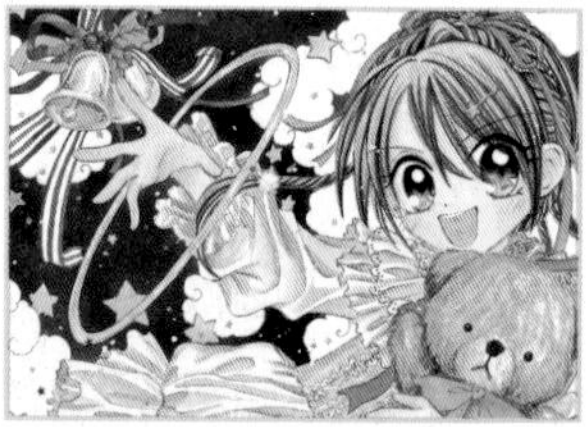

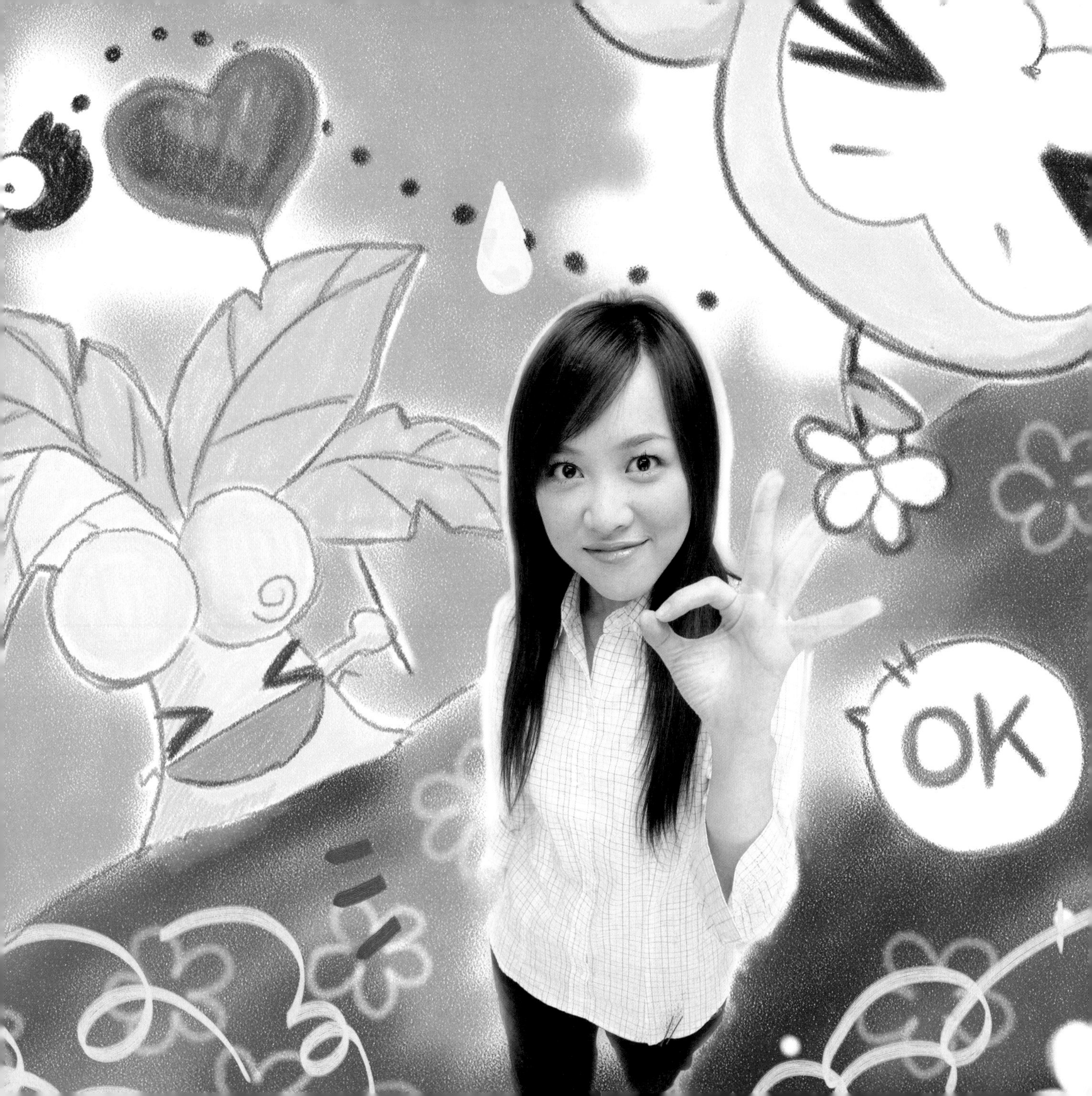
OK

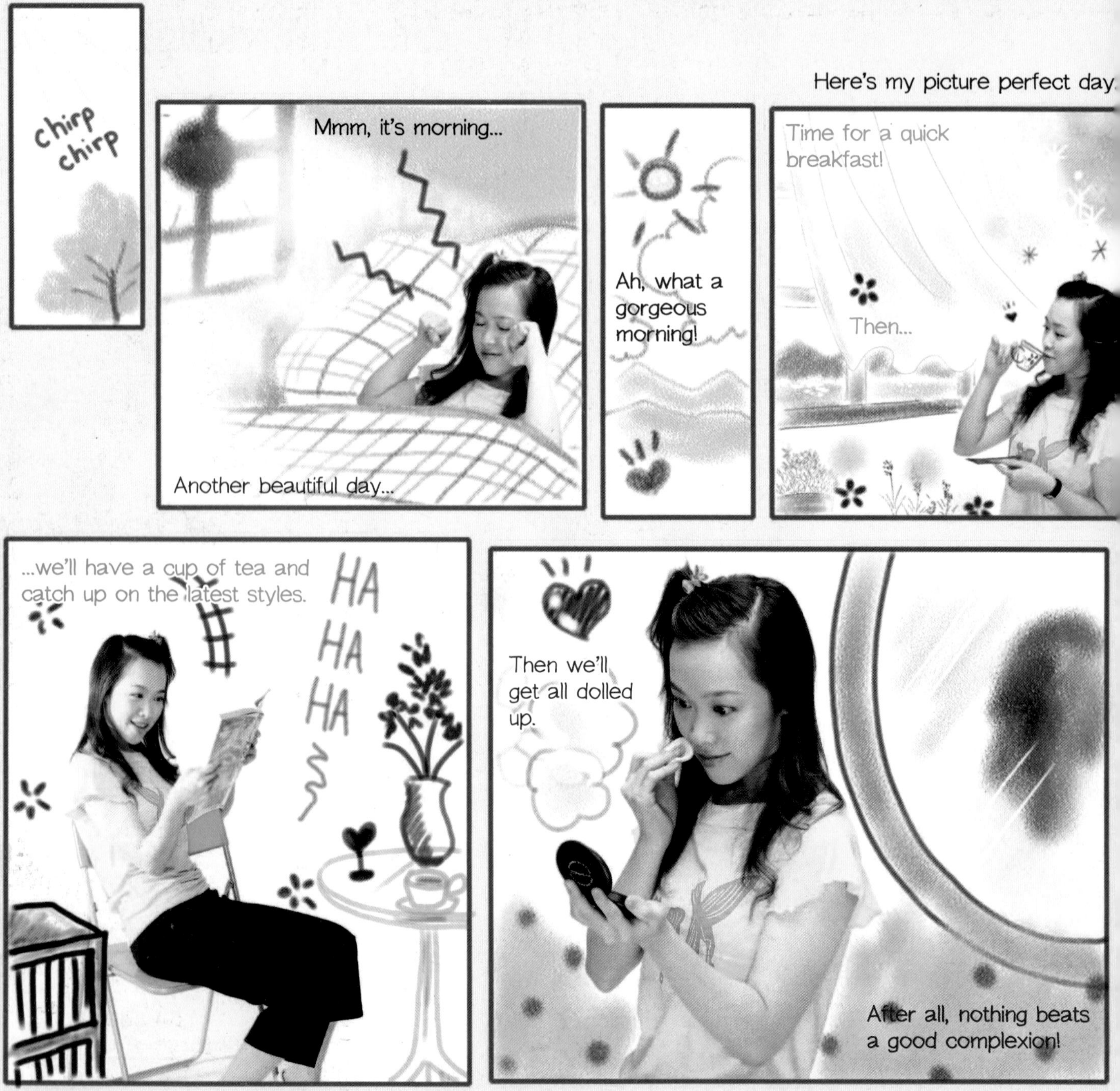
chirp chirp
Mmm, it's morning...
Another beautiful day...
Ah, what a gorgeous morning!
Here's my picture perfect day.
Time for a quick breakfast!
Then...
...we'll have a cup of tea and catch up on the latest styles.
HA HA HA
Then we'll get all dolled up.
After all, nothing beats a good complexion!

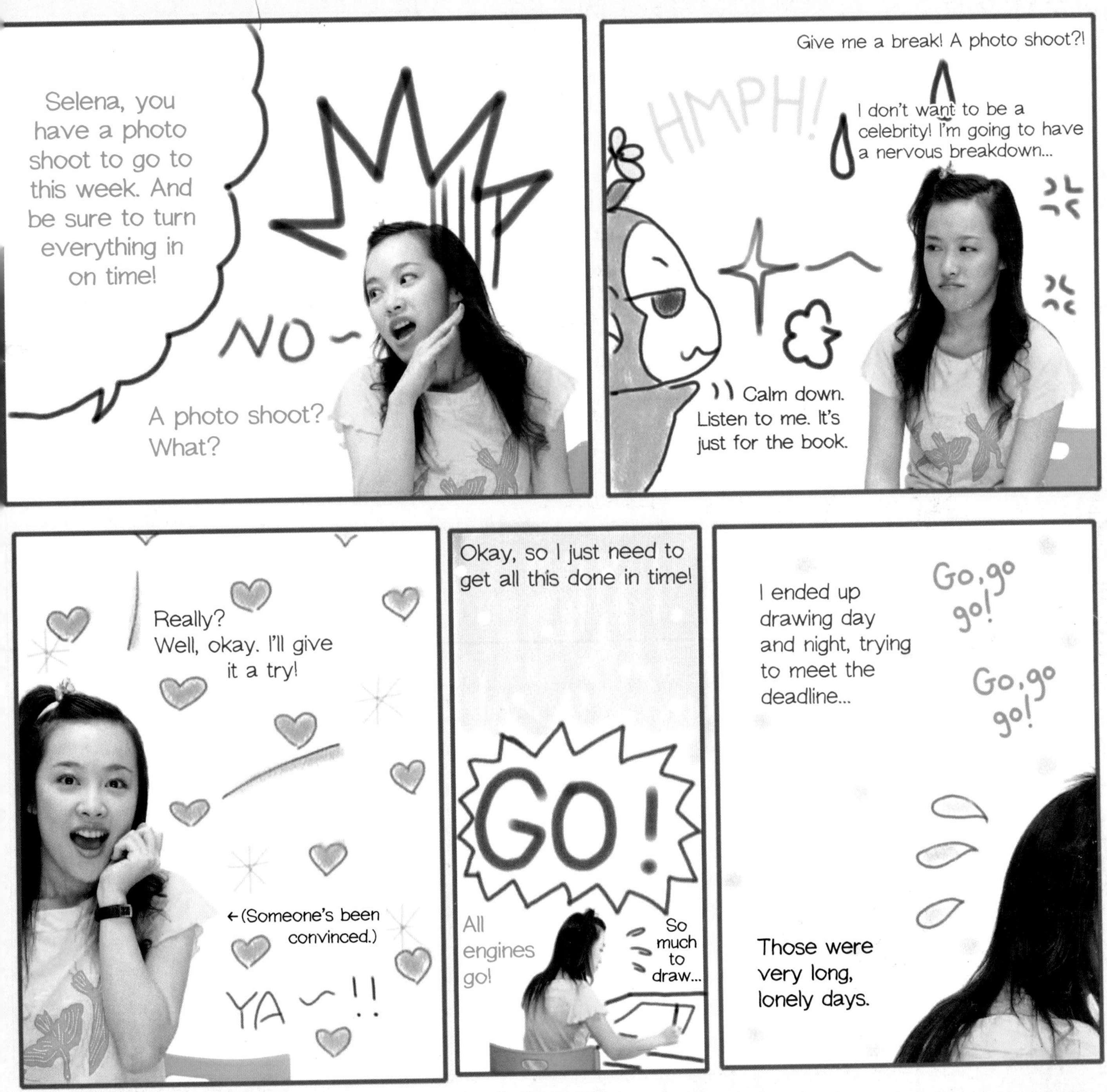
Selena, you have a photo shoot to go to this week. And be sure to turn everything in on time!
NO~
A photo shoot? What?
Give me a break! A photo shoot?!
HMPH!
I don't want to be a celebrity! I'm going to have a nervous breakdown...
Calm down. Listen to me. It's just for the book.
Really? Well, okay. I'll give it a try!
←(Someone's been convinced.)
YA~!!
Okay, so I just need to get all this done in time!
GO!
All engines go!
So much to draw...
I ended up drawing day and night, trying to meet the deadline...
Go, go go!
Go, go go!
Those were very long, lonely days.

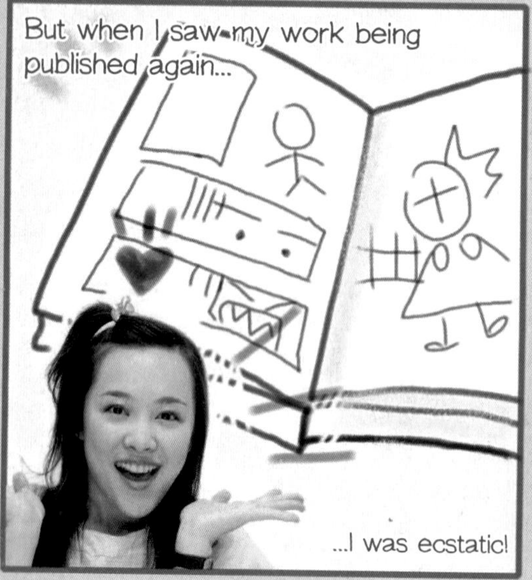
But when I saw my work being published again...
...I was ecstatic!

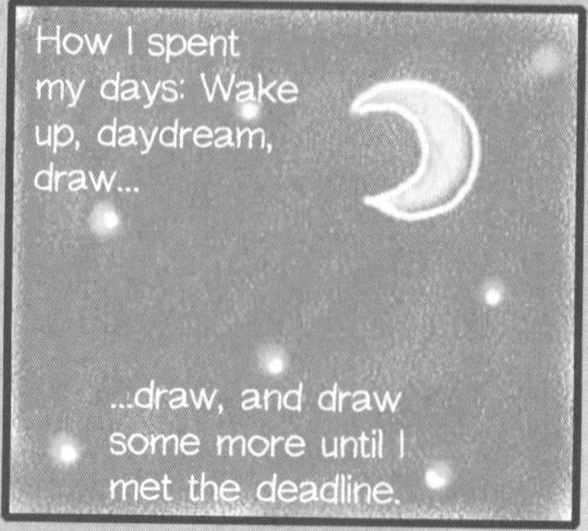
How I spent my days: Wake up, daydream, draw...
...draw, and draw some more until I met the deadline.

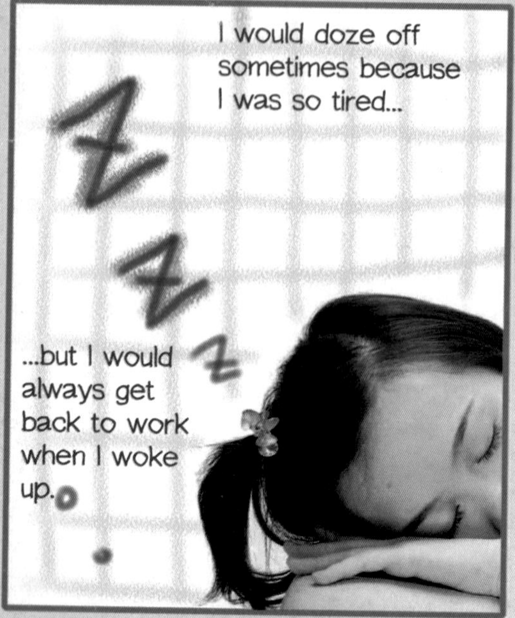
I would doze off sometimes because I was so tired...
...but I would always get back to work when I woke up.

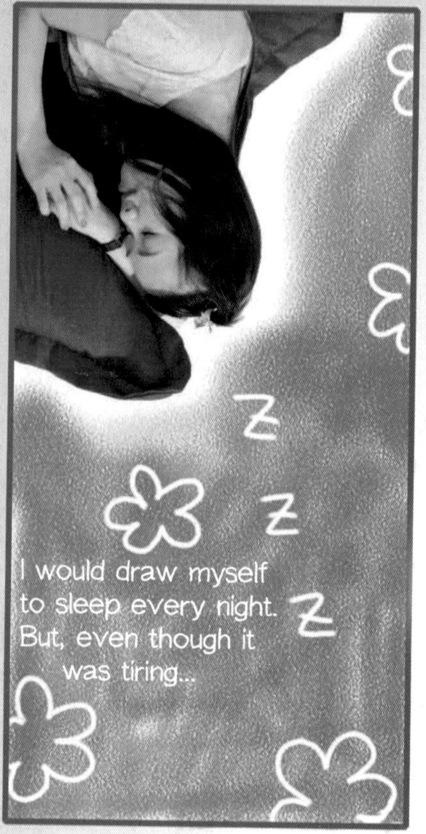
I would draw myself to sleep every night. But, even though it was tiring...

...I never gave up because I knew so many people supported me.

I would like to thank all my friends who have given me their support.

The best to you all!

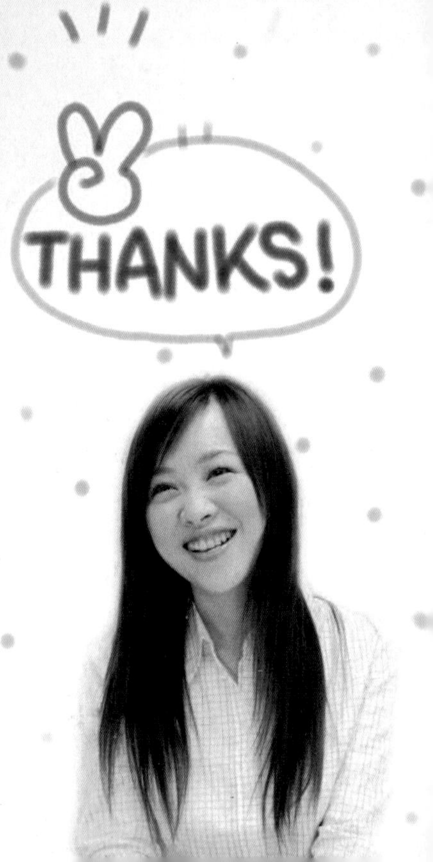
THANKS!

Lesson One

Manga Drawing Tools and Supplies

There are so many tools and supplies on the market that it can be a bit confusing. Which ones should we use to draw manga? How do we use them? It's actually pretty simple. In this lesson, I'll teach you how to choose the tools and supplies that best fit your needs.

Assorted Tools and Supplies

Pentel
2B 0.5
HI-POLYMER
SOFT

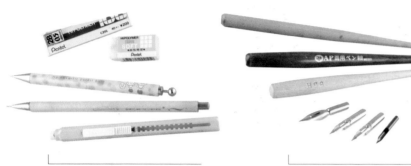

Mechanical pencils, 2B refills, eraser

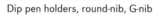

Dip pen holders, round-nib, G-nib

rotring rapidograph
rotring rapidograph
rotring rapidograph

0.1 mm, 0.3 mm, 0.5 mm technical pens

NEOPIKO Line 0.05
NEOPIKO Line 0.5
NEOPIKO Line 0.3
NEOPIKO Line 0.2
NEO PIKO Line 1.0

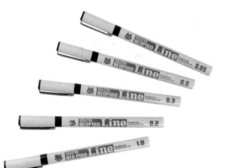

0.05 mm, 0.3 mm, 0.5 mm, 1.0 mm felt tip pens

Black brush pen, black marker

Tone burnisher, file clipper, lighter (File clippers are not readily available in the US, but paper clips or removable tape can be used instead.)

Hobby knife

Snap blade knife

Extra blades

Tacks

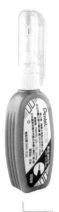

White-Out

アイシー/COMIC
SUPER BLACK

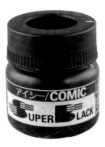

Water-resistant superfine pigmented black ink

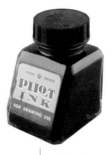

PILOT INK
FOR DRAWING USE

Drawing ink

THE 修正 INK

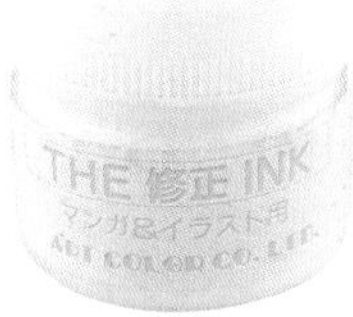

Correction fluid for manga

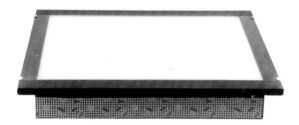

Light table

ECOLINE
ECOLINE
COLINE
ECOLINE

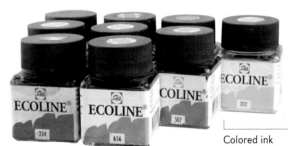

Colored ink

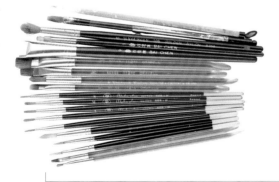

Watercolor brushes (your choice)

17 cm (6"), 23 cm (9"), 30 cm (12"), 40 cm (15") drawing rulers

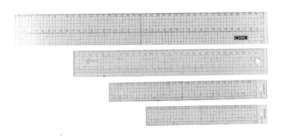

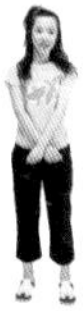

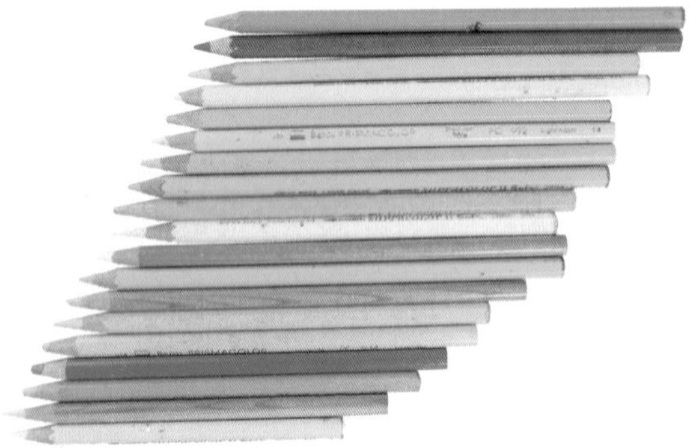

Colored pencils

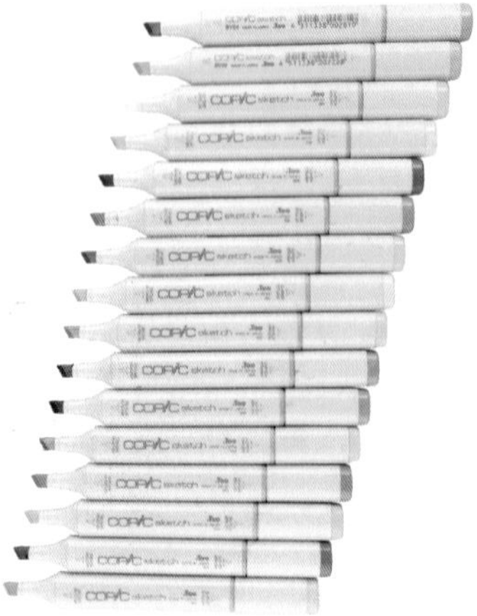
COPIC sketch

Copic markers

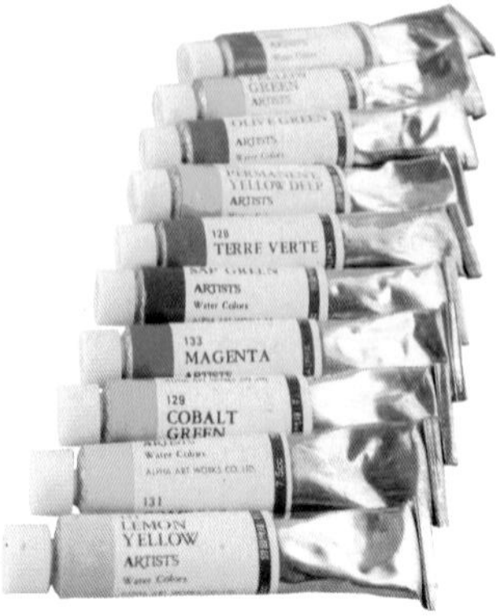
PERMANENT YELLOW DEEP
ARTISTS
126 TERRE VERTE
133 MAGENTA
129 COBALT GREEN
131 LEMON YELLOW
ARTISTS
Water Colors

Watercolor paint

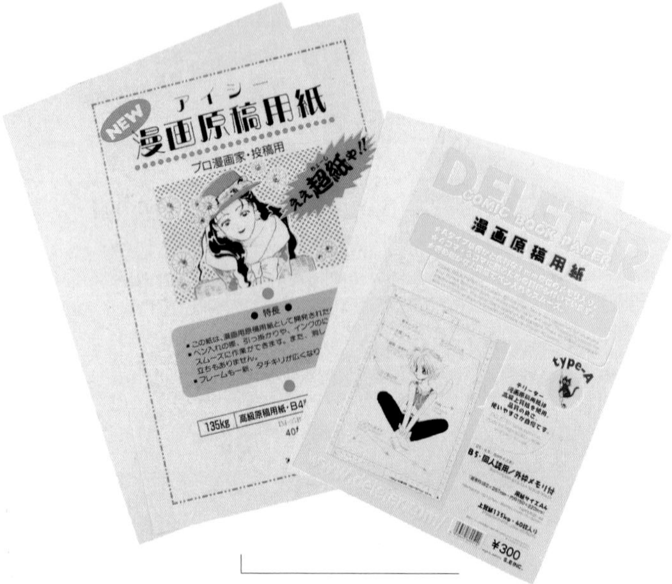
NEW
アイシー
漫画原稿用紙
プロ漫画家・投稿用
ええ超紙や!!
特長
135kg
DELETER
COMIC BOOK PAPER
漫画原稿用紙
type-A
¥300

Manga/Comic paper

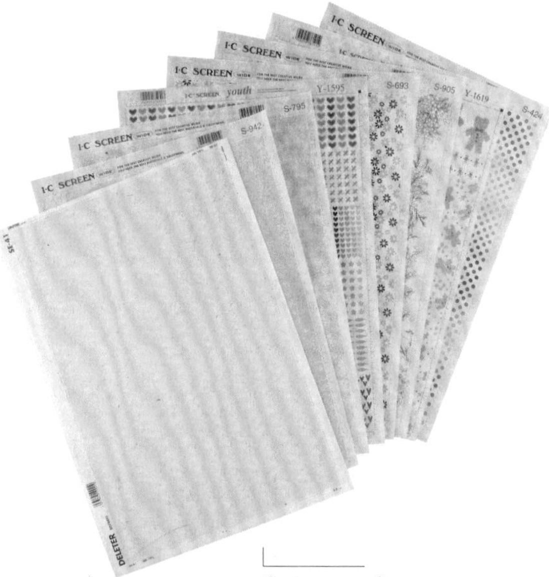
I-C SCREEN
youth
S-795
Y-1595
S-693
S-905
Y-1619
S-424
S-942
DELETER

Screentone sheets

Water container for brush washing

Palette

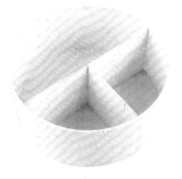

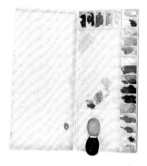

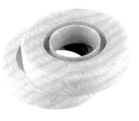

Magic tape (3M brand, blue)

A4 (approx. 8.5" x 11"), B4 (approx. 10" x 14") printer and tracing paper

Watercolor paper and other drawing papers

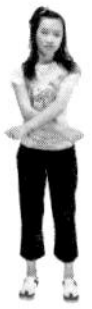

How to Use Dip Pens

1 Insert the nib into the end of the holder. Be careful! Don't use excessive force while doing this, or you might end up damaging the nib.

2 New nibs have a protective coating of wax to prevent rust. Before using a new nib, use a lighter to melt the wax (takes about 2 seconds), and wipe it off while it is warm and soft. If this isn't done, the nib won't hold ink properly. Be careful not to burn the nib while heating it!

3 Now your pen is ready for use. Dip 1/4-1/3 of the nib into the ink. Don't dip too much or it may drip on the paper.

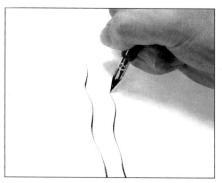

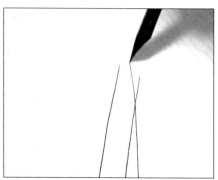

4 G-nib pens are often used to draw contours and defining lines. Depending on how much pressure you apply, a G-nib pen can render thick or thin lines.

5 Round-nib pens are often used to render details, such as hair and eyes. To prolong the life of your nibs, don't apply too much force when using them. Be gentle!

Helpful Hint

Why won't my dip pen work?
Making sure your ink flows onto the paper properly is important! If the ink on the nib has dried out or if the nib is too dirty, your pen will not work properly. Keep a small container of water or alcohol handy so you can wipe the nib to keep it clean. This will ensure that it performs properly.

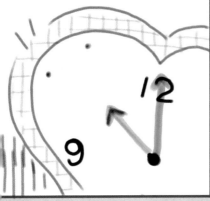

BING BONG!

GASP!

Uh-oh! It's already 10 a.m.!

Oh no! I can't make it to the department store before the doors open! OMG!

I need to hurry! Throw on something pretty to shop in!

No, none of these will do...

Oh, dear. What should I wear?

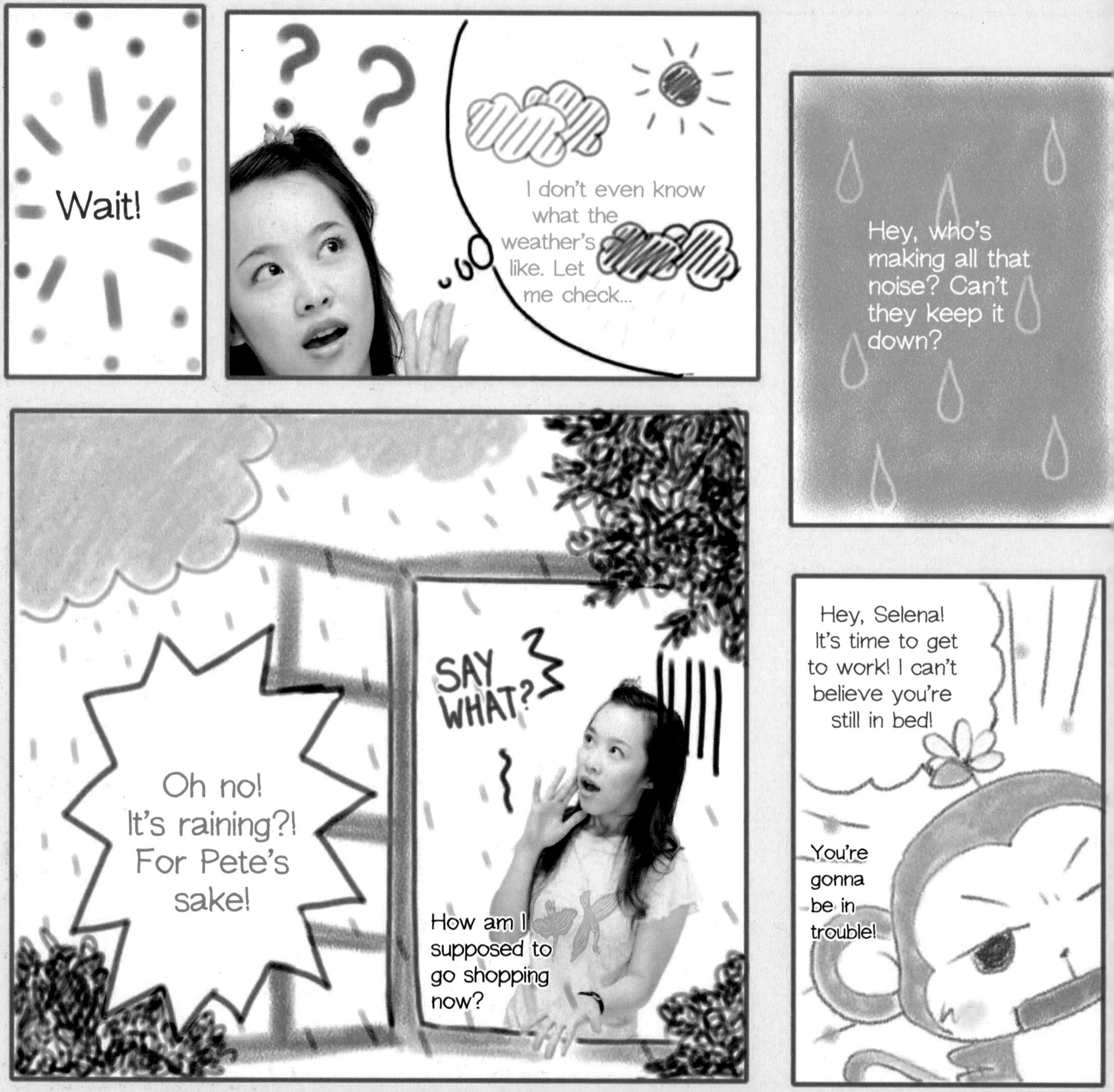
Hey, Selena! It's time to get to work! I can't believe you're still in bed!
You're gonna be in trouble!
Hey, who's making all that noise? Can't they keep it down?
Wait!
I don't even know what the weather's like. Let me check...
Oh no! It's raining?! For Pete's sake!
SAY WHAT?
How am I supposed to go shopping now?

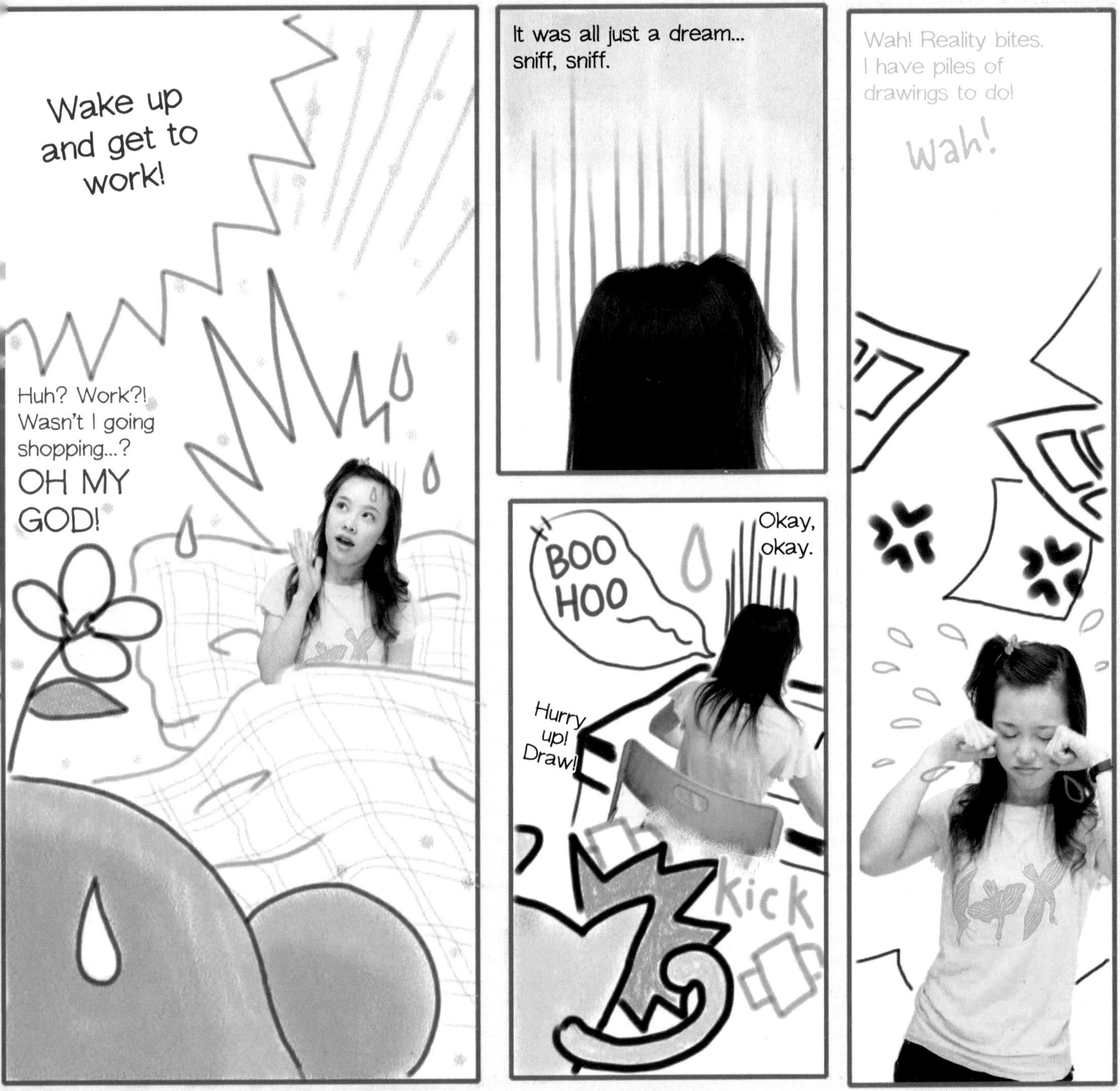

Wake up and get to work!
Huh? Work?! Wasn't I going shopping...? OH MY GOD!
It was all just a dream... sniff, sniff.
BOO HOO
Hurry up! Draw!
Okay, okay.
Kick
Wah! Reality bites. I have piles of drawings to do!
Wah!

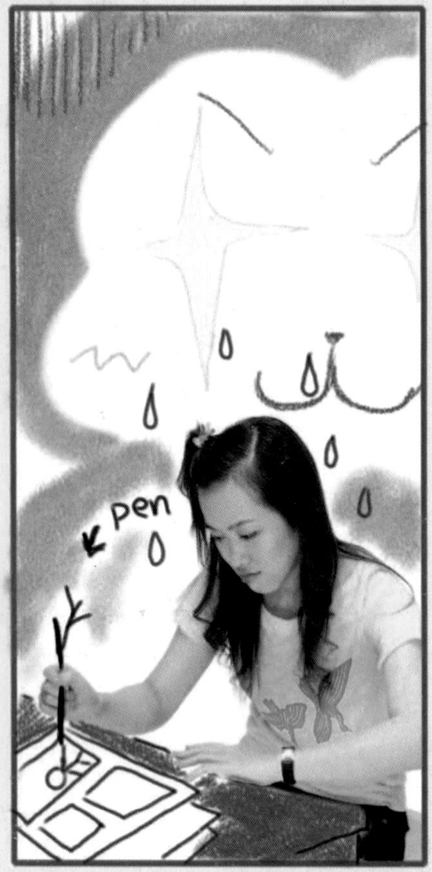
pen

Sigh.
Well, I can't do anything about it except keep on working. But don't hover over me! It's distracting!

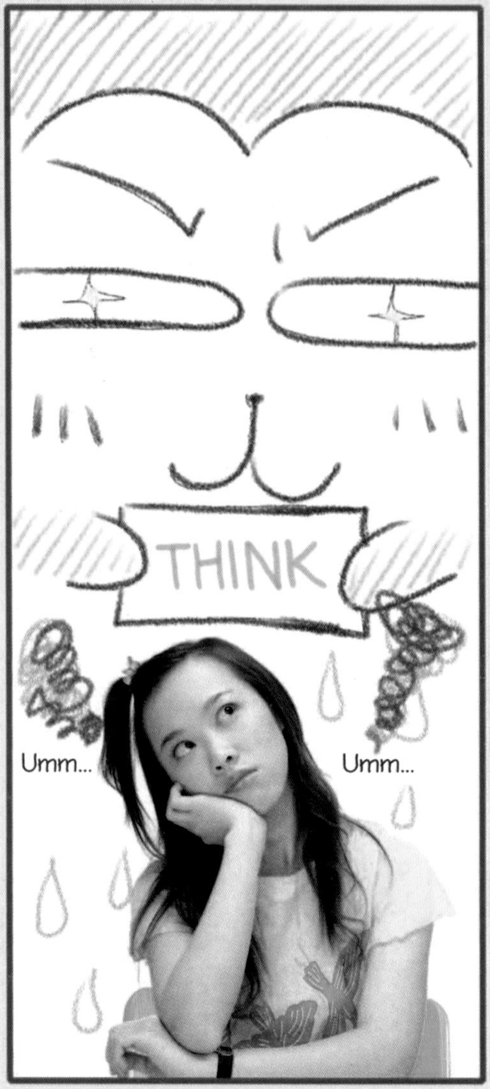
THINK
Umm...
Umm...

↑ Thinking really hard.

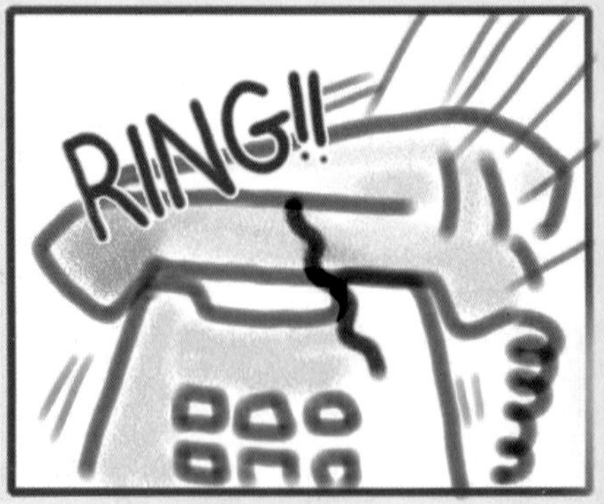
RING!!

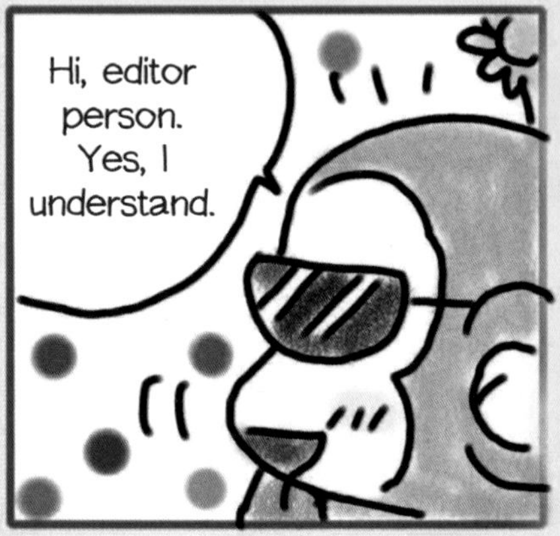
Hi, editor person. Yes, I understand.

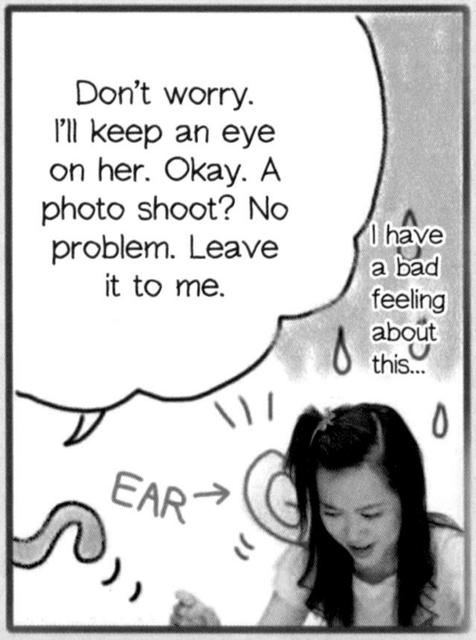
Don't worry. I'll keep an eye on her. Okay. A photo shoot? No problem. Leave it to me.
I have a bad feeling about this...
EAR →

Types of Paper – Their Guides and Usages

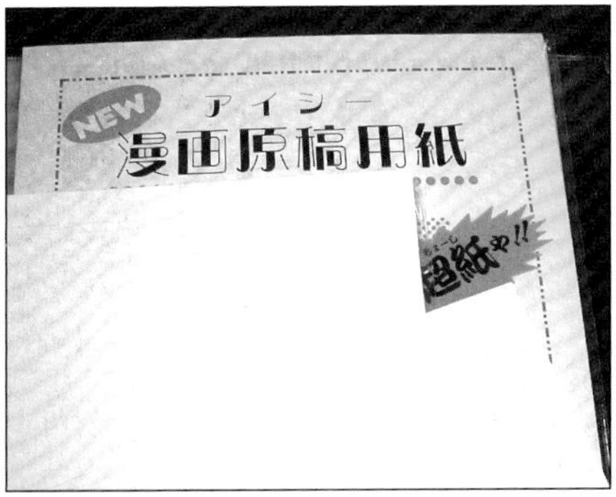
NEW
アイシー
漫画原稿用紙

1 Two common sizes for manga paper are A4 (approx. 8.5" x 11") and B4 (approx. 10" x 14"). The most commonly-used size for drawing manga is A4, but the larger B4 size is more professional.

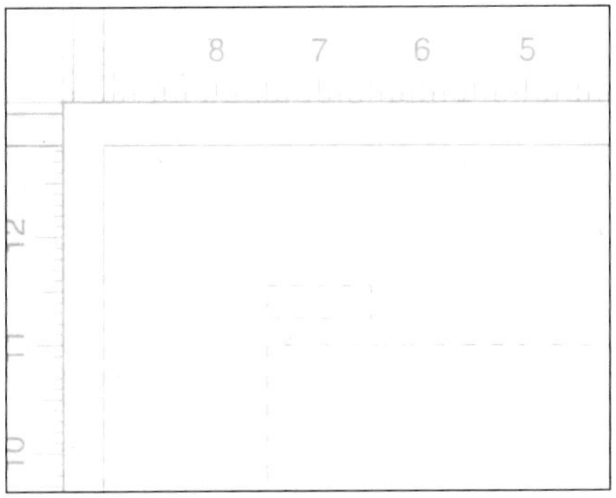

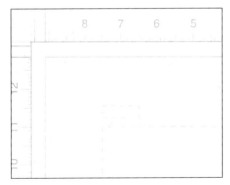

2 You'll see blue boxes printed on both A4 and B4 manga paper. What are they for?

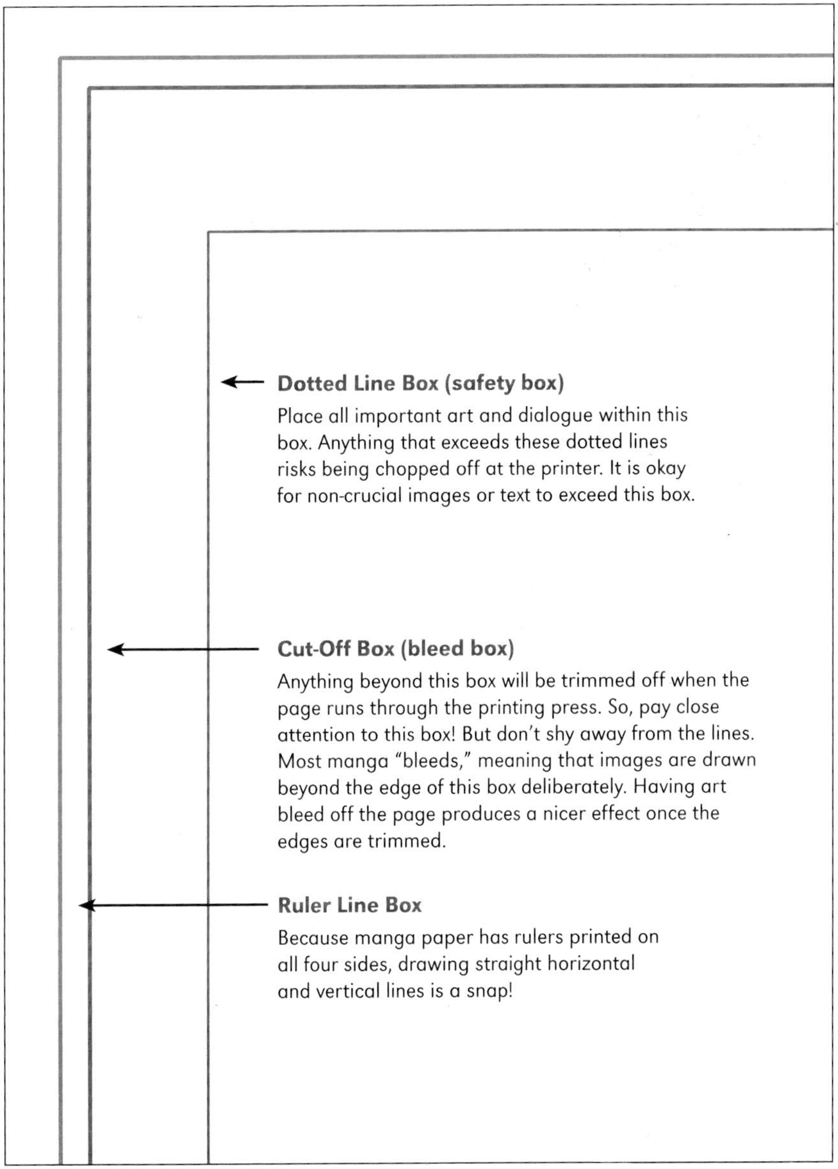

Dotted Line Box (safety box)

Place all important art and dialogue within this box. Anything that exceeds these dotted lines risks being chopped off at the printer. It is okay for non-crucial images or text to exceed this box.

Cut-Off Box (bleed box)

Anything beyond this box will be trimmed off when the page runs through the printing press. So, pay close attention to this box! But don't shy away from the lines. Most manga "bleeds," meaning that images are drawn beyond the edge of this box deliberately. Having art bleed off the page produces a nicer effect once the edges are trimmed.

Ruler Line Box

Because manga paper has rulers printed on all four sides, drawing straight horizontal and vertical lines is a snap!

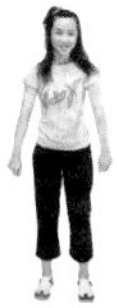

Do-It-Yourself Manga Paper

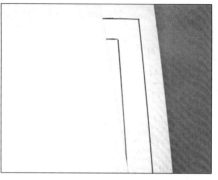

1 Take a piece of manga paper and use a pen and ruler to trace over the safety box, bleed box and ruler line box. (Remember that tracing the lines does not mean making them thicker; thicker lines are less precise.)

2 Take a piece of printer paper that's the same size and place it directly over the manga paper that you just traced. You should be able to see the black lines through the paper. If you can't see the lines clearly, go back to the manga paper and retrace the lines to make them darker.

3 The traced manga paper is reusable. Place it underneath every new piece of printer paper to use it again. From this template, you reproduce as much "manga paper" as you need.

That's really cool!

Helpful Hint ★★★★★

You can buy paper designed especially for drawing manga. But, to be honest, it doesn't come cheap. So why not use this method instead to make your own manga paper? It gives you the same format, but at a much lower price.

Screentone Sheets

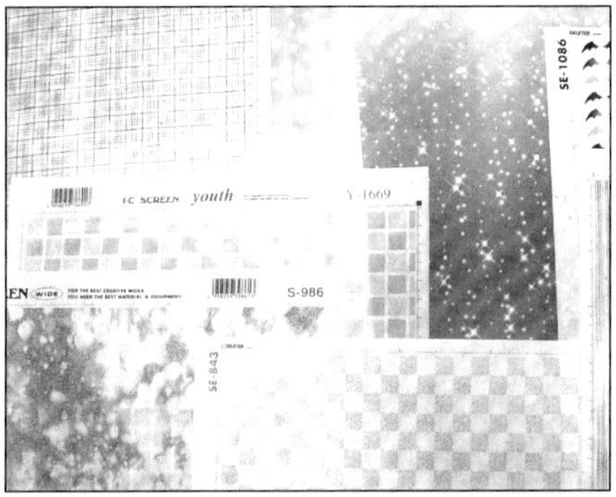
SE-1086
youth
Y-1669
S-986

1 Screentones come in a variety of patterns and brands. Choose the ones that you like best and find the easiest to use. There's no need to base your choices on brand, nor should price be the deciding factor. Asking other people which tones they prefer and why can also help you decide.

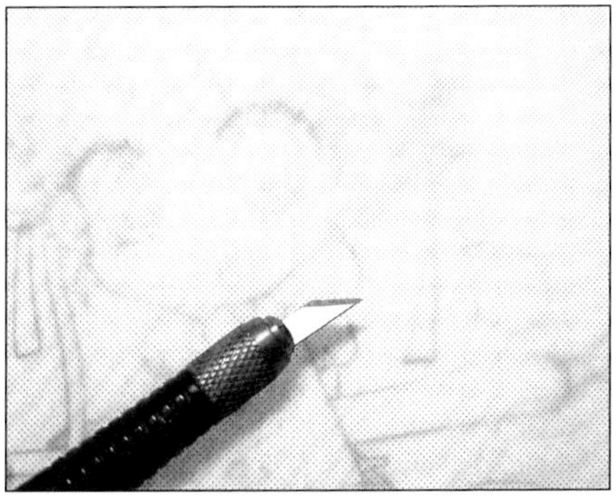

2 A sheet of screentone is like a see-through sticker. When you place it over your drawing, you will be able to see your drawing through it. Before you stick it down, judge the amount of tone you'll need and then cut that amount out.

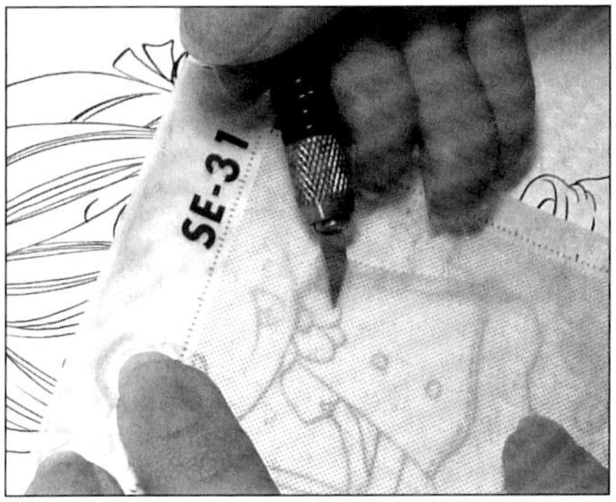
SE-31

3 Carefully use a hobby knife to lift the area you cut out. Try to keep the sticky side clean while doing so. This will help it stick better.

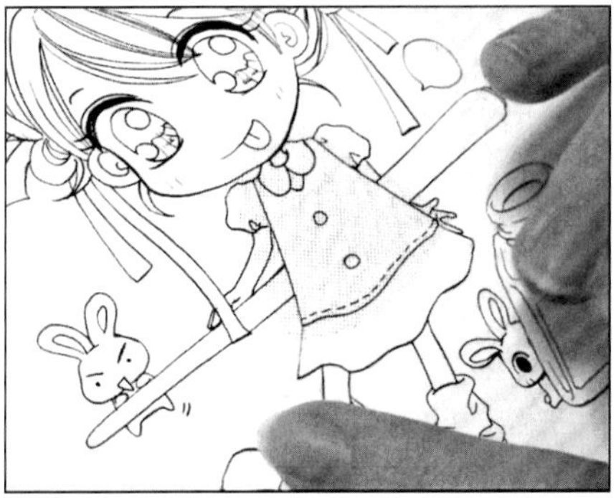

4 Gently place the piece of sheet over the designated area on your drawing. Cut away any unnecessary bits.

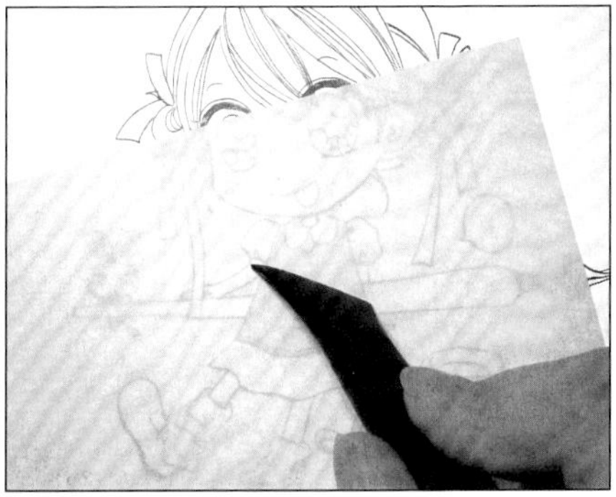

5 Place a piece of paper over the sheet. This will help secure the sheet in place and protect the page while you flatten the area with a burnisher.

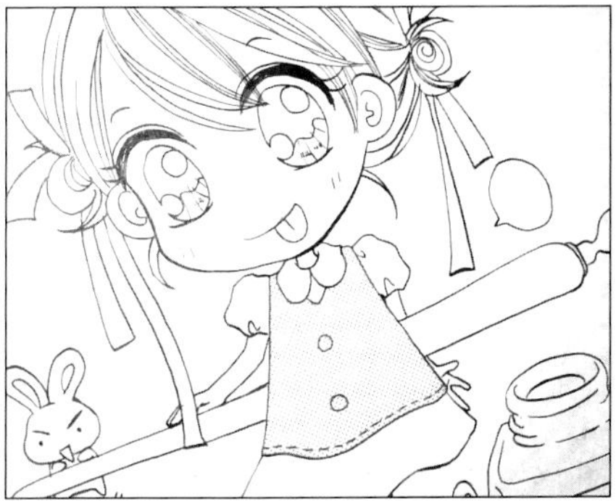

6 You have now toned part of your drawing. Toning is a process that takes time and practice. You can use the rest of the sheet for practice. (Most toning is done by computer now, so this is mainly just an exercise.)

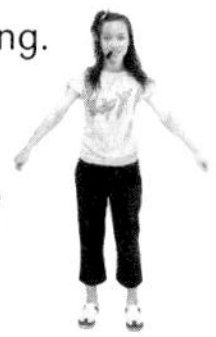

Inks and Effects

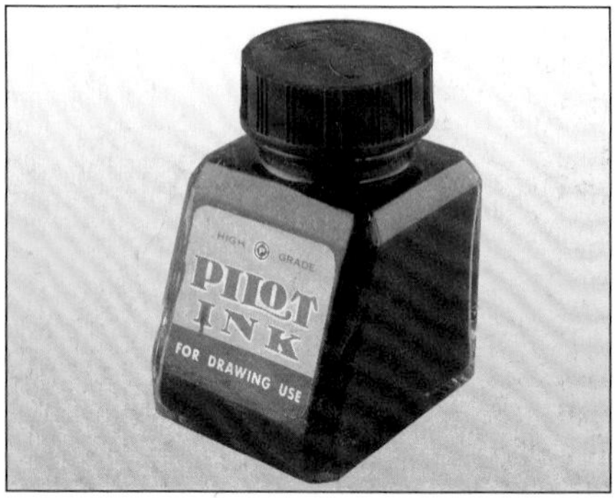
HIGH GRADE
PILOT INK
FOR DRAWING USE

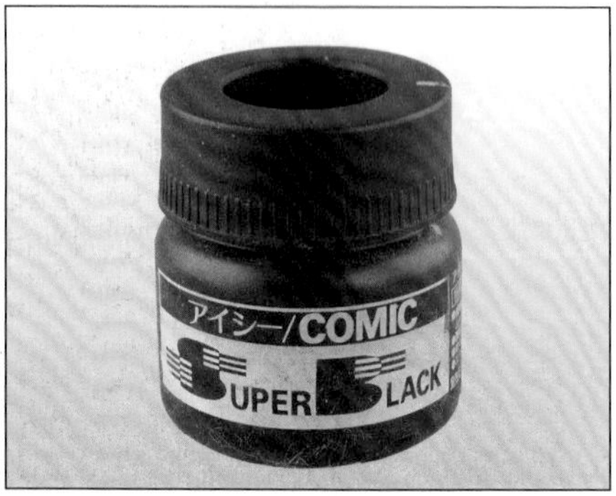
アイシー/COMIC
SUPER BLACK

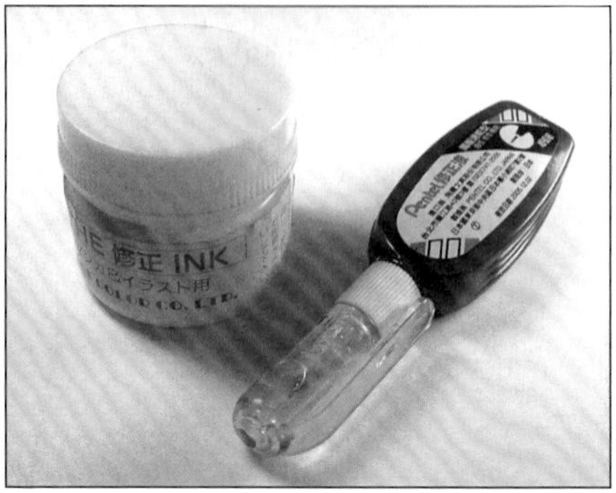

1 Drawing inks are thin, so that they won't clog the pen nib during the inking process. That's why drawing ink is the ink of choice for most artists.

2 Water-resistant superfine pigmented black ink is very dark, dries fast and is waterproof. It's very convenient, since it doesn't bleed when you're using watercolor. But because it is water-resistant, you'll need to use alcohol to clean the nib.

3 There are both water-resistant and regular correction fluids. They are used to make small changes during the final stages of revisions. White-Out works too.

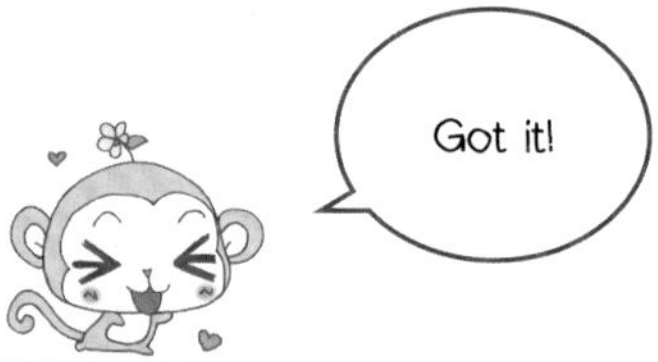
Got it!

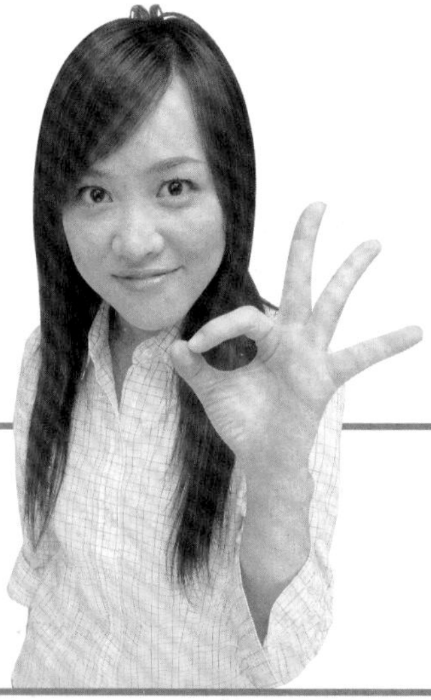

Friendly Reminder ★★★★★

You can actually use the calligraphy ink that is sold in many stores to ink your drawings. The only disadvantage is that calligraphy ink tends to give off a peculiar smell after sitting for a while. The choice is up to you, really.

Lesson Two

Getting Ready to Draw

Now that you've been introduced to the basic manga tools and supplies, I'm sure you can't wait to get started drawing your manga. But let's not rush into things. I'll show you step-by-step what you need to do before you begin, what reference books you need to have at hand and some ideas you can use when creating a story. Ready to unleash your creativity?

Creating a Story

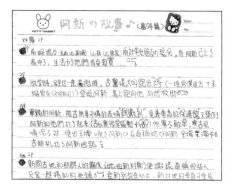

1 Make it a habit to write down ideas and thoughts from your everyday life, the novels and comics you've read, and the movies you've watched.

中國建築形態與文化
建築攝影藝術
中國建築的門文化
中國園林藝術
歷代家具圖錄大全
巧聯妙對

2 Whether you decide to write a period or contemporary piece, start researching information pertaining to that specific place and time. This step is very important because the more information you have, the easier it will be to create and expand your story.

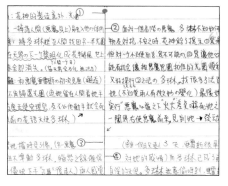

3 String all your ideas together in a logical sequence divided by chapters. Decide how the story will start and how it will probably end. Once you've done this, you'll find that the middle chapters will unfold more easily.

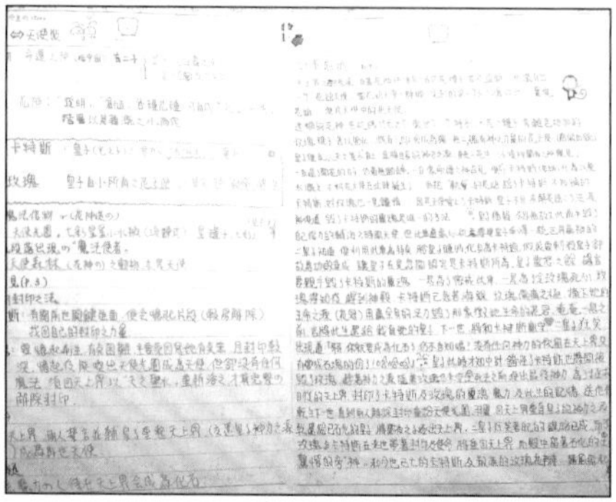

4 Think about further details for each chapter. You can even include what the characters are doing and what they are saying.

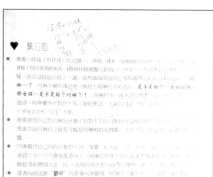

5 Decide what needs to be added and what needs to be removed. In the end, you'll find that you have a workable story. (There is no such thing as a one-size-fits-all outline format. You have to create an outline that works for you, and works for your story. When you're starting out, you'll find you have to revise a lot, but you'll get the hang of it eventually!)

Helpful Hint

The more detailed information you can provide the reader about a certain place and time, the more convincing your story will be. Of course, figuring out all those details can be tricky business! So, if you're new to manga, it's a good choice to tell a contemporary story; after all, the information you need is all around you.

Characters and Personalities

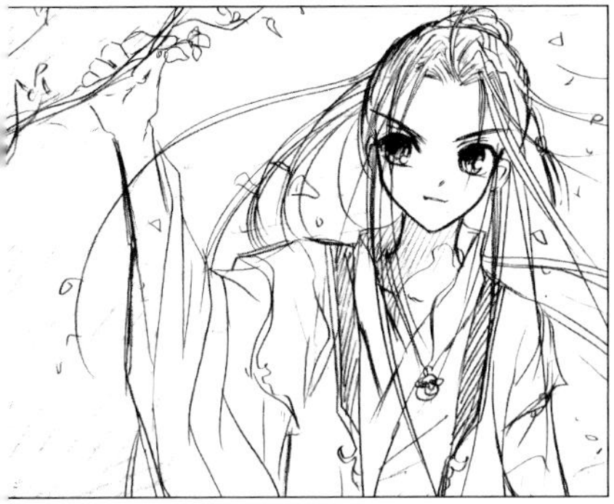

1-1 Design your hero and/or heroine the way you want them to look in your story. Draw the other supporting characters as well.

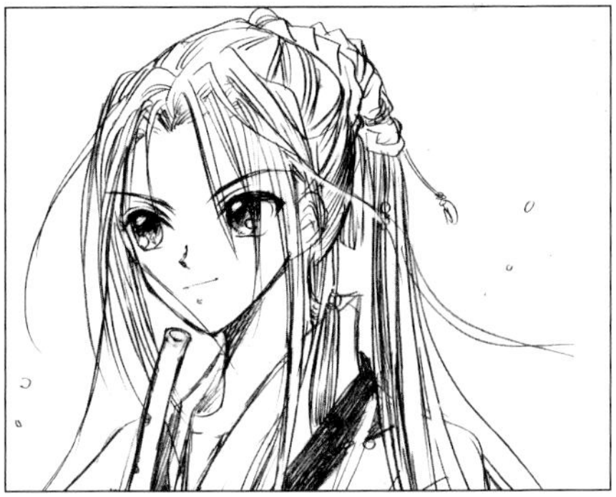

1-2 Draw the hero in a way that appeals to you. Although his image might not appeal to everyone, it is important that you like what you draw. It makes the process much more enjoyable.

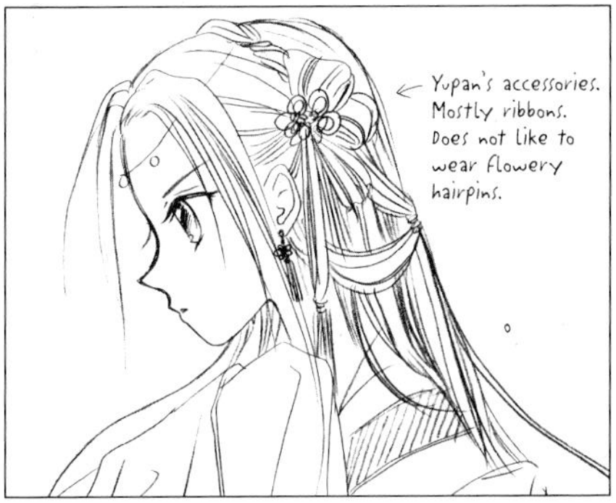
Yupan's accessories. Mostly ribbons. Does not like to wear flowery hairpins.

1-3 Draw the heroine in a way that accentuates her unique personality and sets her apart from the other characters. Let her be the center of attention whenever she appears.

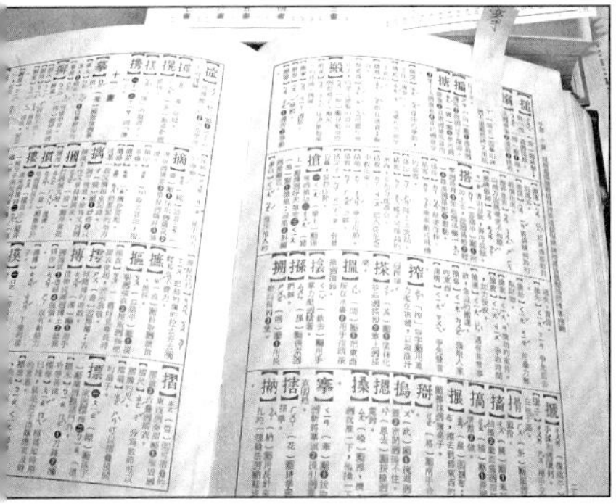

2 After "casting" all the characters, look up names in a baby naming dictionary. Find the names that best suit them.

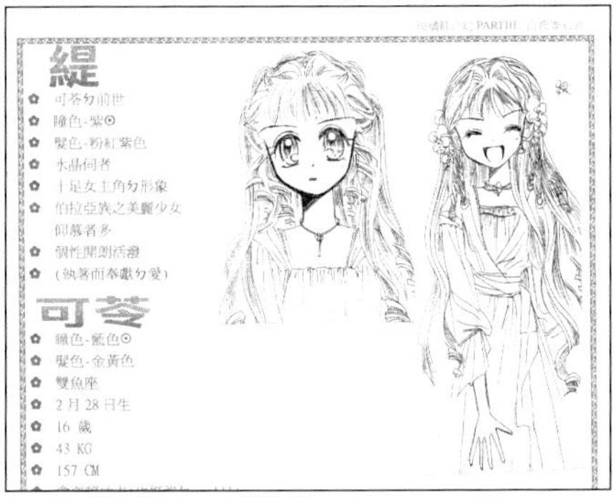
緹
可苓ㄉ前世
瞳色-紫⊙
髮色-粉紅紫色
水晶伺者
十足女主角ㄉ形象
伯拉亞族之美麗少女 仰慕者多
個性開朗活潑
(執著而奉獻ㄉ愛)
可苓
瞳色-藍色⊙
髮色-金黃色
雙魚座
2月28日生
16 歲
43 KG
157 CM

3 Write down the personality and unique qualities of each character before you start drawing the story. This will keep the characters consistent throughout the drawing process, preventing any deviation from your original concept should the story take a long time to finish or if the plot gets complicated.

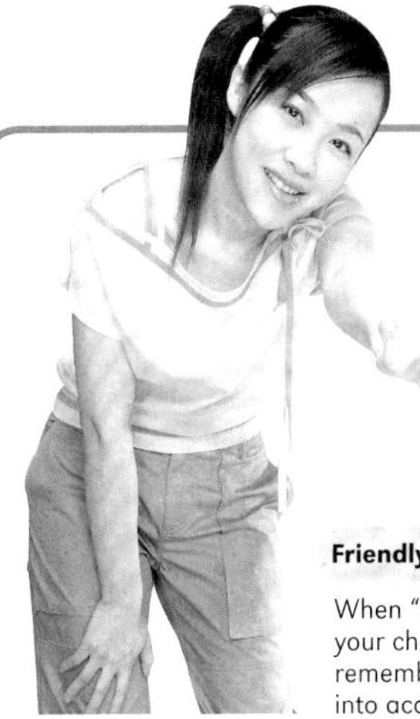

Friendly Reminder

When "fitting" your characters, remember to take into account the specific styles and clothing that pertain to the time and place your story is set. For example, if your story is set in a certain Chinese dynasty or in a certain European empire, remember to research the clothing and style of that period.

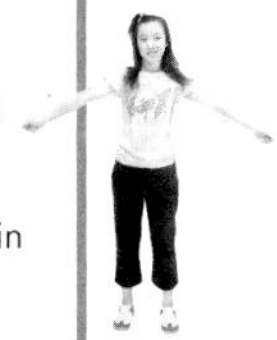

Character Wardrobe and Accessories

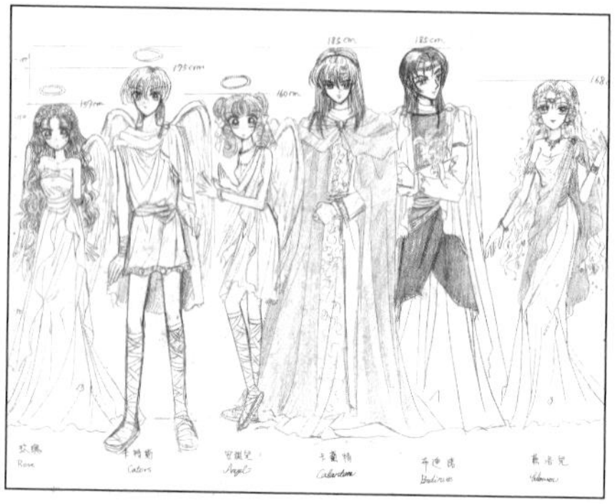

1 When characters appear next to each other, it's important to show a consistent difference in height. Do so by making a chart comparing their relative heights.

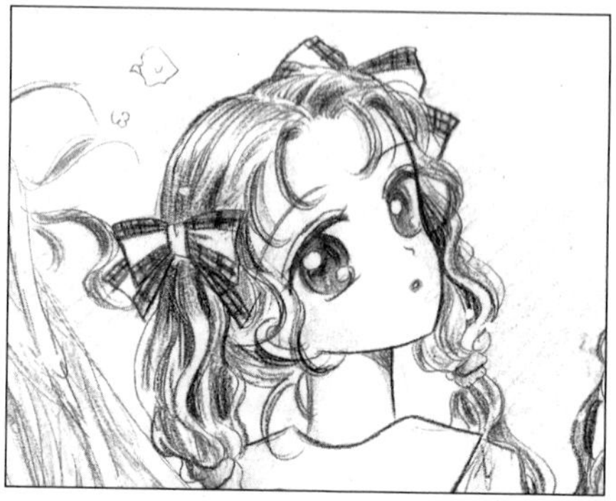

2–1 Once you've drawn the height chart, you can begin to provide each character with a distinct wardrobe and set of accessories.

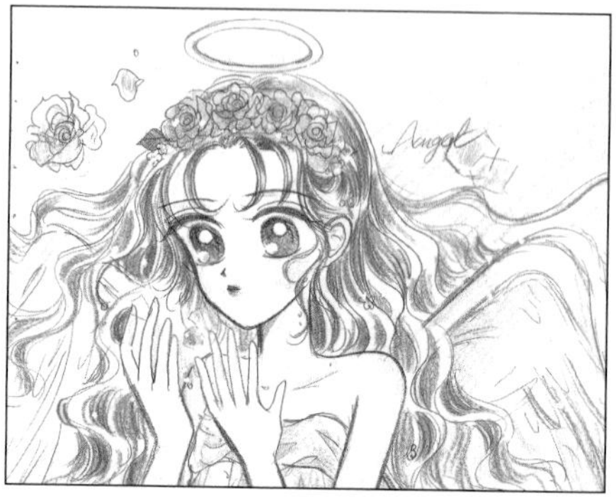

2–2 For example, if you had a character who was an angel, you would design their wardrobe to correspond to the ideas of an angel for the culture, time and place of your story.

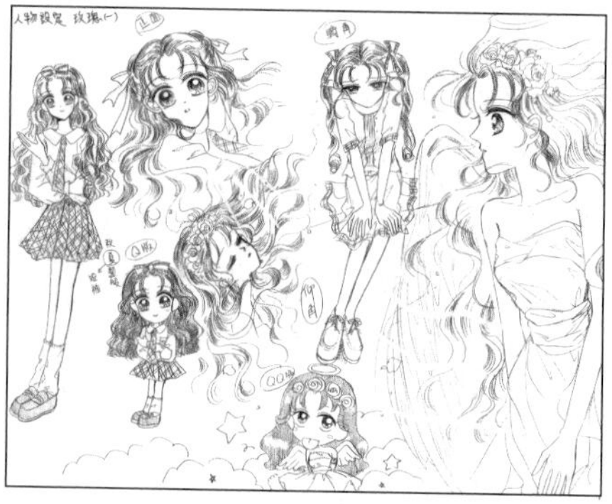

2–3 Once you have an idea of what a character will look like, try drawing the character in different ways (e.g. from the front, the side, head to toe, waist up, a chibi version, etc.).

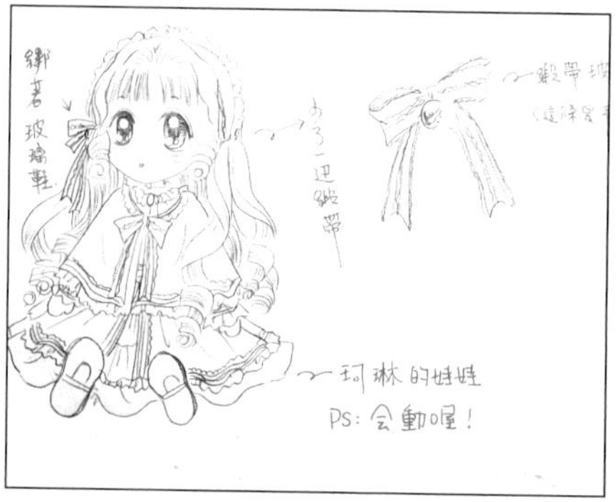
珂琳的娃娃
PS: 会動喔!

2–4 Don't forget to make your characters unique. You can do so by designing a set of different accessories for each of them. That way, your readers will have an easier time recognizing them.

Note: In Asian cultures, it is a common belief that blood type indicates a person's personality, similar to the western belief in the Zodiac.

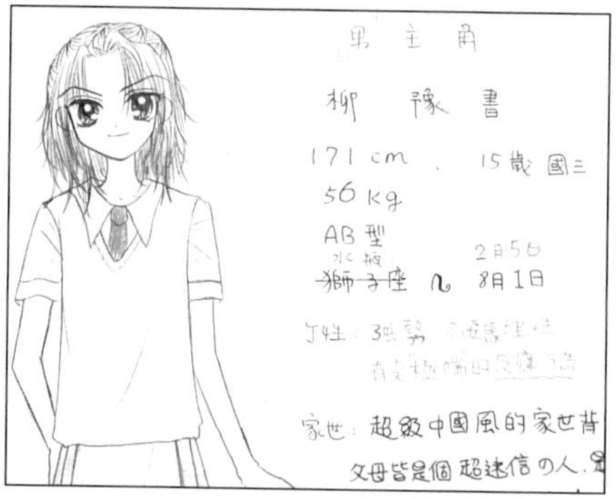
男主角
柳豫書
171 cm
15歲 國三
56 kg
AB 型
8月1日

2–5 Besides giving your characters names, don't forget to fill in other personal information. For example, you can decide their date of birth, sign, and blood type. This is a very good way to help you better grasp each character's personality.

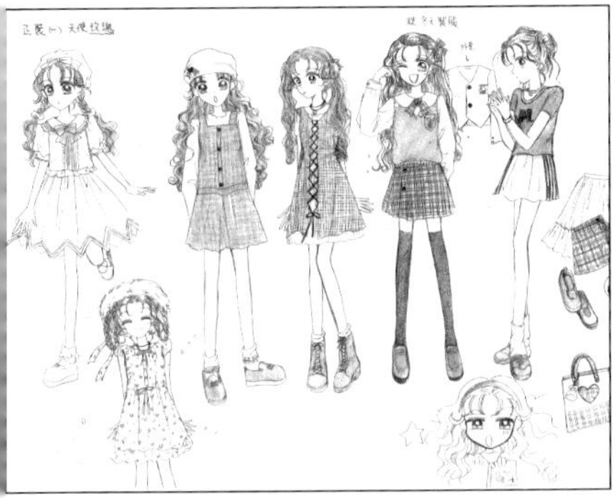

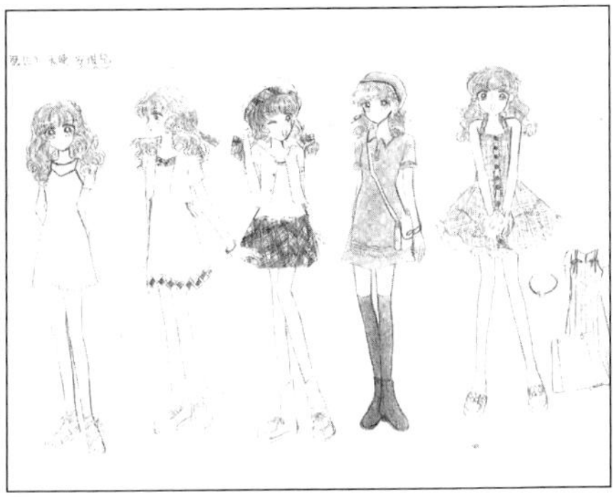

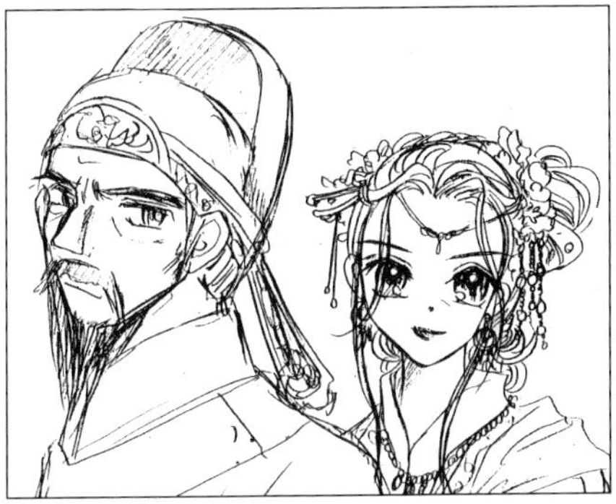

2-6 If you're drawing something contemporary, it's easier to decide what your characters will wear as you draw along. For example, do you want your heroine to look cute or mature? Do you want your hero to look dashing or casual?

2-7 Supporting characters may only play side roles, but their style of clothing is just as important. They should have a distinct style that corresponds to their personalities.

3 Characters have different social statuses and their style of clothing should reflect that. For example, aristocrats wouldn't dress like commoners. But don't forget to incorporate their individual personalities into their styles as well.

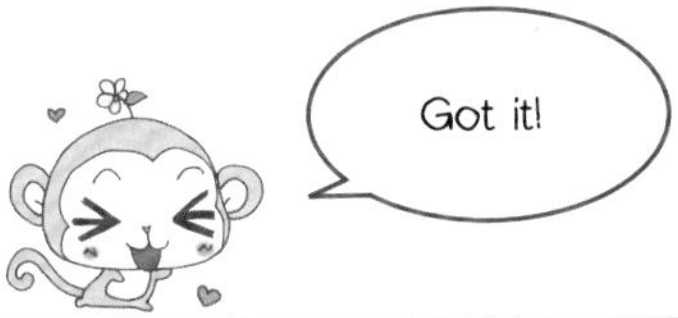
Got it!

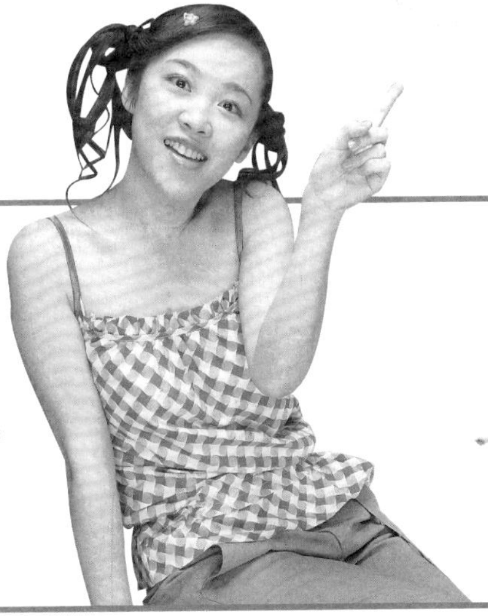

Friendly Reminder

Once you determine a character's personality, it will be much easier to design a series of outfits for the character. Now that you've decided on characters, personalities, heights and wardrobes, you're basically done with the character design stage.

We've covered how to create an outline and the basic manga tools and supplies; we have a plot and characters; we have reference information collected. So what are we waiting for? On the following pages, I'll show you how to draw your own manga step-by-step. Are you ready?

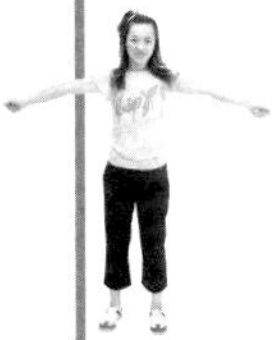

Paneling

I'm sure you've heard of manga having "panels." It sounds like all you need to do to create a manga is put all the panels together on a page. But, in fact, you can't just place them anywhere. The way you place your panels determines whether or not your story will work. So what is "paneling"?

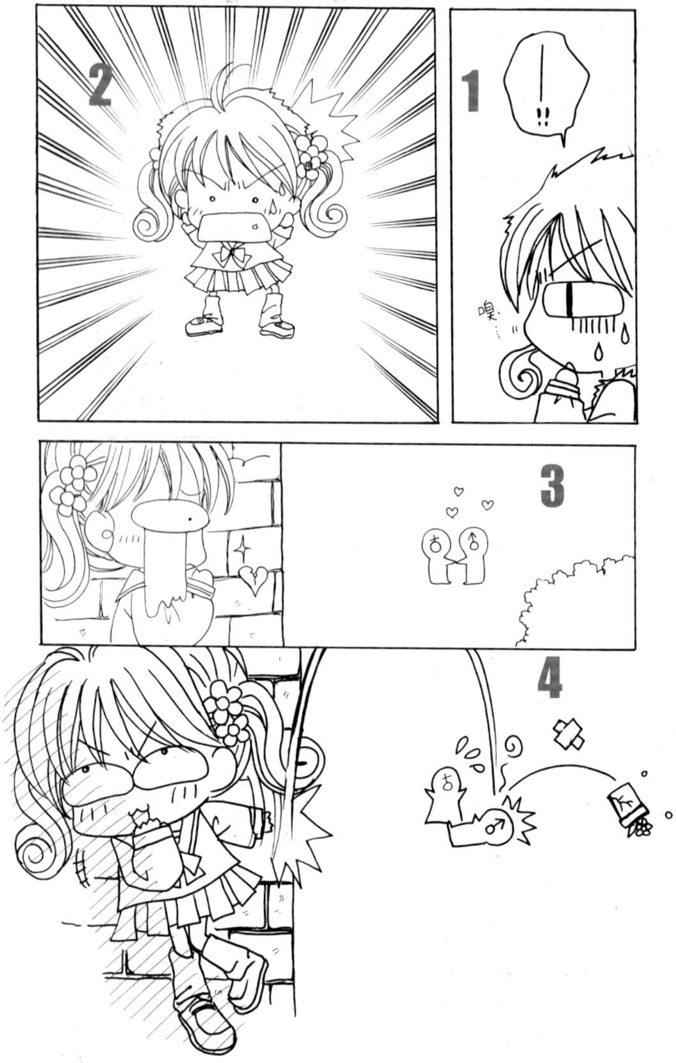
! !!

1 In manga, a sequence of actions and conditions is told through panels.

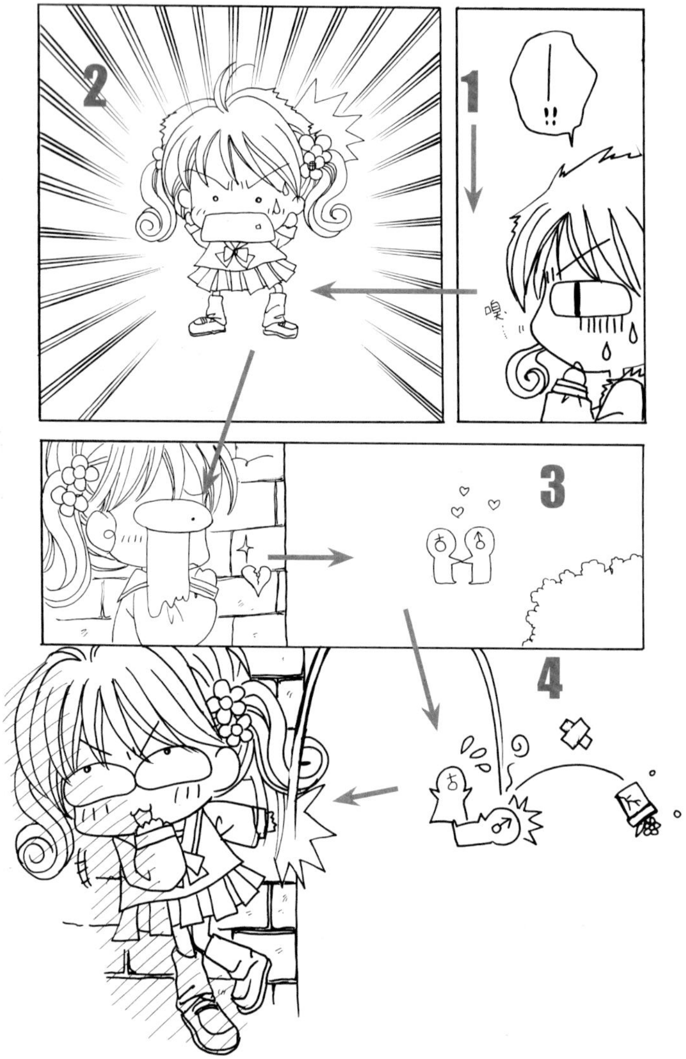
! !!

2 Each panel employs a different visual perspective.

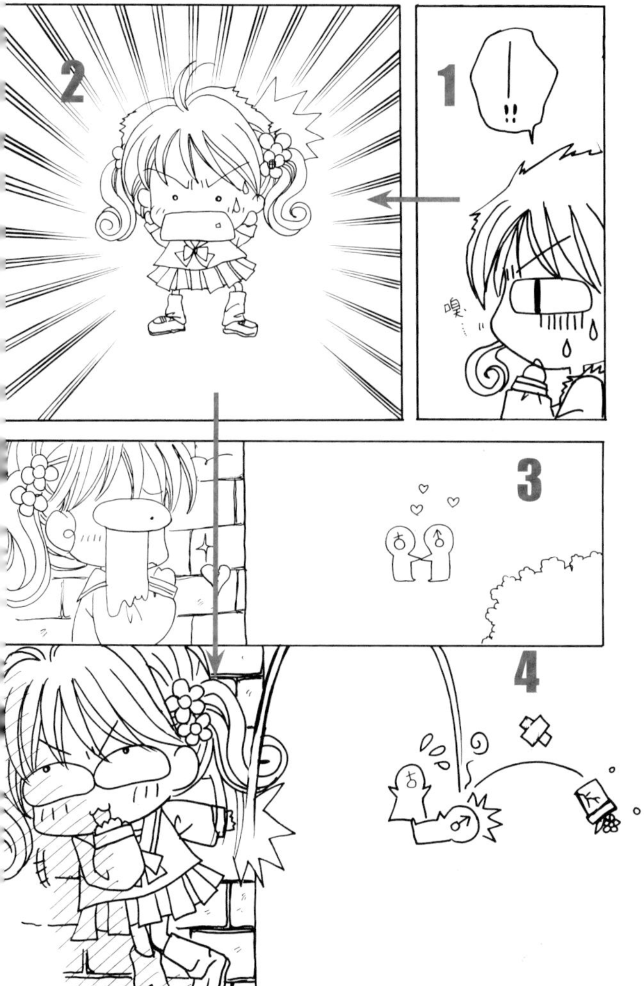
!!
嗅…

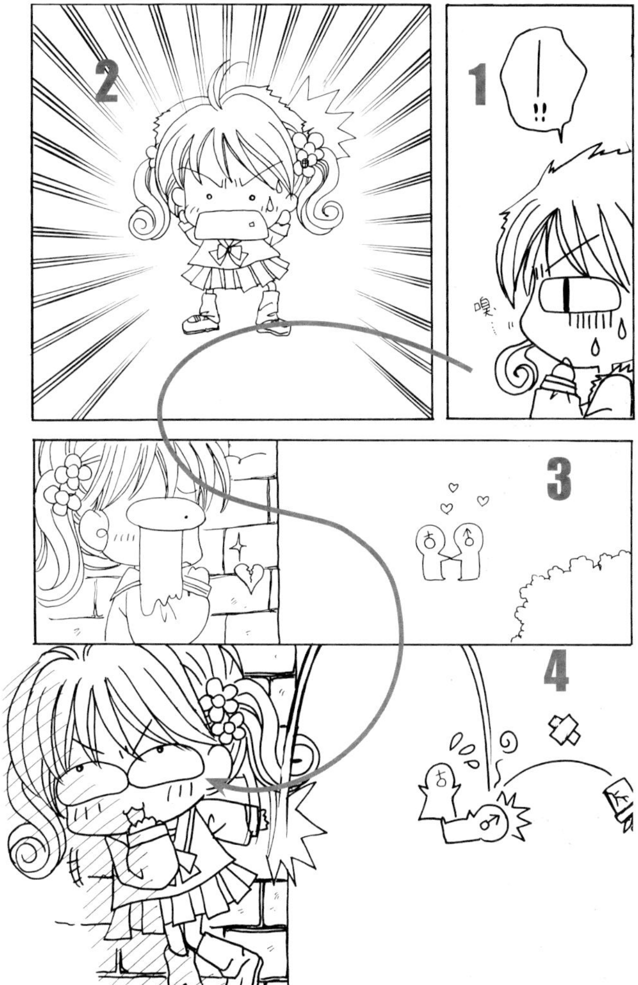
!!
嗅…

3 Paneling shows changes in a character's emotions and should explain why a character's mood changes.

4 Panels determine how your eye travels over a page. If you follow the directions the panels guide you on this page, you'll notice you're traveling an "S" shape.

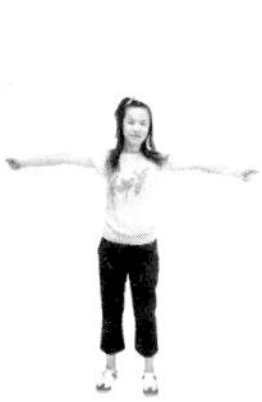

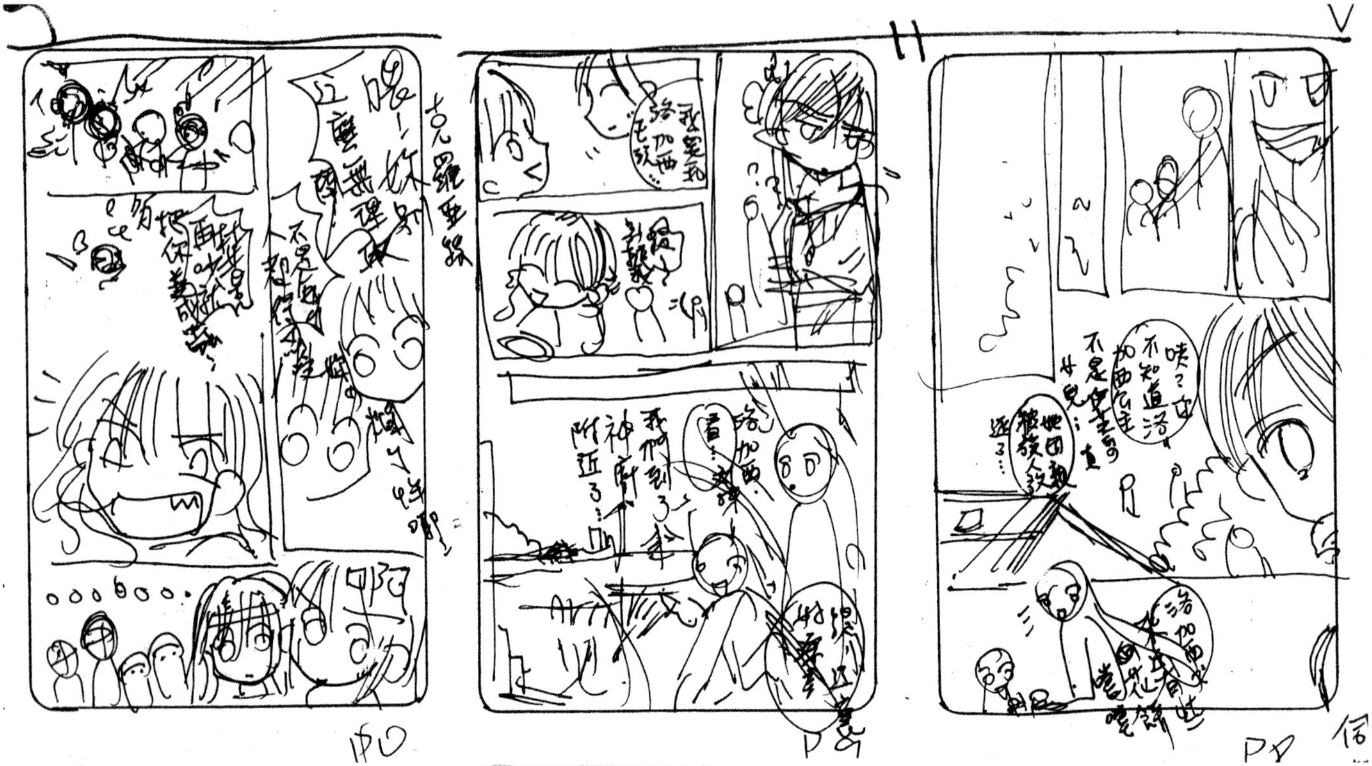

5–1 First, you'll create a thumbnail draft to decide where to place your panels. In this stage, you're just looking to see if your story will flow smoothly, so don't spend time drawing the details of the characters. As soon as you've thought of how the story should flow, quickly draw your ideas in a way that makes sense to you.

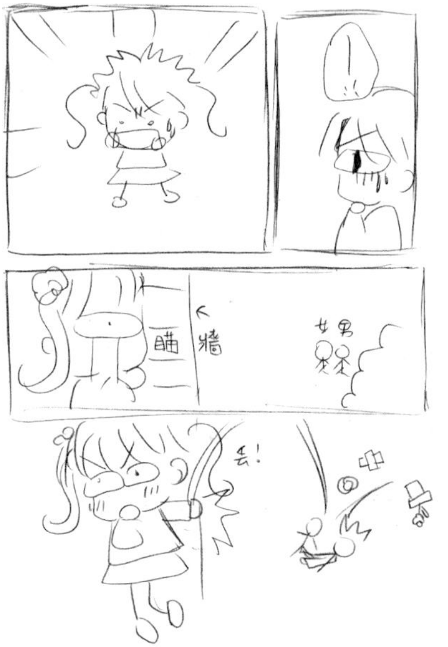

5–2 The thumbnails above show how a longer sequence is usually done. It is a bit more complicated to follow. The thumbnail on the left is a lot simpler, using just a few different expressions to show the progression of the character's mood.

Paneling Tips

The kind of panels you use usually depends on your target readers and their age group.

READ R TO L

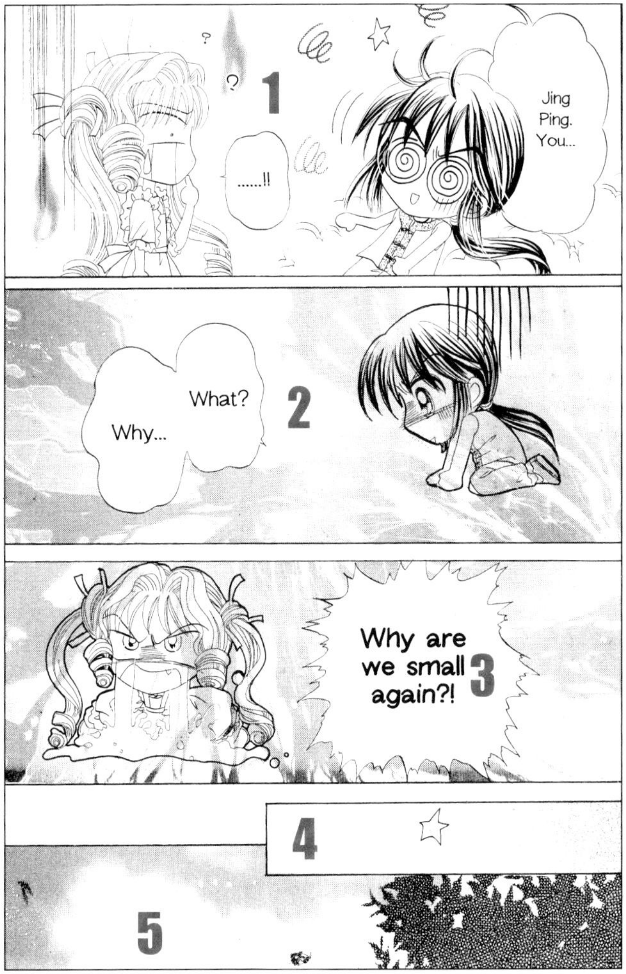
Jing Ping. You...
......!!
What?
Why...
Why are we small again?!

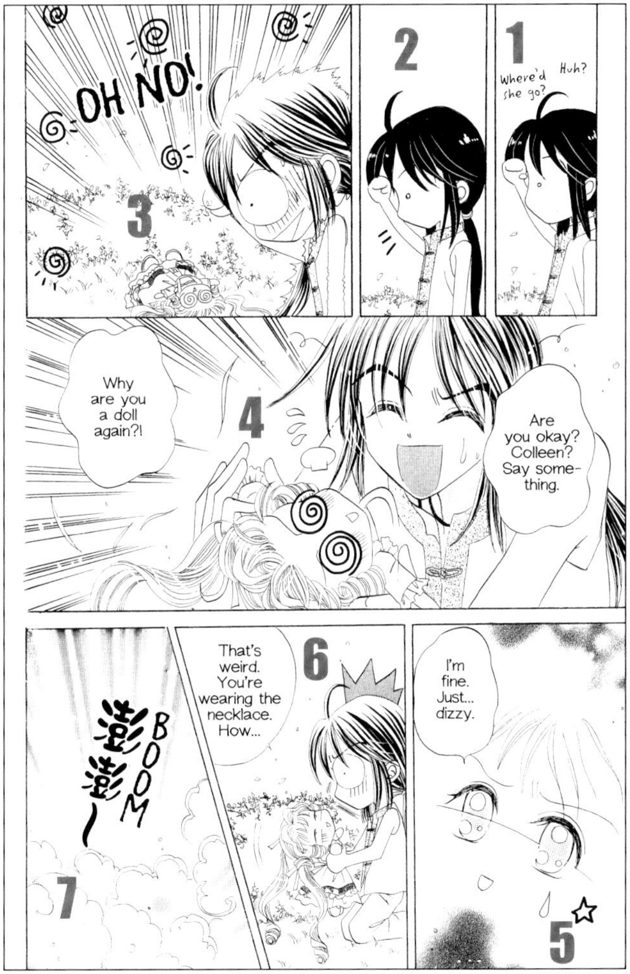
Huh?
Where'd she go?
OH NO!
Are you okay? Colleen? Say something.
Why are you a doll again?!
I'm fine. Just... dizzy.
That's weird. You're wearing the necklace. How...
澎澎~
BOOM

1-1 | Keep track of the number of panels you use when paneling. Usually a page consists of 3-7 panels.

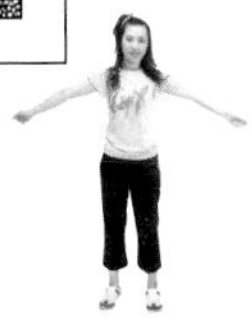

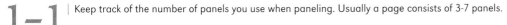

READ R TO L

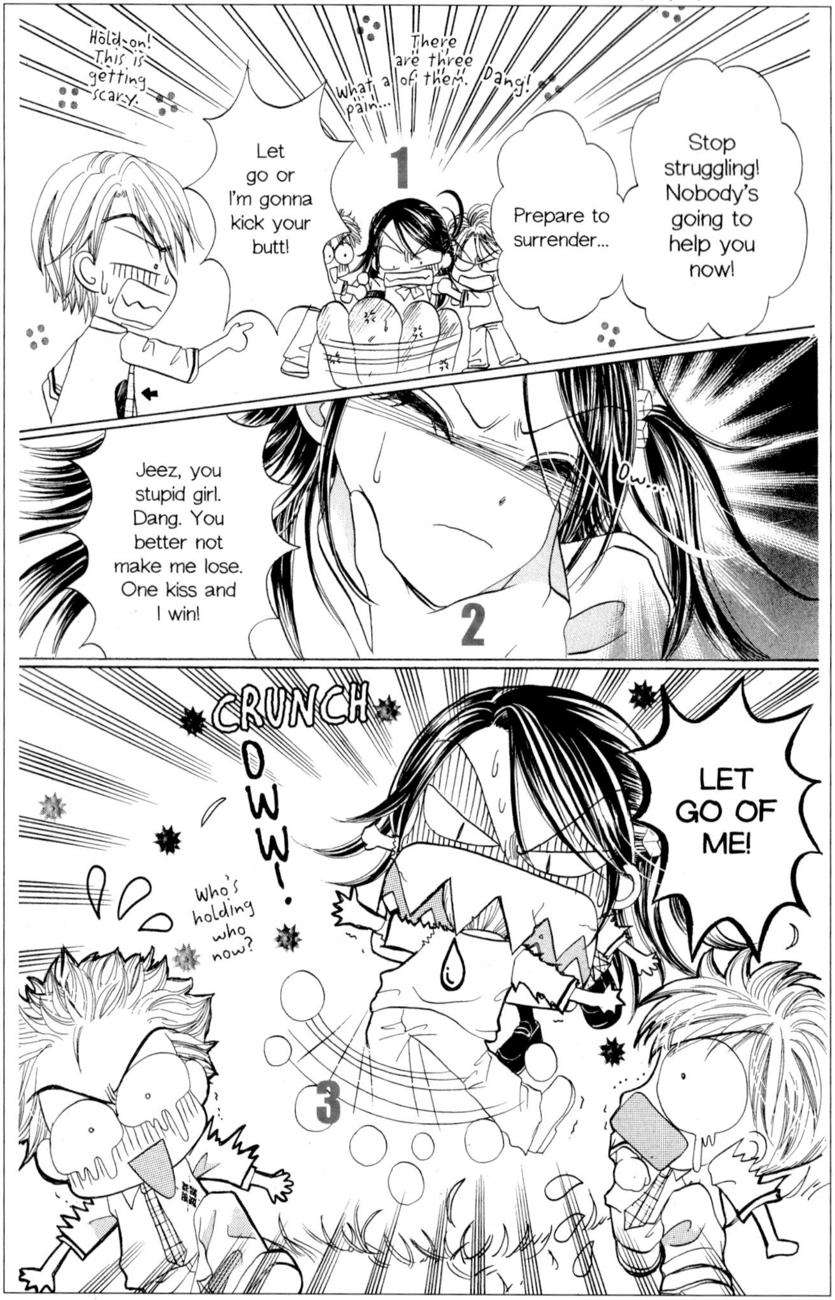
Stop struggling! Nobody's going to help you now!
Prepare to surrender...
Dang!
There are three of them.
What a pain...
1
Let go or I'm gonna kick your butt!
Hold on! This is getting scary.
Ow...
Jeez, you stupid girl. Dang. You better not make me lose. One kiss and I win!
2
LET GO OF ME!
CRUNCH
OWW!
Who's holding who now?
3

1–2 The ideal number of panels per page is 3-7. Visually, it's the most convenient number to follow because the reader can easily find the emphasis of each panel.

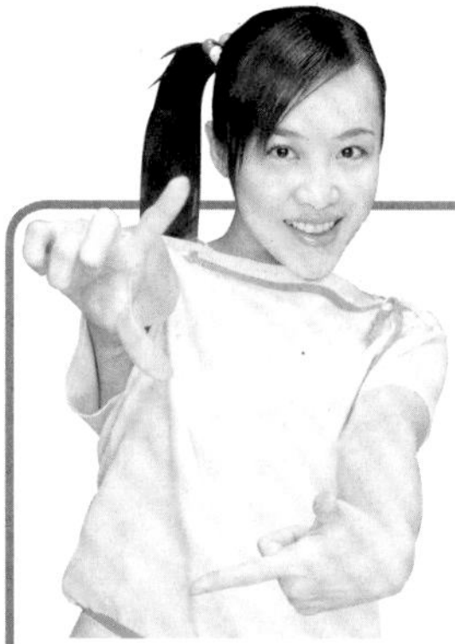

Helpful Hint

Paneling can seem difficult when you're new to drawing manga. But don't worry. Observe what other artists do to express the progression of the story and the moods of the characters. You'll get the hang of it in no time!

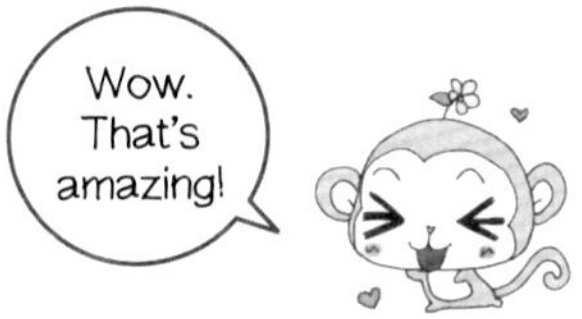
Wow. That's amazing!

READ R TO L

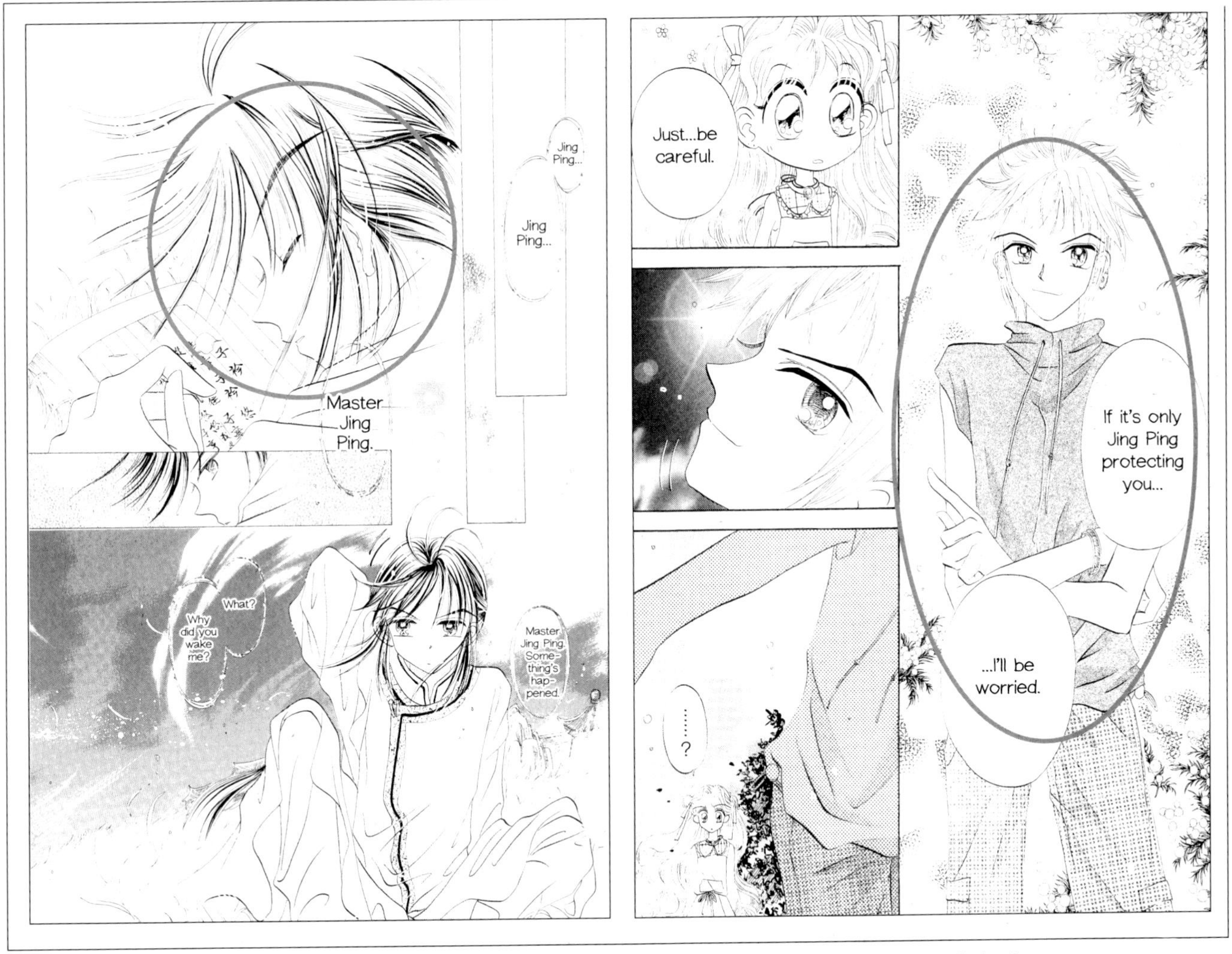
If it's only Jing Ping protecting you...
...I'll be worried.
Just...be careful.
......?
Jing Ping...
Jing Ping...
Master Jing Ping.
Master Jing Ping. Something's happened.
What?
Why did you wake me?

2 Remember that panel sizes aren't accidents. There's a reason for the different sizes: to create emphasis. It might be the text or it might be the drawing that you're emphasizing. Also note how every page of manga has one main panel that is the focal panel.

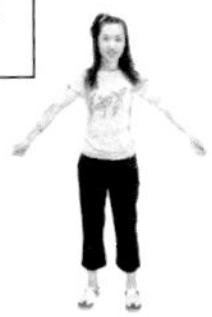

READ R TO L

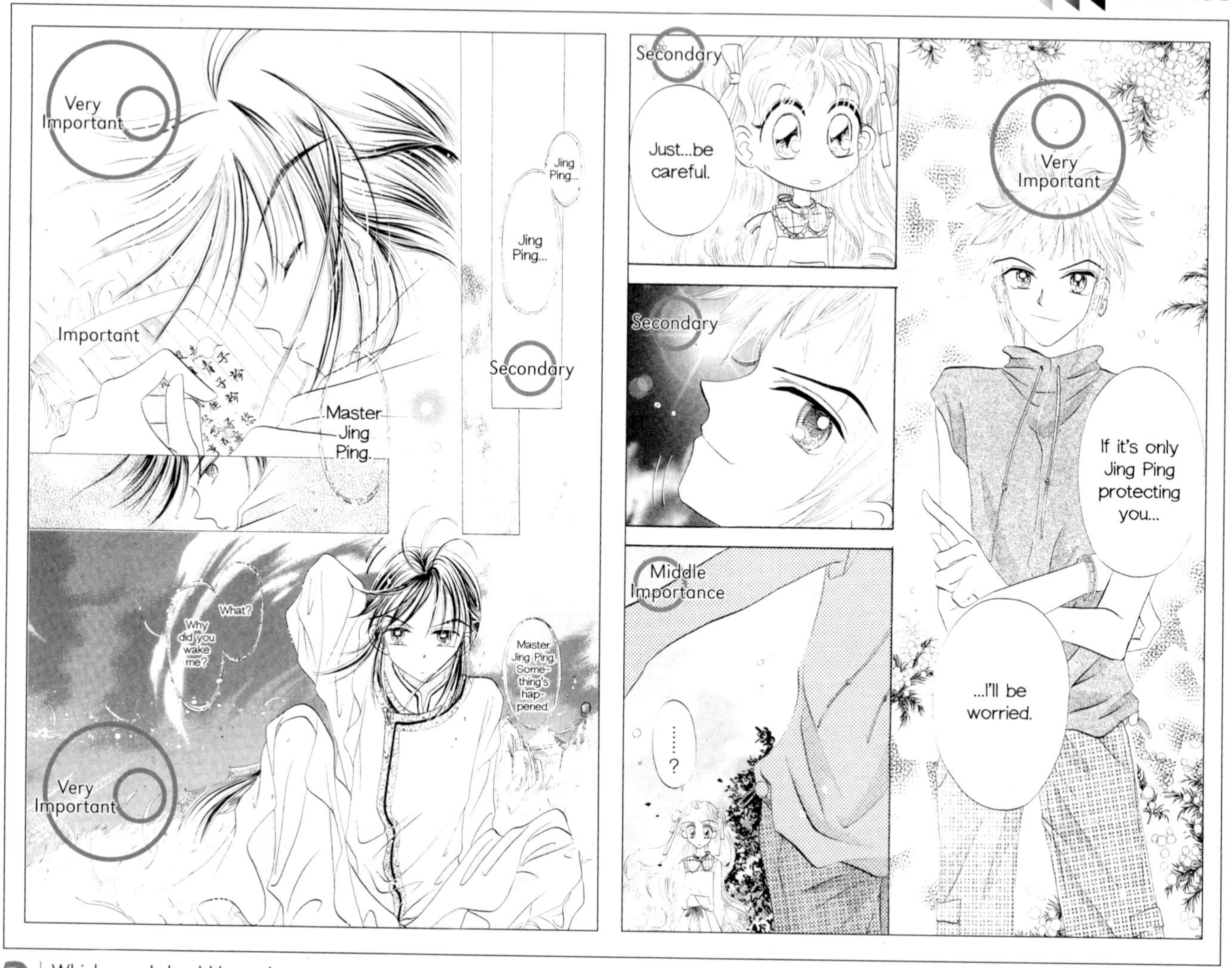
Very Important
If it's only Jing Ping protecting you...
...I'll be worried.
Secondary
Just...be careful.
Secondary
Middle Importance
......?
Jing Ping...
Jing Ping...
Secondary
Very Important
Important
Master Jing Ping.
Master Jing Ping. Something's happened.
What?
Why did you wake me?
Very Important

3 Which panel should have the most emphasis? It should be the one that expresses the character's emotions the clearest. Usually we try to make this panel as obvious as possible among the 3-7 panels on the page.

READ R TO L

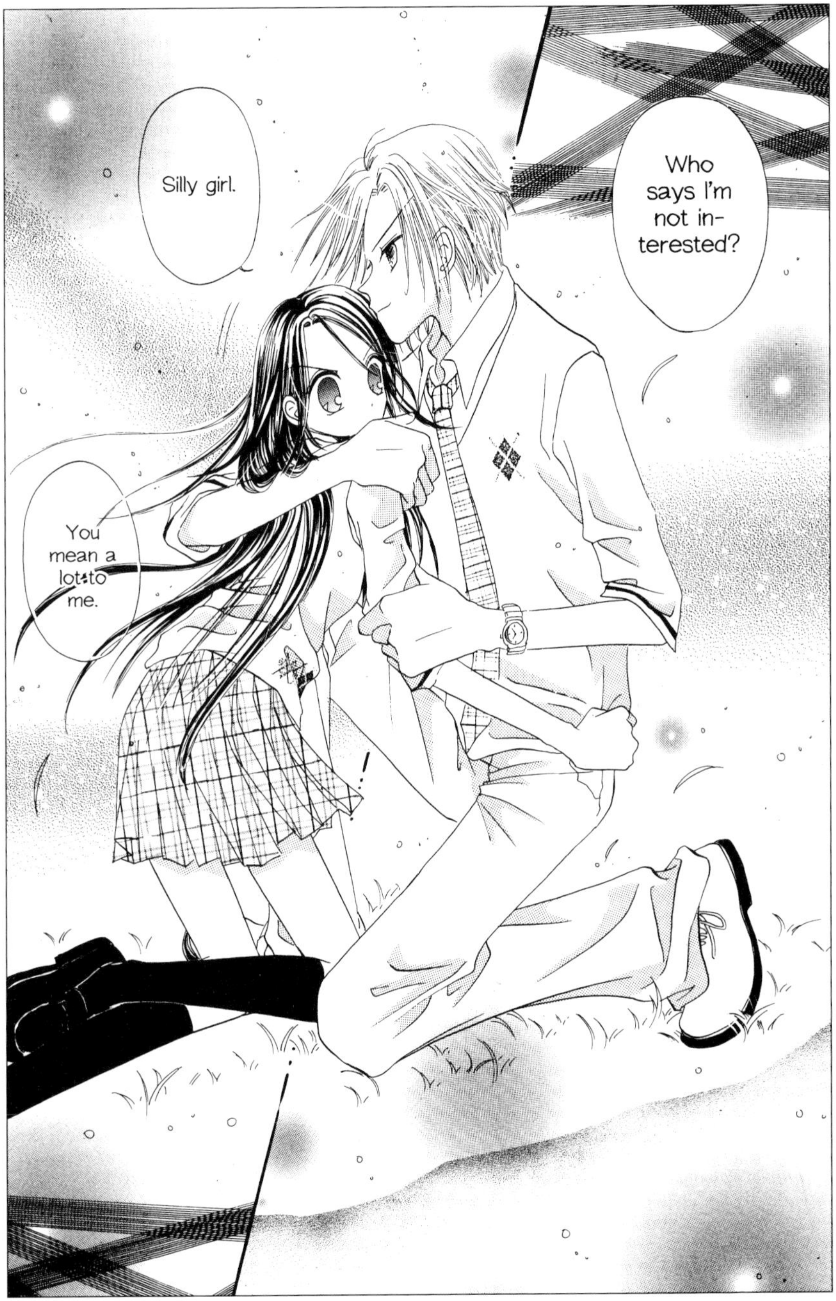
Who says I'm not interested?
Silly girl.
You mean a lot to me.

4–1

There are many ways to make the main panel the most obvious. Usually, it's the largest panel. When we want to leave an even deeper impression, we might use a whole page or a two-page spread for the main panel. The examples shown here each have a clear main panel and clear dominant mood. These allow the story to progress in a logical manner.

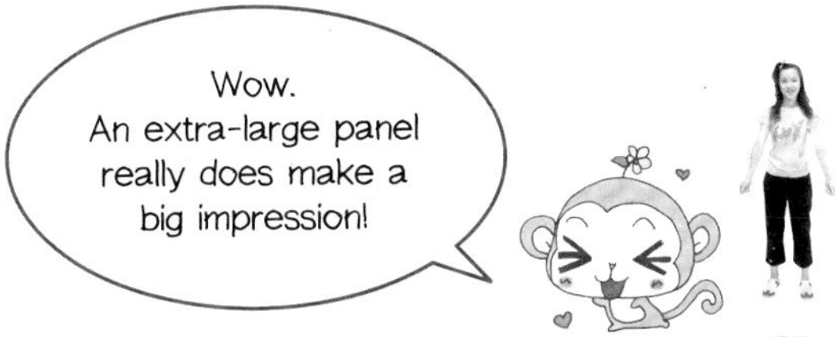
Wow. An extra-large panel really does make a big impression!

READ R TO L

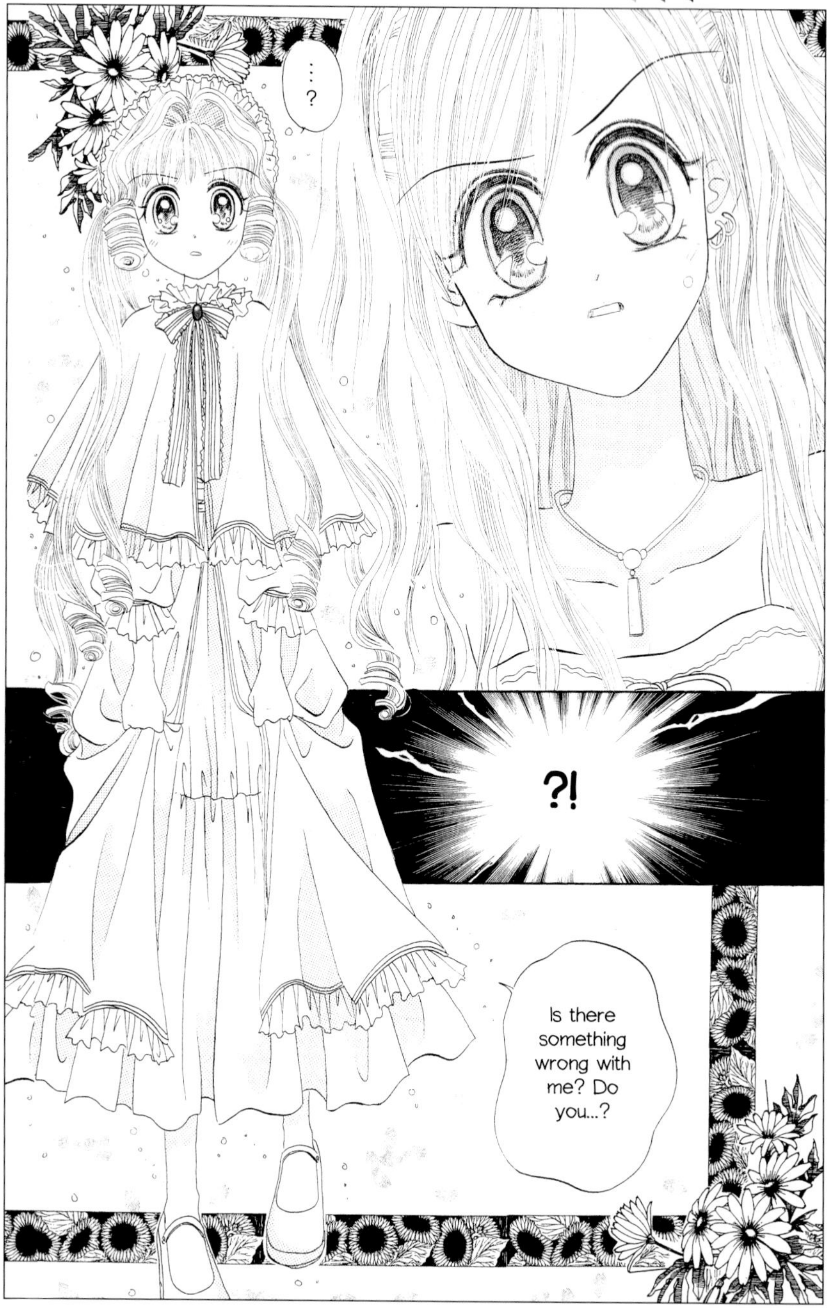
?!
Is there something wrong with me? Do you...?
...?

4–2 Another technique for creating emphasis, besides utilizing an entire page, is to vary the distance of your "camera" from the character or scene. Varying how far away or close your character is creates emphasis and contrast on the page. Utilize full-body shots, close-ups and everything inbetween.

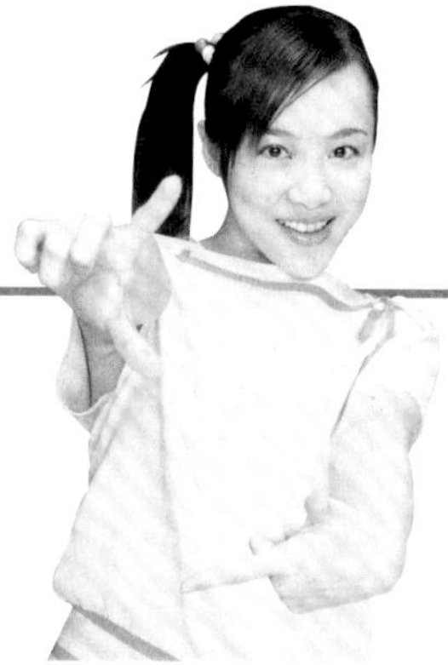

Reference Your World

- Manga's not the only medium that uses paneling!
- Every TV show, movie, cartoon or commercial consists of a series of continuous shots. Every shot is a panel.

Creating a Rough Draft

Panels compose the skeleton of your manga. Thumbnails are a diagram of that skeleton, and they also hint at its muscles and nerves.

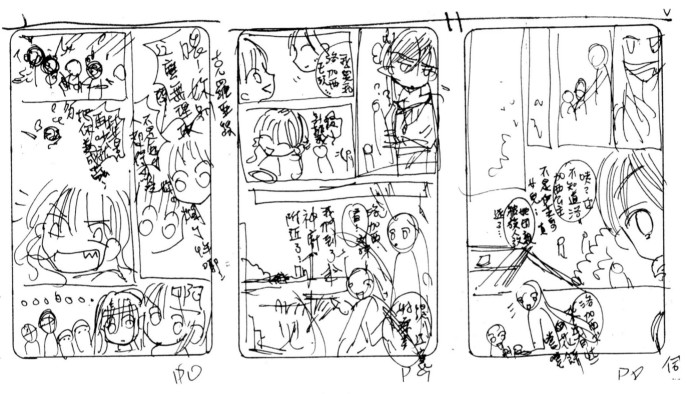

1 The thumbnail stage doesn't provide us with fully drawn panels or characters. It mostly consists of basic sketches and dialogue.

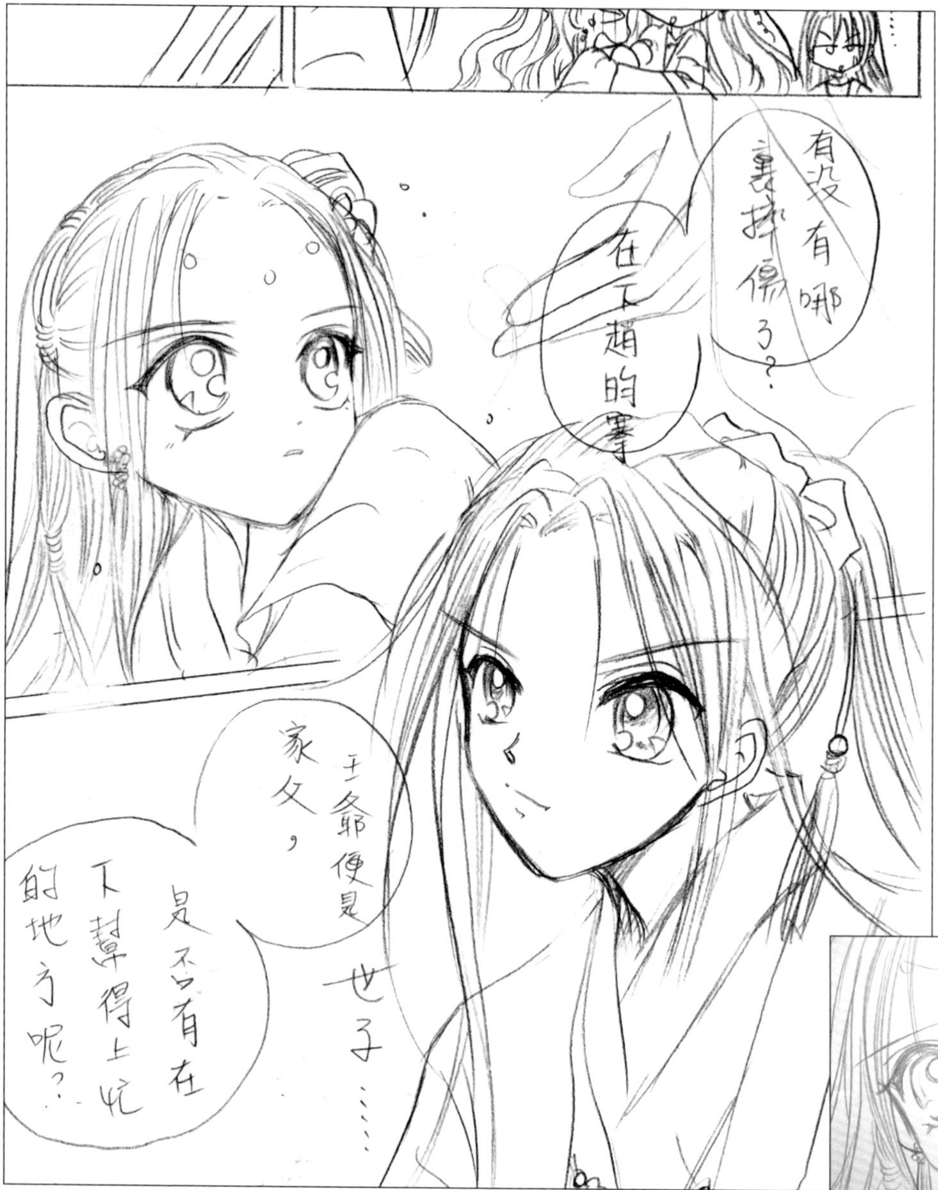
有沒有哪裏摔傷了？
在下趙昀
家父，王爺便是
世子……
是否有在下幫得上忙的地方呢？

2 Using your thumbnails as reference, take pieces of your do-it-yourself manga paper and redraw the pages with more detail. Use the guidelines you drew to help you draw the panel lines that you outlined in your thumbnail sketches. (Look back to the last chapter to learn how to make your own manga paper!)

3 How detailed should your drawings be at this stage? Some people like to make them as detailed as possible, some don't. It's really up to you.

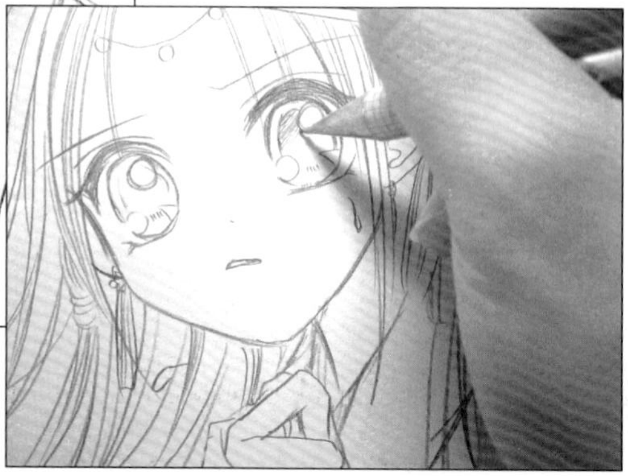

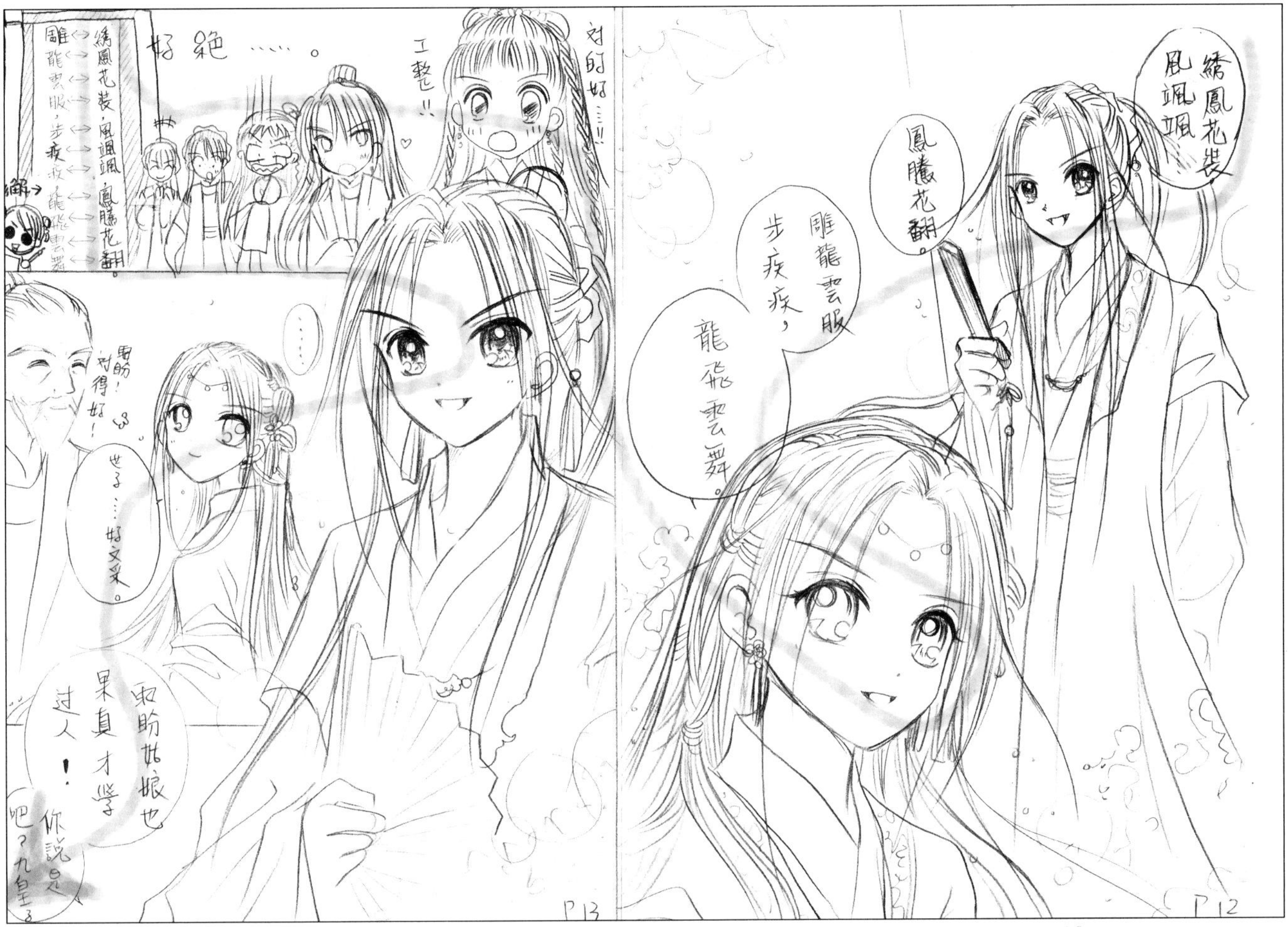
繡鳳花裳 風颯颯
鳳騰花翻。
雕龍雲服 步疾疾，
龍飛雲舞。
對的好!!!
工整!!
好絕……。
雨盼!對得好!
好文采。
雨盼姑娘也果真才學過人!
P13
P12

4 | The pencils should provide you with a clear picture of your story.

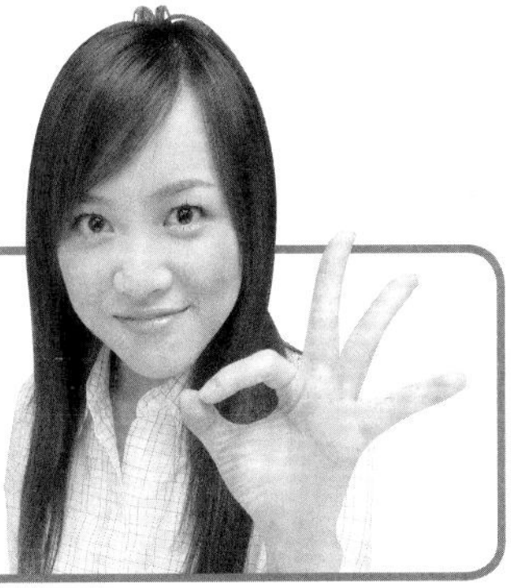

Friendly Reminder

Try to view your work from an outside perspective at this stage. Go over it a few times to see if any adjustments need to be made, such as to the dialogue, the flow of the story, or the clothes and accessories. If there are none, you have completed the rough draft stage.

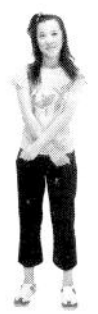

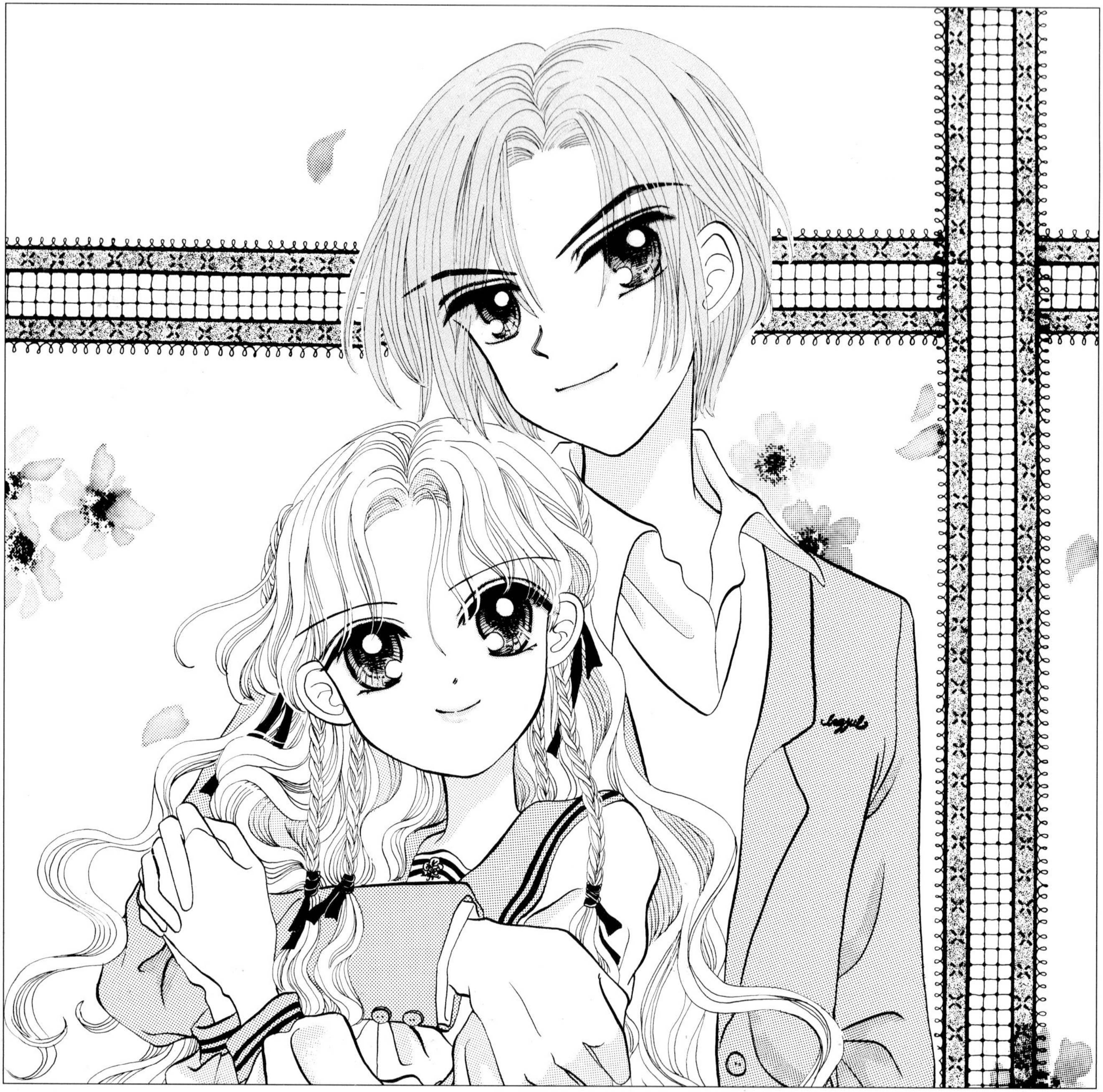

Lesson Three

Creating Finished Work

In the last lesson, we talked about the process of getting ready to draw your manga: creating an outline, inventing the characters, paneling and drawing your basic story out in thumbnails and pencils. By now, you should have a better understanding of the basic process of drawing manga. In this lesson, I'll show you how to finalize your pencils so that your drawings are even more detailed. Ready? Let's begin.

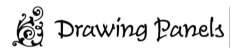 # Drawing Panels

Could those pencils you just created be considered a final manga product? Actually, if drawing manga is just a hobby, they'd certainly be good enough to be filed away in your own manga library. But if you're thinking about pitching it to a publisher for publication, you'll need to finish your manga professionally.

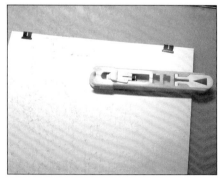

1 Before you proceed with finishing your pages, secure your pencil page underneath some manga paper with a file clipper. (Make sure the paper sizes match! If your pencils are on a piece of A4 paper, use a copy machine to enlarge it to fit the manga paper.)

2 Use a 0.5-0.8 technical or felt tip pen for tracing.

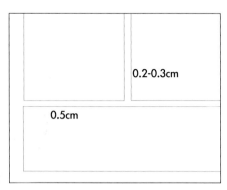

3 Place the overlapping pieces of B4 paper and manga paper over a light table. The pencils should easily show through the manga paper. However, the panel boxes on your pencil draft might not be completely square.

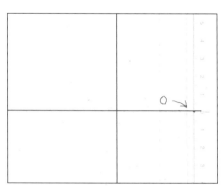

4 There are two ways to correct those wonky panels on the manga paper. The first one is to use the rulers printed on the manga paper to draw horizontal and vertical lines. Because there are measurements printed on all four sides of manga paper, your boxes are sure to be square.

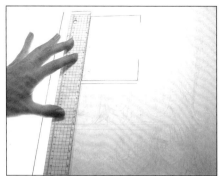

5 Another way is to use the measurements on your ruler. You can also use any straight-edge to check if the vertical and horizontal lines of a box make a proper right angle and if the lines of the boxes are indeed parallel.

6 To create good visual flow, vertical panels are usually spaced 0.5 cm (0.2") apart and horizontal panels spaced 0.2-0.3 cm (0.1") apart.

Inking

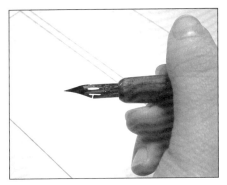

1 | Once you've traced the panels, use your dip pen to start inking.

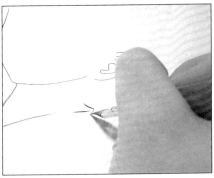

2 | You can start with the most important lines. Use a G-nib pen for this. You can also use any pen that gives you the same flexibility between thick and thin lines as the G-nib. Important lines include facial contours and clothes. You can use different thicknesses to render objects closer or further away.

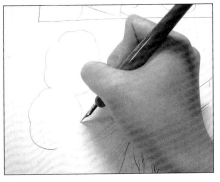

3 | Then choose a nib for the dialogue balloons. I usually stick with the G-nib, but you can choose a different nib for whatever effect you want to achieve.

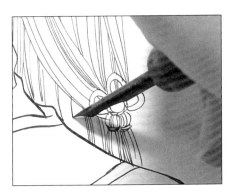

4 | After tracing the big, eye-catching lines, use a round-tip pen to trace the finer details, such as hair and eyes.

5 | The inking stage is complete once you've traced all the lines.

If it's your first time drawing with a dip pen, it's normal to feel awkward. Watch that you hold the pen at a 45 degree angle up from the paper. Watch your grip, and things will improve with time.

Drawing Effects

I'm sure you want to be able to draw eye-popping effects. Here's how to do it!

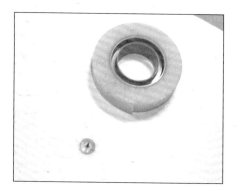

1 Place two strips of 3M Magic tape over a tack as shown in the photo (any tape that can be peeled off without damaging the paper is okay, too).

2 The tack will serve as the visual focal point, so place the tack where you want the focal point to be. In other words, this is where you want the readers to look, so it is very important where you place the tack.

3 For example: If you want the readers to focus on the face, place the tack on the face. If you want the readers to first focus on what's behind the character, place the tack behind the character. And so on and so forth.

4 Use a ruler with a ridge. That means that all along the small side an extra piece will stick out from the ruler. Place the ridged side next to the tack and start drawing. Remember to press firmly when you begin drawing and ease up as you finish.

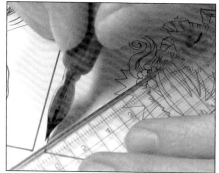

5 Use the D-nib, which is especially designed for drawing effects. Try it out first on another piece of paper. Then place the ruler against the tack and start drawing lines in a fan-like manner.

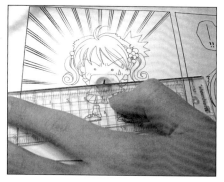

5-2 If you're a right-handed person, move the ruler counter-clockwise as you draw. That way, if there is any residual ink on the ruler, it won't smudge onto the paper.

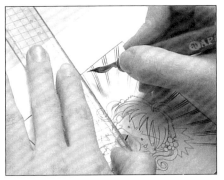

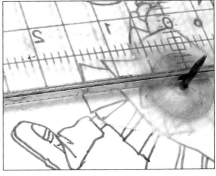

6 | Turn the paper as well. Start drawing from the upper right corner, proceeding to the upper left, then lower left, and finally back to where you began.

7 | Remember to draw using the side of the ruler that has a ridge, or the ink will seep under the ruler and smudge the paper.

8 | The density of the lines is all up to you. Once the ink has dried, you'll have achieved a stunning focal effect.

Try to keep your hand steady while drawing effects!

Helpful Hint ★ ★ ★ ★ ★

Make sure you keep your pen at a steady angle while drawing effects. If you're not careful, excess ink might seep underneath the ruler and smudge the paper.

Applying Screentone

We've pretty much finished drawing. Now let's talk about toning, which is a more advanced technique and a little more difficult to grasp.

I·C SCREEN
I·C SCREEN WIDE
I·C SCREEN WIDE
I·C SCREEN youth
Y-1595
S-795
S-942

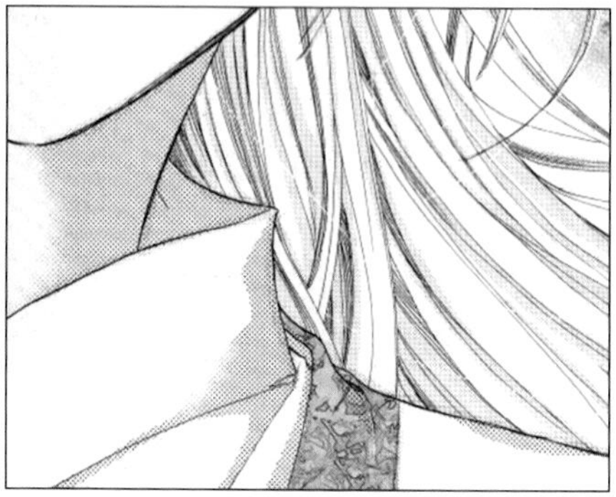

1 There are a variety of screentone sheets on the market. Some have darker tones; some have lighter tones; some are densely patterned; some are loosely patterned.

2–1 Adequate contrast is important for black and white printing. By using different tones, we can create the proper contrast. A scale of grayscale values has been standardized, for the use of toning.

2–2 You will create your final work on B4 size manga paper. If your work is printed at a different size later, the shades will appear denser and darker as a result. Please keep this in mind when choosing tones.

From left to right, grayscale values number 31, number 41 and number 51.

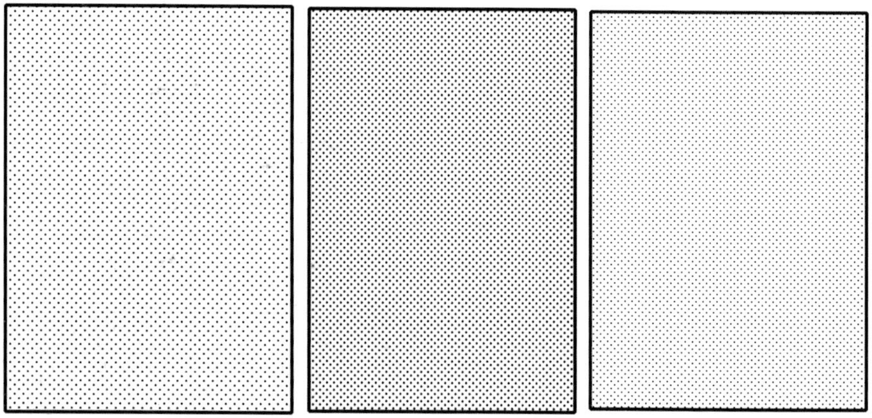

3 It's actually not that difficult to understand how to use sheets of screentone. Just think of one as a see-through sticker. We've already touched upon the basics of their usage in Lesson One. Please refer back to page 21 if you still need help. When you're toning a character, you'll use a grayscale value that varies depending on panel size; common values vary from number 30 to number 40 to number 50.

From left to right, grayscale values number 61, number 71 and number 92.

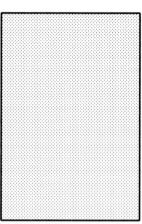

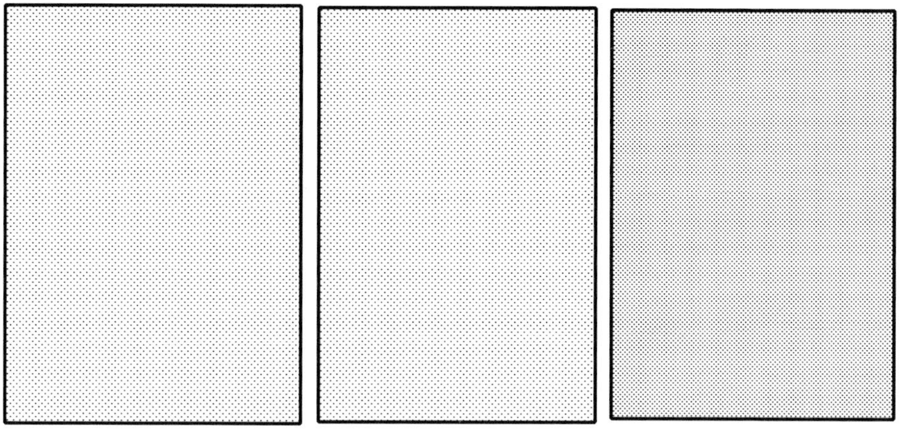

4 Grayscale values of objects tend to range from number 60 to 90. But the ultimate decision of how an object should be rendered lies with you. Choose what you think best reflects your style.

Friendly Reminder

When experimenting with different shades to see which looks best on your drawings, apply both lighter and darker tones to see their different effects. Then compare their differences after enlarging or reducing the size of the page. This should help you decide what best suits your work.

Scraping

1 Scraping away tone with a knife is a technique often used in manga to achieve a fading effect. It's important to decide what screentone and scraping technique to use because each will have different results.

2 Choose a screentone sheet that you would like to scrape to create a fading effect. Apply the sheet over the part of your drawing you would like to have shaded. Avoid using tones that are too dense or dark because this will look less natural. Remember to firmly press the sheet against your drawing: you want this to stick!

3 Use a hobby knife with a sharp blade. Try using a knife similar to the one in the photo. I find this kind to be the most effective.

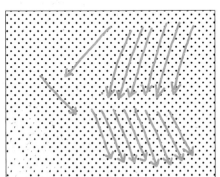

4 Observe the natural direction (the grain) of the tone pattern. Follow it with your knife, but in a slightly more slanted direction. Start scraping in a criss-cross manner.

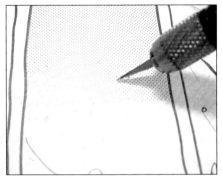

5 Hold the knife at a tilted angle while scraping. Scrape the knife towards you. You should hear an obvious scraping sound, but make sure not to scrape too hard and damage the paper.

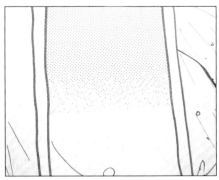

6 Scrape until you see a natural fading effect. Now you've learned scraping.

More Ways to Use Screentone

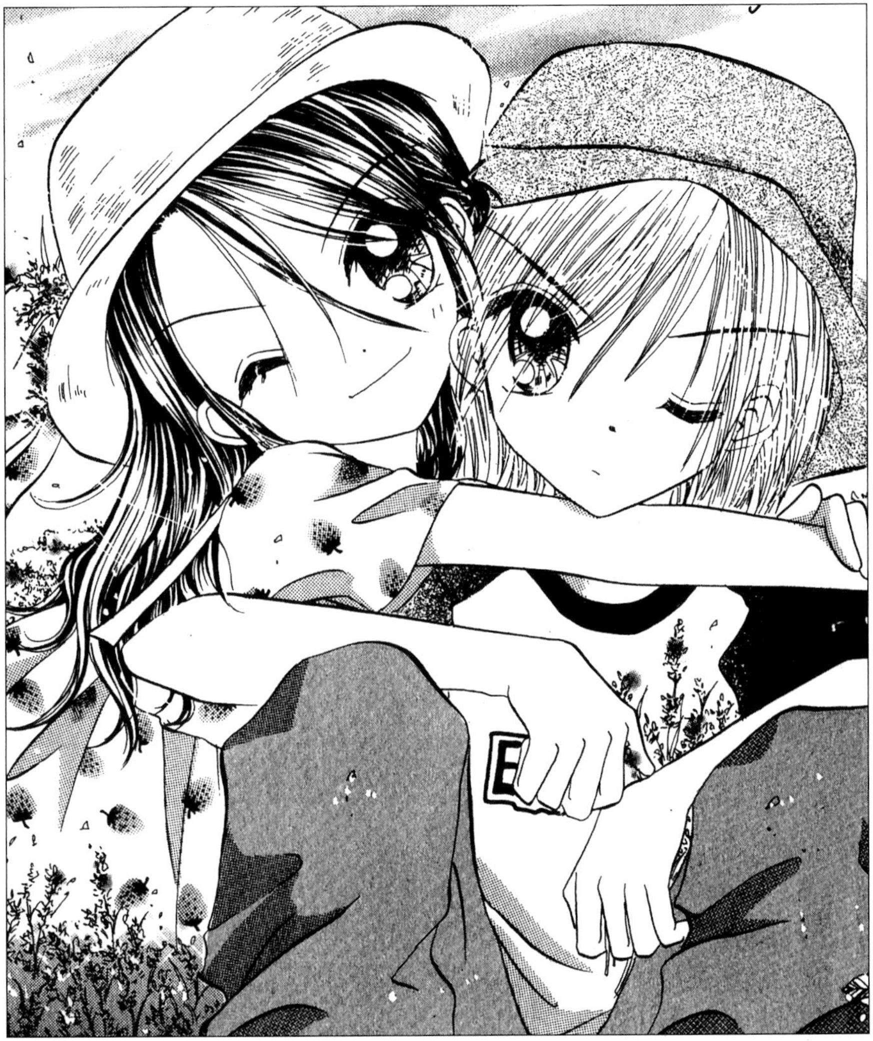

1 You can achieve a livelier toning effect by placing two sheets on top of each other. This will give the drawing even more contrast. (Notice the boy's pants.)

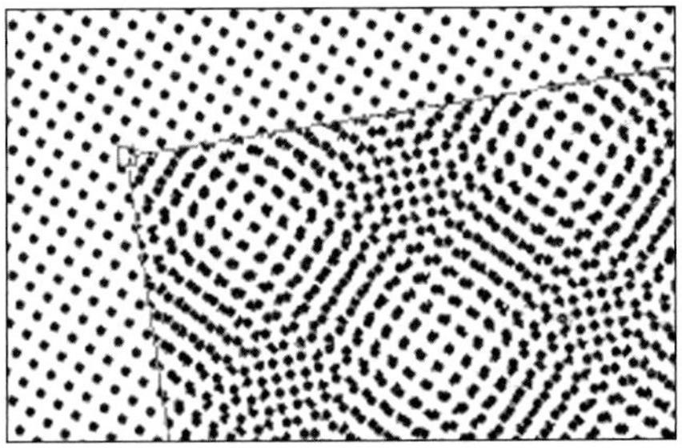

2 When you place two sheets of the same tone pattern over each other, the overlap will result in snowflake-like patterns.

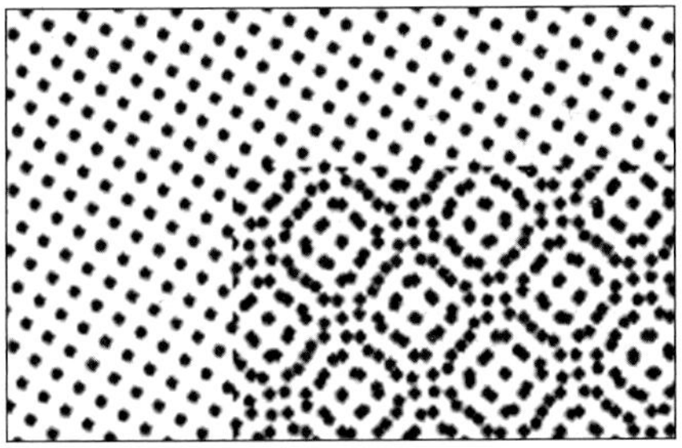

3 If you do not wish to see snowflakes, try to overlap the sheets at the exact same angle. But snowflakes do come in handy if you want to give your drawings an alternative feel. It all depends on you.

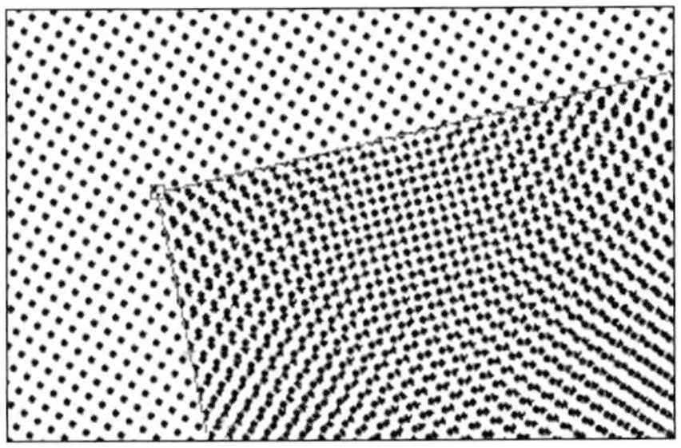

4 Once you've decided on an angle, you'll see the enhanced contrast. Overlapping different tones achieves different contrasting effects. I recommend that you use dot patterns for overlapping.

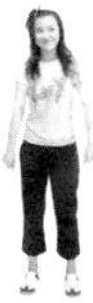

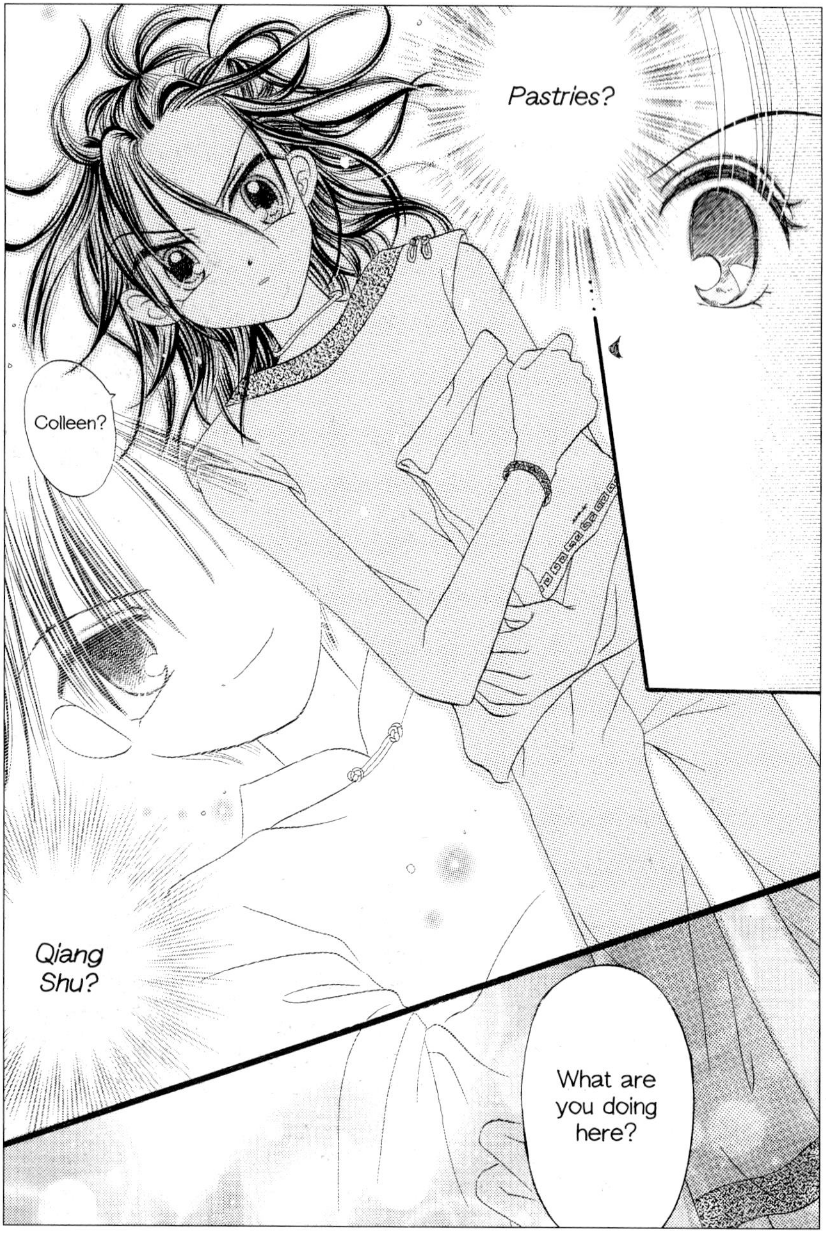
Pastries?
Colleen?
Qiang Shu?
What are you doing here?

1 To express memories, try using lighter tones and lots of scraping.

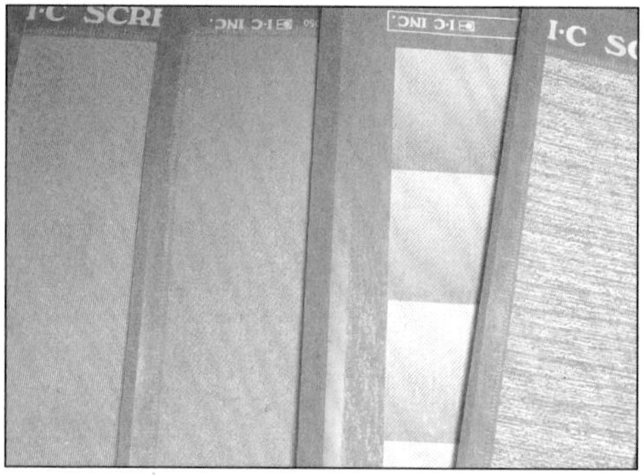
I·C SCR
I·C INC.
I·C INC.
I·C S

2 Besides sheets used to add shades of gray to a white background, there are also screentone sheets for adding shades of gray or white to a dark or black background. These are known as highlighting sheets and can be used in the same way.

Corrections and Highlights

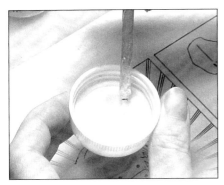

1 | Finishing a page involves correcting mistakes. We can use correction fluid to do this.

2 | Dip the correction brush in water and mix it with the correction fluid. The fluid should be just thick enough to cover the black lines.

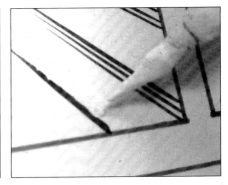

3 | If the fluid is too thick, it might clump together and be difficult to brush on.

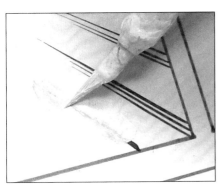

4 | If it is too thin, it will not provide proper coverage and might even dissolve the inked lines, soiling the paper.

5 | Add highlights with correction fluid to enhance the contrast in hair and eyes, or to provide contrasting lighting effects.

6 | White-Out is also a handy tool. It can help brighten up the image. Try it out and use it as much or as little as you like.

Favorite Tones

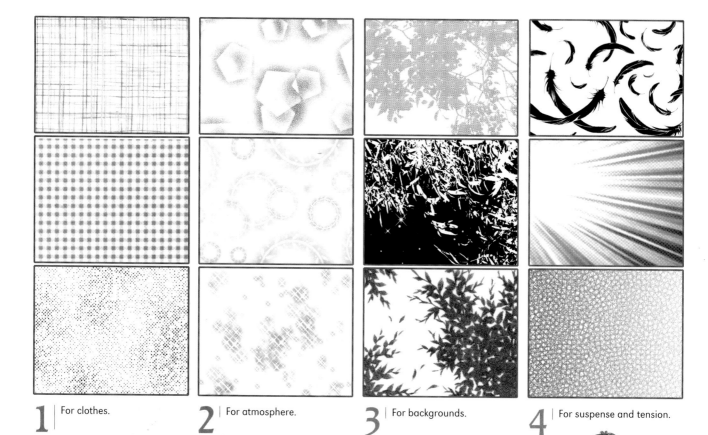

1 | For clothes.

2 | For atmosphere.

3 | For backgrounds.

4 | For suspense and tension.

Helpful Hint

There are so many different patterns of screentone out there. You should choose the ones that fit your style and give your drawings dimension and life. If you observe how different manga artists use toning effects, you'll notice that each artist has his or her own preferences when creating certain emotional or background effects.

Dialogue Balloon Tips

I told you about it before. Remem-ber?

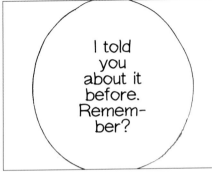

1 This balloon is too narrow. It crowds the characters.

I told you about it before. Remem-ber?

2 This balloon is too round for the vertically laid out text. Visually, the two don't go well with each other.

I told you about it before. Remem-ber?

3 This oval-shaped balloon has an only slightly wider middle, making it just right for the text.

Friendly Reminder

Different dialogue balloons can create very different visual effects. When creating dialogue balloons, make sure the text you want to put in them will fit. These three examples represent good and bad fits. There are many different ways to draw a dialogue balloon. Just remember that your text must fit in them. I remember when I first started out, my editor would often comment that I wrote way too much text for my balloons and it looked awkward. Avoid that beginner's mistake by planning your balloon sizes in advance and sticking to them.

Writing Dialogue on Tracing Paper

So far we've covered creating an outline, paneling, finishing and toning effects. Your manga is almost finished now. All we need to do is put in the dialogue. Let's begin.

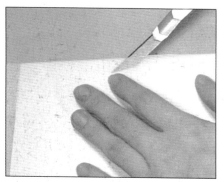

1 Cut A3 (approx. 11 x 17") size tracing paper to fit the width of your B4 size manga paper. (All that matters is that the width fits.)

2 Place the tracing paper over the manga paper. Any excess length of tracing paper should be on the top. Fold the excess behind the manga paper.

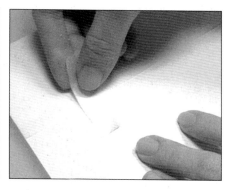

3 Use tape to secure the folded part onto the back of the page.

4 After securing the tracing paper, you can start writing in your dialogue.

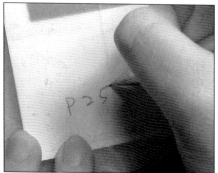

5 Finally, don't forget to check for any mistakes or omissions. Plus, don't forget to put in the page numbers! And voilà, your very first manga!

Helpful Hint

We've gone through all the steps to drawing manga. Creating your own manga isn't that hard after all, is it? If you're still not comfortable with all the techniques, just practice. Practice makes perfect. Don't give up!

Computer Graphics – The Basics

If you're interested in doing your finishes on a computer, I'll show you the basics of how I usually do it.

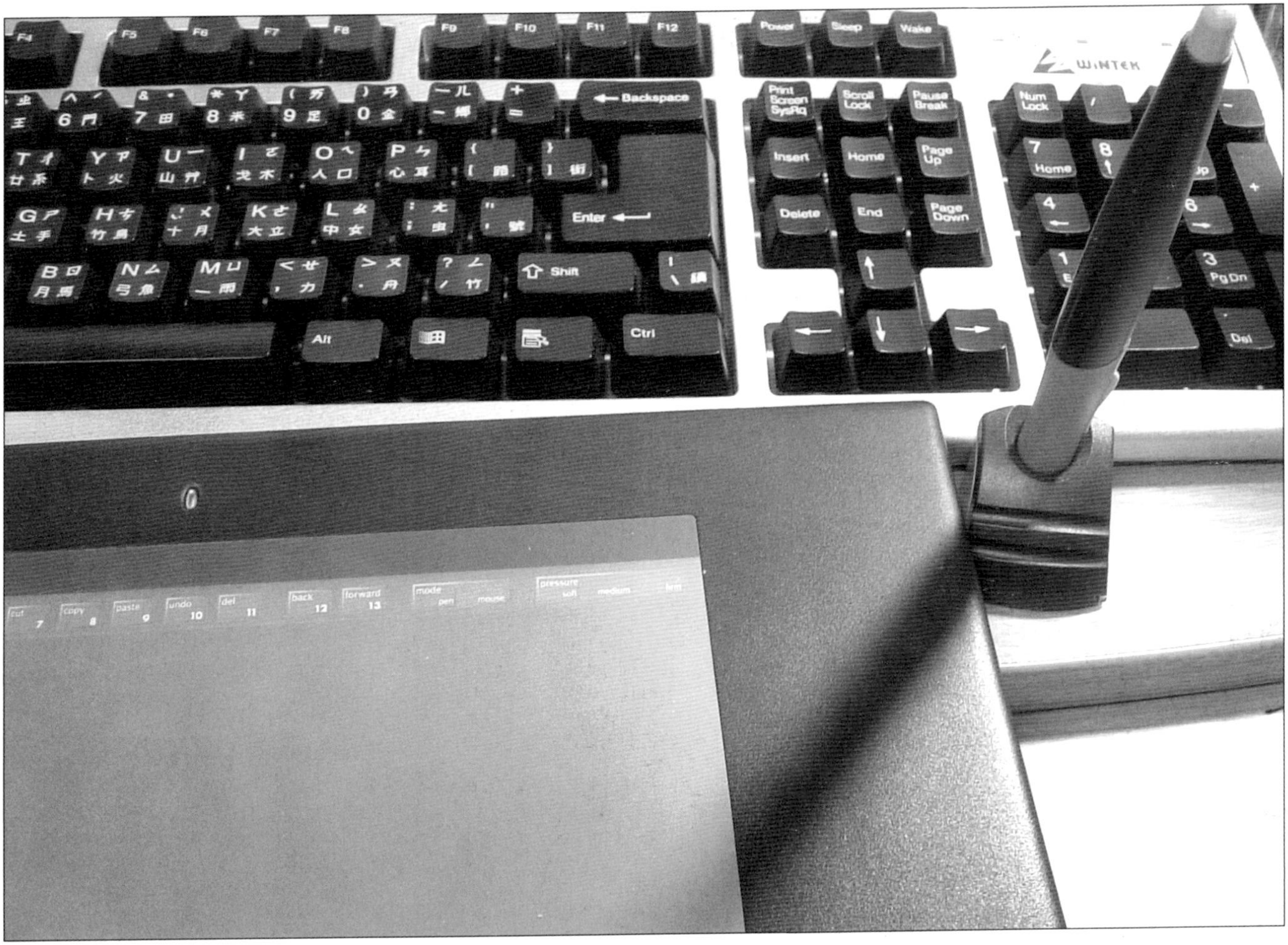
Power
Sleep
Wake
Backspace
Enter
Shift
Alt
Ctrl
Insert
Home
Delete
End
Page Up
Page Down
Num Lock
Del

* All instructions are based on use of a standard desktop PC.

Besides a PC that meets basic system requirements, and Photoshop, you may also want a scanner and a digital drawing tablet. If you plan to print your drawings, you'll need a printer, too. Once you have everything, you're ready to create finished work on the computer.

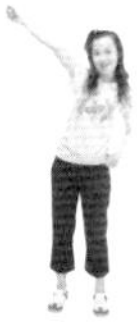

Computer Graphics – Scanning

EPSON TWAIN
EPSON

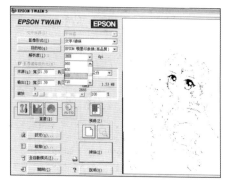

1 How do you scan your inked drawing? Place the page in your scanner. Prepare to scan.

EPSON TWAIN
EPSON

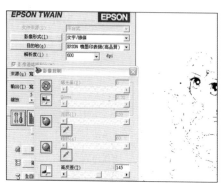

2 Set the resolution to 600 dpi or higher for black-and-white inked drawings.

EPSON TWAIN
EPSON

3 Scanning applications have options for different scanning output modes. The mode chosen here is Line Art. In this mode, the scanner will only scan black and white: no color, no gray.

EPSON TWAIN
EPSON

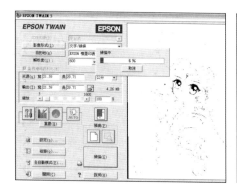

4 Choose the advanced scanning option in your scanner application. Adjust the values for resolution and quality.

5 When you open the file in Photoshop, it will appear as a bitmap file.

6 Now you can choose Image>Mode>Grayscale and convert the image into a grayscale image.

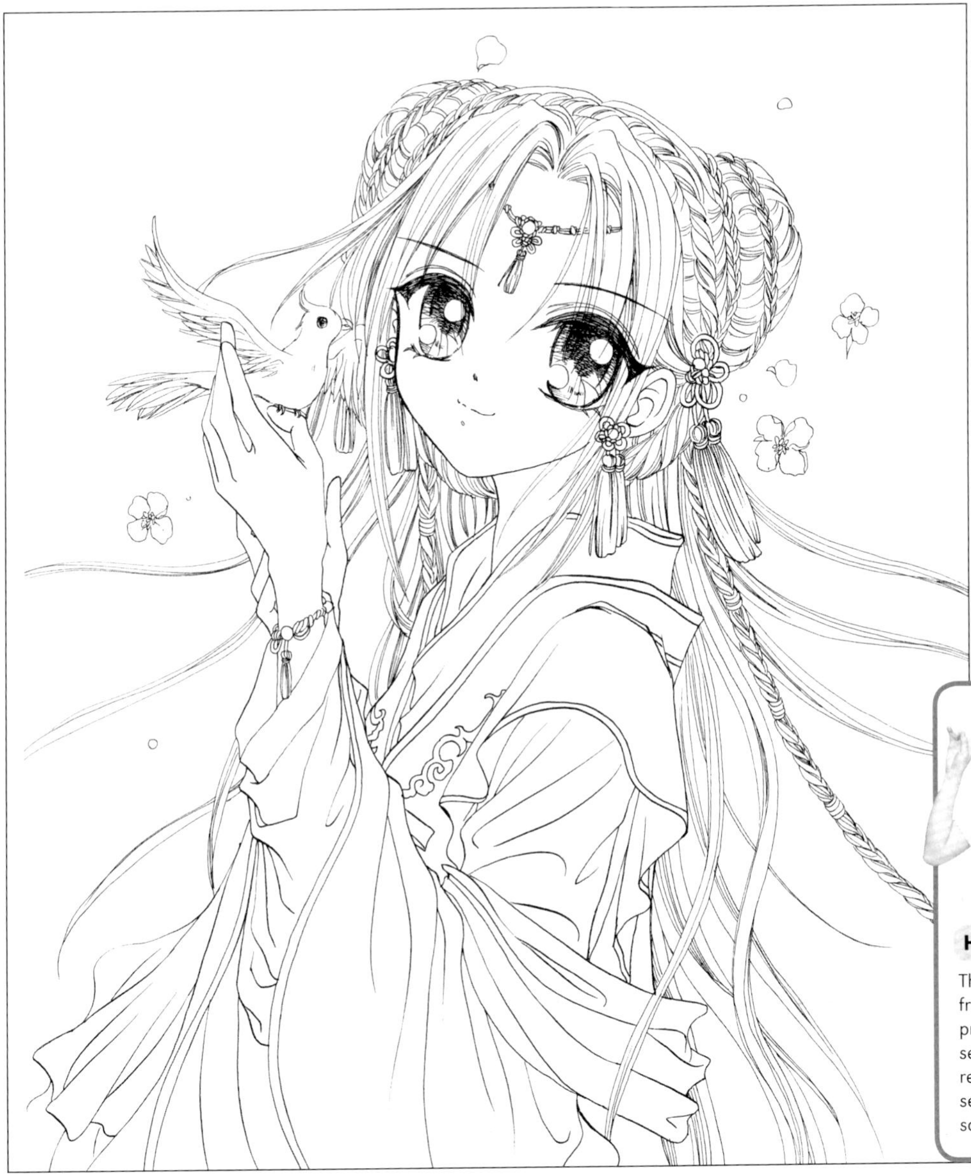

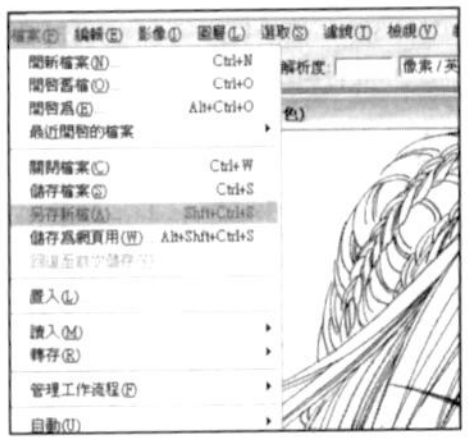

檔案(F) 編輯(E) 影像(I) 圖層(L) 選取(S) 濾鏡(T) 檢視(V)
開新檔案(N) Ctrl+N
開啓舊檔(O) Ctrl+O
開啓爲(E) Alt+Ctrl+O
最近開啓的檔案
關閉檔案(C) Ctrl+W
儲存檔案(S) Ctrl+S
另存新檔(A) Shift+Ctrl+S
儲存爲網頁用(W) Alt+Shift+Ctrl+S
置入(L)
讀入(M)
轉存(R)
管理工作流程(F)
自動(U)
解析度

7 Once you're satisfied with the resolution and quality, save the file. This file is your back-up. Then click Save As to save a second file that you will actually work off of. Name the file something indicating that it is "undergoing finalization." We can now proceed with computer toning on this new grayscale file.

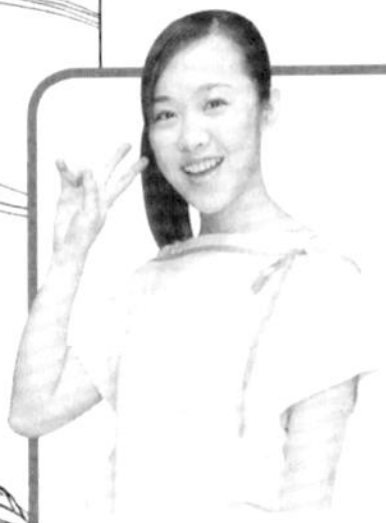

Helpful Hint

The actual scanning results might differ from what you see in your scanner's preview mode. Experiment with different settings until you arrive at the ideal resolution and quality. Remember those settings and use them every time you scan your inked drawings.

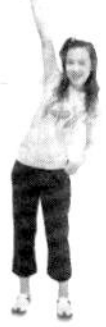

Computer Graphics – Creating Tones

We now have an inked drawing on file, but we don't have ready-made tones on the computer. How do you create tones with a computer?

Adobe Photoshop

1 Open a new grayscale file. Set the resolution at 600 dpi and the size as 36 cm x 25 cm (approx. 14" x 9").

2 Select the color black from the color window. Go to the Color Picker and set the value of K (black) to 10%.

3 Use the Paint Bucket tool to fill in the image.

Adobe Photoshop

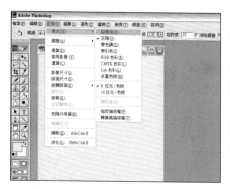

4 Go to Image>Mode>Bitmap. You'll see a window with a number of options.

5 Under Resolution, the input and output values should be the same, so we will put in 600 dpi for the output value. Under Method choose Halftone Screen. This will give us an effect very similar to tone sheets.

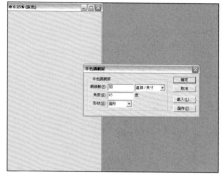

6 If you want to create a number 41 tone, put in 50 for Frequency, 45 for Angle, and choose the most common Round for Shape.

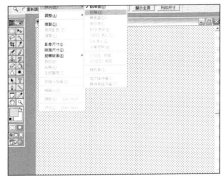

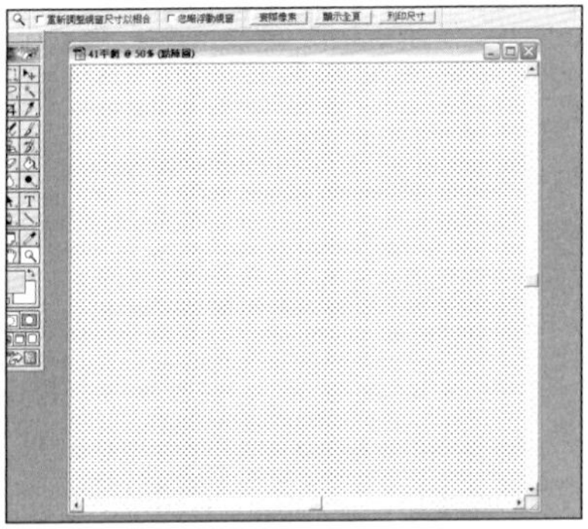

7 Click OK. Enlarge your image. You'll see that it looks exactly like a number 41 tone sheet.

8-1 Because we mostly work with grayscale at the finalizing stage, save your tone file as a grayscale file. This will save you the trouble of having to convert it to a grayscale file before you use it the next time. Now you have a number 41 tone file ready for use. Pretty convenient, isn't it?

Yay! Now I'll have an endless supply of screentones!

Friendly Reminder ✱ ✱ ✱ ✱ ✱

You can create many different screentones using your computer. But not all of them are suitable for manga. On the next page I've listed a number of commonly used screentone settings for your reference.

Screentone Settings

If you want to make different screentones, all you have to do is follow the steps I showed you on the previous pages. Just change the values and frequency to achieve different tones. Here is a list of settings that will give you the same effects as some of the most commonly used screentones.

SCREENTONE NUMBER	FREQUENCY (LINES/INCH)	ANGLE	K VALUE % (BLACK)	COMMON USAGE
10	30	45	5%	background/effects
20	32.5	45	5%	background/effects
22	32.5	45	20%	background/effects
30	42.5	45	5%	large shade
31	42.5	45	10%	large darker shade
40	50	45	5%	standard lighter shade
41	50	45	10%	standard shade
42	50	45	20%	large darker shade
50	55	45	5%	small lighter shade
51	55	45	10%	small shade
52	55	45	20%	small darker shade
61	60	45	10%	shade/filling
91	85	45	10%	metal
92	85	45	20%	filling

Computer Graphics – Toning

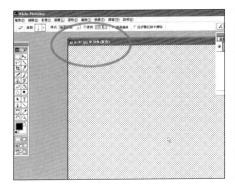

1 We've finished making our tones. Now let's choose one to use as an example. I'll show you how I usually tone, but everyone has own their method, so feel free to make adjustments.

2 I recommend that you create a new layer every time you use a different screentone. Change the layer mode from Normal to Multiply. Click the layer to start working on it.

3 Select the Pencil tool from the Paint Brush/Pencil button.

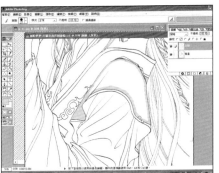

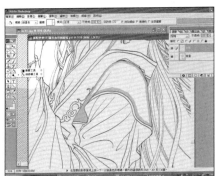

4 Choose a black with the K value that corresponds to the tone you want to apply. It will look gray. Brush the gray onto the area you want to tone.

5 For larger areas, use the Pencil or Paint Brush tool to outline the area. Make sure the outline of the area is solid (no gaps). Paint all your grey on the same layer.

6-1 Select the Paint Bucket tool (as shown in the example).

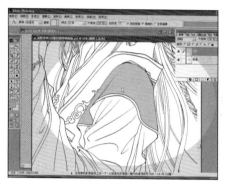

6-2 Fill in the outlined area with the same gray. Remember to check that only the area you want to tone is filled.

7 After filling in the area, hold down Ctrl and select the Layer 1 thumbnail.

8 You'll see that the area we just colored gray has been selected.

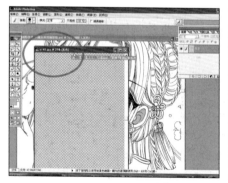

9 Open the files for the tones we just made. We'll choose number 41, the screentone often used for basic shading. Now we're going to copy the tone for placing over the selected gray area.

10 Open file number 41. Select all (Ctrl+A) then copy (Ctrl+C).

11 We just selected and copied screentone number 41. Now we'll place it on the page.

12
Go to Edit>Execute>Paste Selected Area or simply hold down Ctrl+Shift+V to paste screentone number 41 onto the selected area. You should now see that the tone has been successfully pasted.

13-1
But something doesn't look quite right, does it? Look at your layers menu. There should be an additional Layer 2 above Layer 1.

13-2
Layer 2 is the new layer with the number 41 screentone. But by default, the mode for Layer 2 is set at Normal. This will cause it to cover up some of the lines in your drawing.

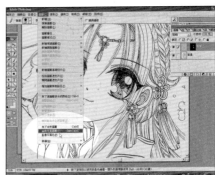

13-3
In Layer 2, change the mode setting from Normal to Multiply. Then you should be able to clearly see the lines of Layer 1.

13-4
There's one more step. The layer with the number 41 screentone has replaced the layer with the selected gray area. The latter is now redundant. You may delete it.

14
Now you have a properly toned image. If you're all finished, you should consider first saving an unmerged version before saving a merged version where you merge all the layers into one. This will make things convenient for future revisions if needed. Go to Layer > Merge Visible to merge your image.

Computer Graphics - Scraping

Not only can you can apply screentones with a computer, but you can also achieve scraping effects. There's no need to use a hobby knife anymore. But how do we "scrape" on a computer?

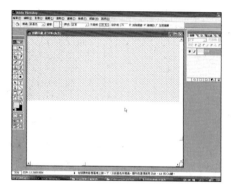

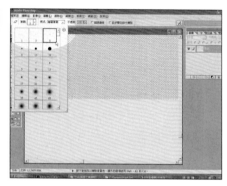

1 There are many ways to achieve a fading effect on a computer screentone, but if you want your effect to have that natural handmade feel, try using the Eraser tool.

2-1 First you need to set the eraser so it will behave like a hobby knife.

2-2 For the hobby knife effect, set the size so that the tip is slightly larger than the screentone dots. (I personally like to set it between 1-5 px.)

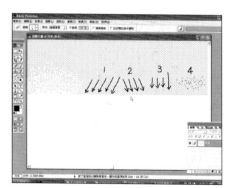

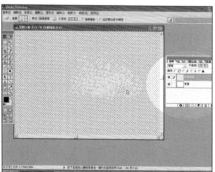

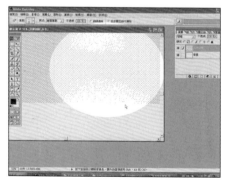

3-1 Use the eraser and crisscross it over the tone like you would with a hobby knife. This is how you scrape on a computer.

3-2 Remember that this needs to be done on an unmerged tone layer. If you use it on a merged page the lines in your drawing will also be erased.

3-3 Try to make the scraping effect look as natural as possible. Now you've just mastered scraping on a computer!

Computer Graphics – Dialogue

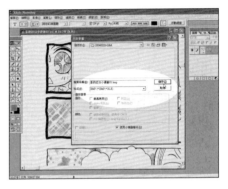

1 If you directly type the dialogue onto your art and save it as a merged file, problems might arise when you turn your final pages in. Different publishers have different font styles. Also, once the drawings are resized they may require different font sizes.

2–1 In order to keep things convenient for our editors, we can keep our text layer and the art layer separate so they can be adjusted. (Or you can also choose not to type in the dialogue and let the publisher handle that.)

2–2 Once the page has been finalized, we can merge all the layers and save it as a bitmap file.

2–3 Now print out the final pages and write in the dialogue. Turn in the file and the printed manuscript to the publisher. They'll get everything ready for the press.

Helpful Hint

Every publisher has a different set of guidelines for handing in final pages. For quality purposes, most publishers prefer to use professional layout software to type in the dialogue. They should be very happy if you provide them with an electronic file of the dialogue. But, it's best to ask first.

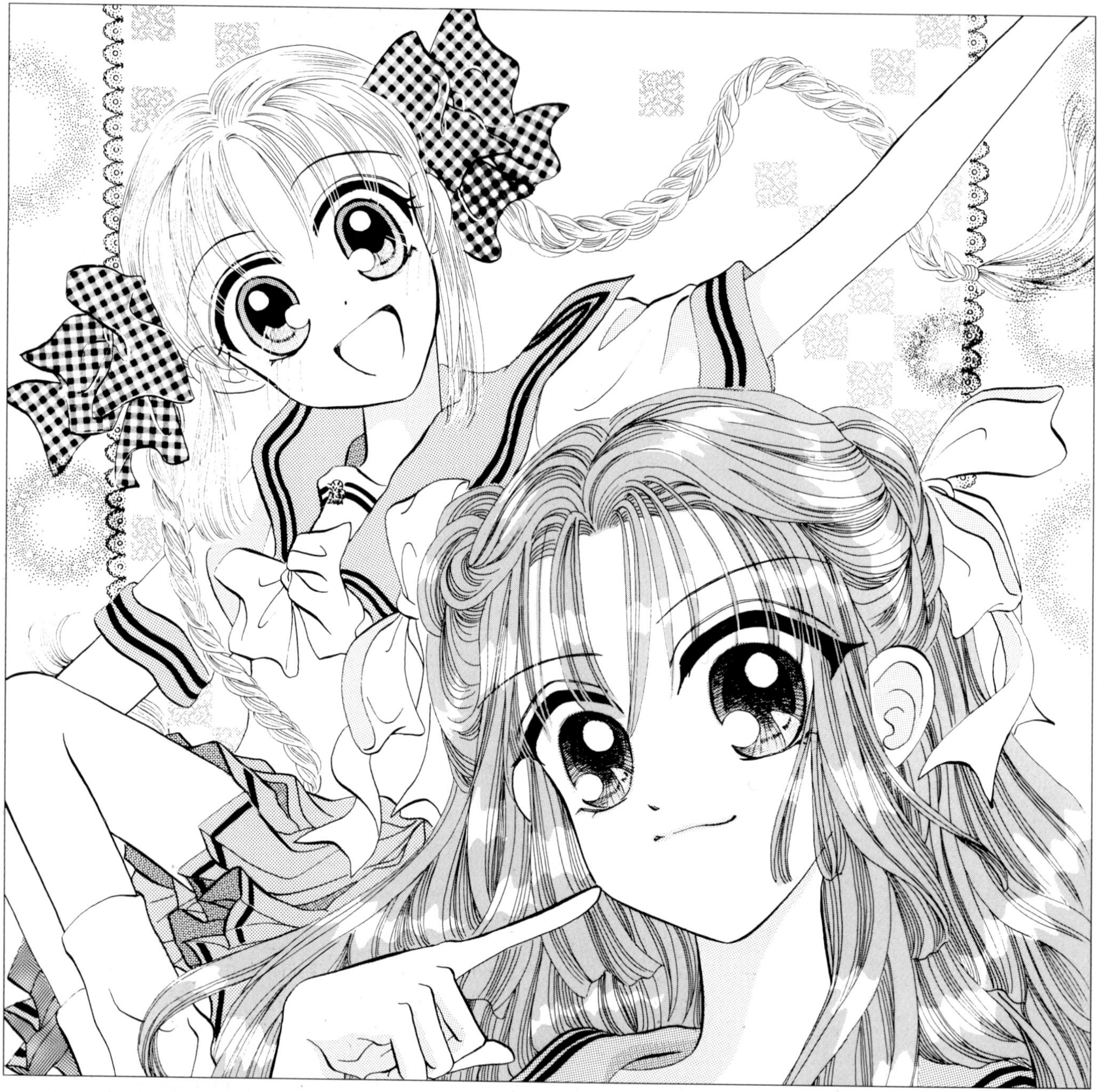

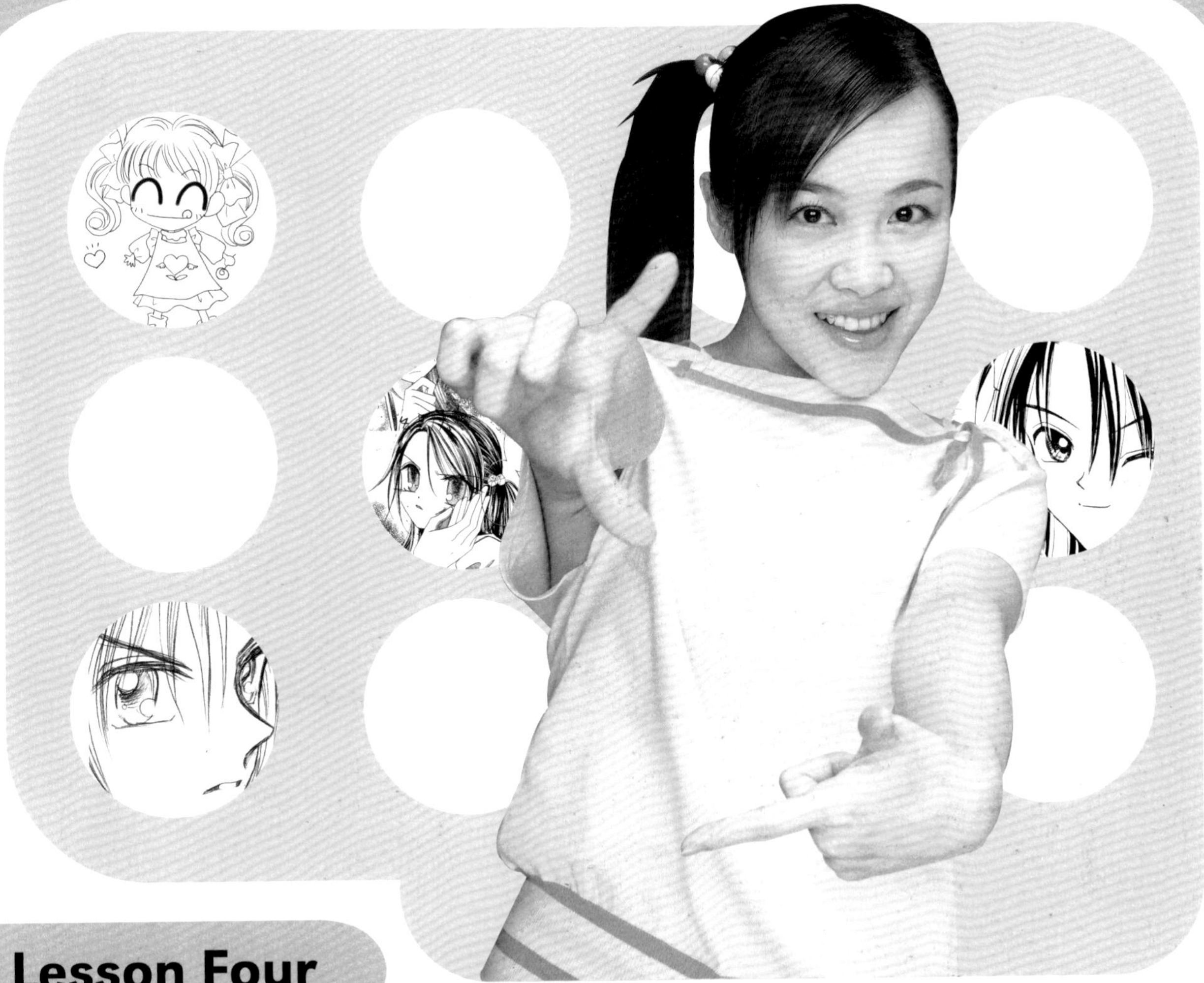

Lesson Four

Special Techniques for Manga Creators

Drawings are extensions of our thoughts and ideas. Because they express a subjective point of view, many artists develop specialized ways of achieving effects. In this lesson, I'll share some of my techniques with you. I hope this will be helpful to you in developing your own personal style.

 Hair Colors

Black-and-white manga characters can have different hair colors, too. But how do you differentiate hair colors in black and white?

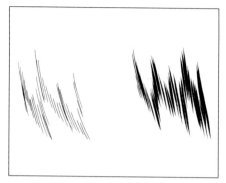

1-1
Drawing blond hair is actually similar to drawing black hair. It uses the same technique: a light touch for the first stroke and heavier pressure before you lift the pen away.

1-2
The difference is that when drawing blond hair, we don't need to use a brush. We can just use a round-nib pen or fine point pen to create the thin and soft texture of blond hair.

2
Now let's talk about hair color. If the color of your character's hair is dull or light (such as light brown, light gray or ginger), then you don't need to worry too much about coloring the hair with tone. Just use tone to show shadows.

3-1
If the character has shiny or dark hair (such as dark red, brown, gray or blue), apply a gray tone across all of their hair. The following are examples of tones often used for hair color.

3-2
If you don't want to darken the hair for fear that it will look too heavy, you can use very light tones. As long as the tone is applied across the whole head, the look is the same.

3-3
You can also use textured tones to create a variety of effects. The above example uses a heavier gradient tone.

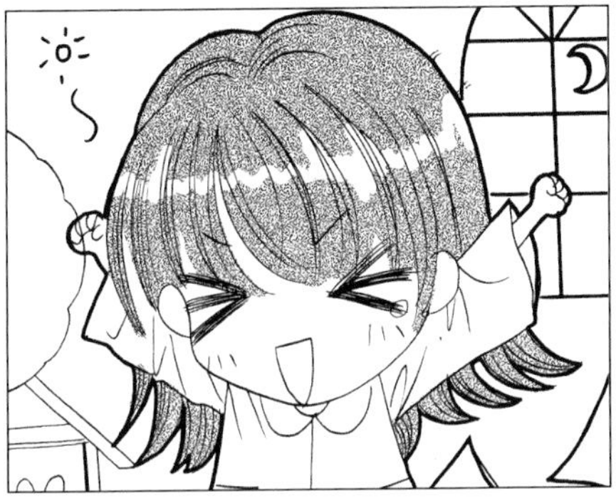

3–4 If you want the hair strands to stand out, try using a medium textured tone.

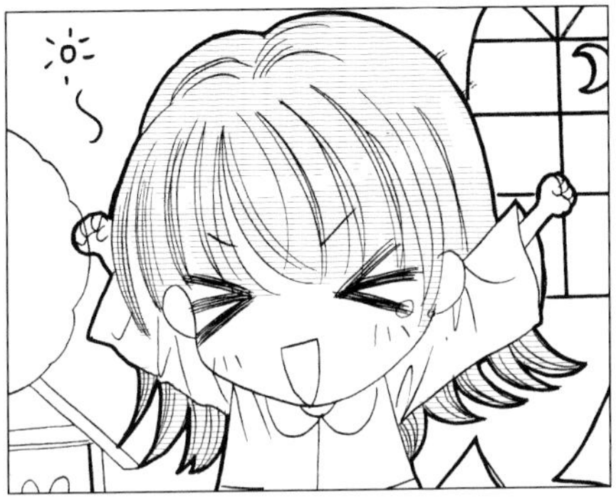

3–5 You can also choose something even lighter. But when trying out different tones, remember that whatever tone you use will tell a lot about what the character is feeling and who they are.

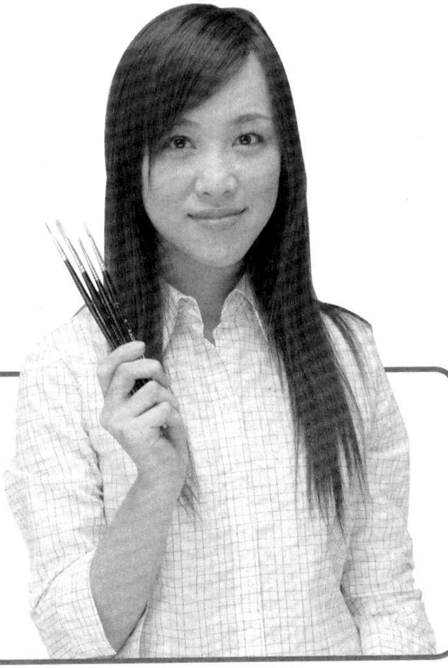

Friendly Reminder ★★★★★

No matter what your preference for hair color is, remember this: do not make everyone in your manga have the same hair color! When readers open to the first page, they immediately look for the most striking image. If the lead character has the same hair color as everyone else, he or she is going to be easily overlooked. So choose carefully!

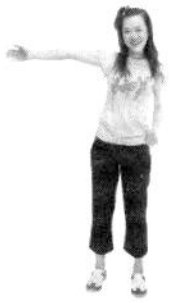

 Hairstyles

When we're creating our characters, we also create hairstyles that suit their personalities and the setting. But how do you create a hairstyle?

1 If you're drawing something contemporary, information on hairstyles is much easier to find. Bookstores carry lots of hairstyle magazines. You can also reference the hairstyles that models wear in fashion magazines.

2–1 Of course, you can always design your own hairstyle for a character.

2–2 For example, braids or buns look particularly well on a character who has a cute and innocent personality. Bright hair colors are also recommended for such characters.

2–3 If your character is charismatic, let his or her hair down. This is true for girl or boy characters! However, for boys, you'll also want to darken their hair color.

2–4 Doing something unexpected is another approach. Try giving your character a hairstyle from a different era. It will make your story more unique.

3–1 You can draw on a character's culture or ethnicity when designing a hairstyle. By including accessories unique to that culture, you can make your character more authentic.

3–2 As you can see in this example, a girl living in the middle ages or in a particular Chinese dynasty will wear her hair in a certain way.

3–3 Reference as many different hairstyles from as many different eras as possible. Also consider the attire and social status of your character. You'll be creating variations on basic styles before you know it!

3–4 If you get stumped, you can always default to the basic style of the era for a character of that given era and social status. It will still give your character depth and definition.

 **Friendly Reminder** ★ ★ ★ ★ ★

If you really like a certain time period, don't be afraid to showcase styles from that era in a story set in a different place and time. Use your imagination to wed the styles, and you'll create something entirely original. Your character will really stand out, plus, you'll be working on something that you really like.

Filling in Blacks and Coloring Dark Hair

I like to fill in all the blacks on a page at the same time, and that includes dark hair. But the two techniques are not exactly the same.

First Technique: Filling in Blacks

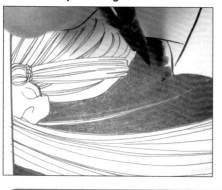  

In the paneling stage, mark off the large areas you plan to fill in with black ink. Use a small watercolor brush, a calligraphy brush or a black marker to color an area black. If you're filling in the area with black ink and you feel that the surface is not smooth enough, wait for it to dry, then apply a second layer—the surface will definitely be smoother after a second coat. When dipping your brush in ink, make sure that it's saturated but not dripping. That's the ideal amount of ink you need on your brush for smooth application. (On the other hand, if your brush is too dry, you're likely to make the area you're filling in look scratched and messy.)

Second Technique: Coloring Dark Hair

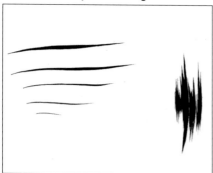  

1 If you want your character to have lustrous black hair, you need to be extra vigilant that the strokes you use create the proper line weight. How do you do that? Begin your brush stroke by lightly touching the surface of the paper, gradually adding pressure and then pulling away lightly. This is the key to making beautiful hair.

2 Apply the strokes in this manner to the character's hair.

3 The strokes you make must follow the natural arches and dips of the character's hair strands. This may seem difficult to do at first. But don't worry. You'll get better with practice!

Tips on Drawing Folds

1–1 Observe the folds in the character's clothing in this example. The places with the most complex folds are around a character's joints. The folds around other parts of the body/limbs are usually simpler.

1–2 In real life as in manga, clothing folds the most around joint areas, because this is where clothing gathers up. Pay special attention to these areas while drawing.

2–1 Different fabrics and textures will have different folds. For example, thick fabrics have fewer folds while thin fabrics have more.

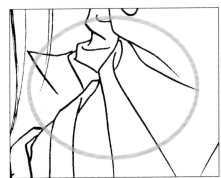

2–2 This example shows an era in which silk fabrics were commonly worn. Because silk is thin and supple, the folds in silk will be denser and longer. Illustrate that, and you'll capture the feel of silk.

3–1 Here's one way to show fabric folding. To illustrate scrunched-up fabric, use a line in the shape of a tilted "2."

3–2 Fabric folds over itself all the time. You can draw overlapping folds like this. You can also reference how other artists draw folds.

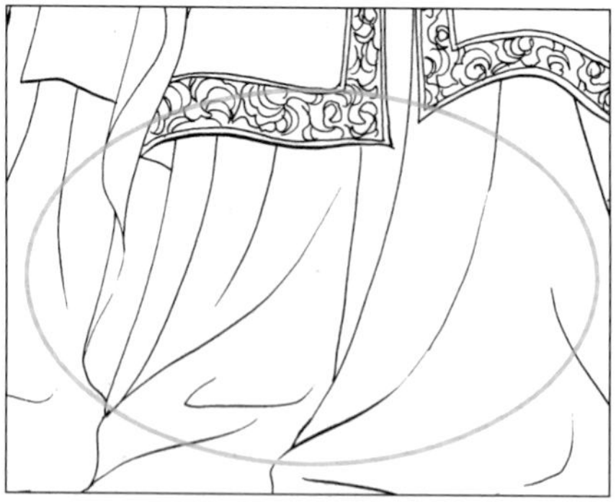

3–3 Large, simple folds can be drawn in this manner.

Friendly Reminder

There are many different techniques for drawing folds. Becoming familiar with how folds look and work in real life is the best way to get better at drawing them. In time, you'll be able to get the exact effect you want when it comes to folds. One of my editors once told me that it was okay to keep it simple, too—if you're having difficulty, just employ the basic lines and keep it simple. That way, at least your drawing will look clean.

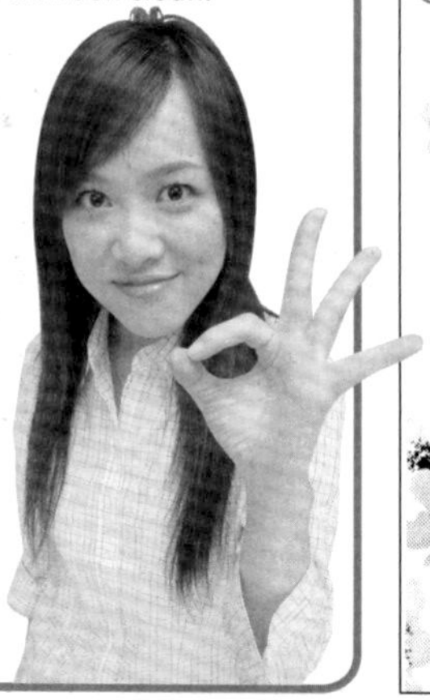

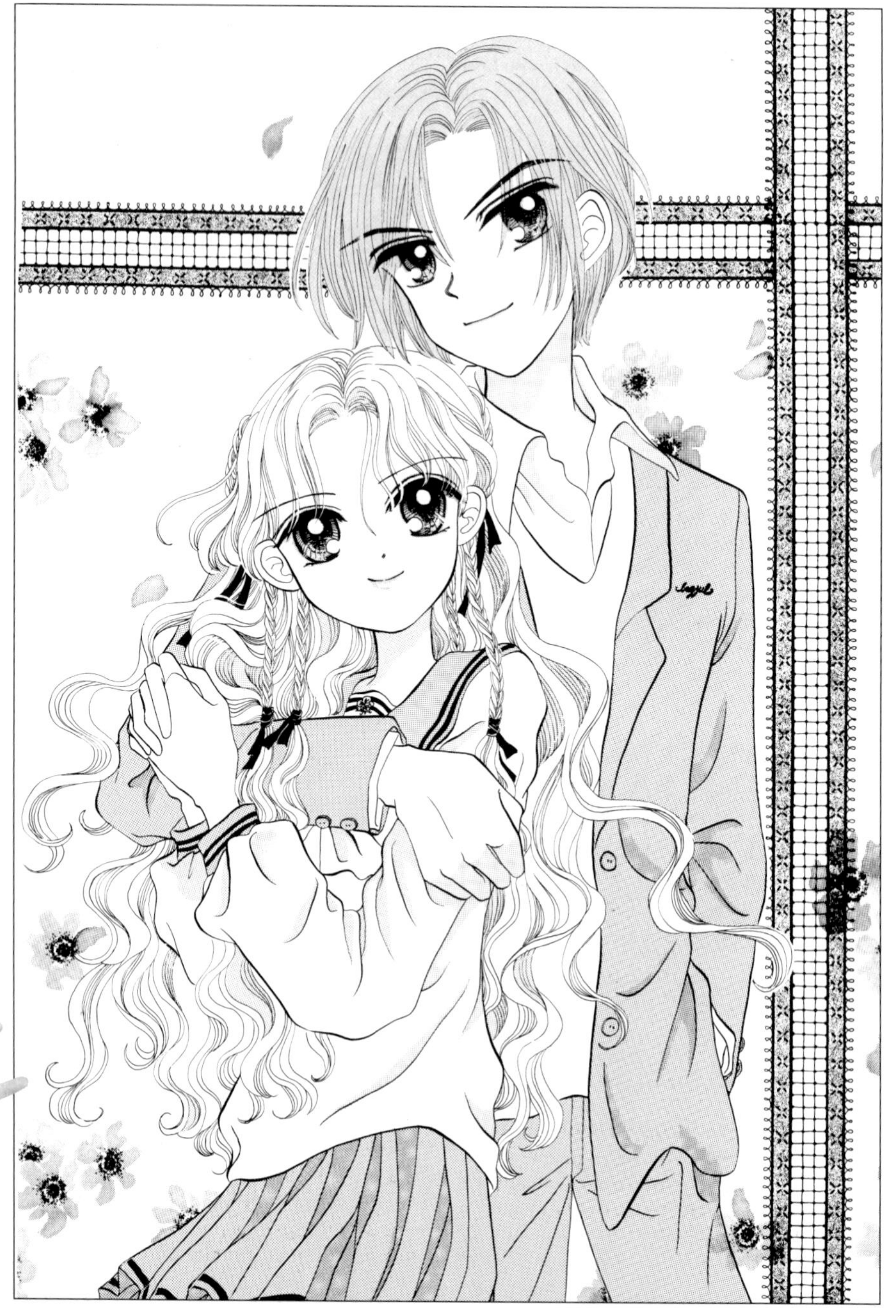

Texture and Tones

Because tones can be used to indicate different shades of gray, we can use different tones and scraping techniques to indicate a variety of fabric textures as well.

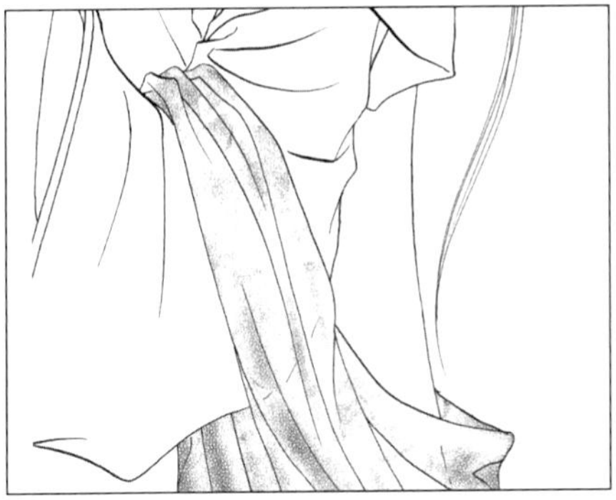

1–1 Tones that are too dark or too heavy are not suited for gauze-like fabrics. For these fabrics, make the highlighted areas as light as possible and that will decrease the overall weight of the fabric.

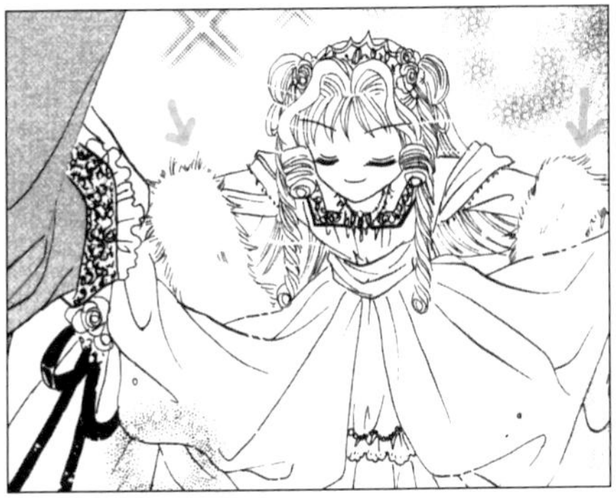

1–2 Fur or knits are often used as accessories. Defining the shapes of these items is often more important than toning them.

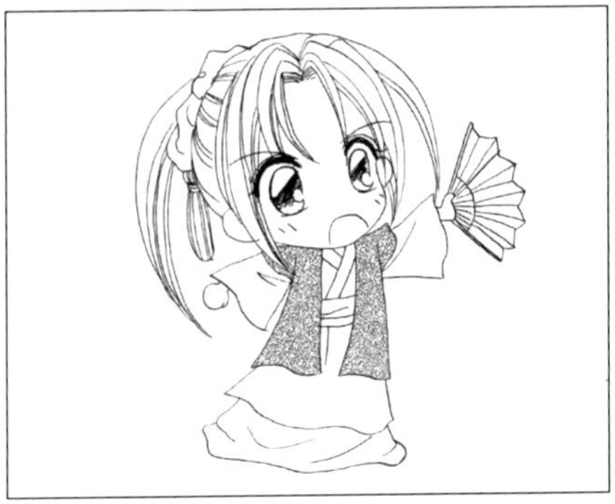

2–1 When it comes to thick fabrics, use sandy textured tones. They have a fuzzy effect and make the clothes look warmer. Darker sand tones are especially good for winter clothes.

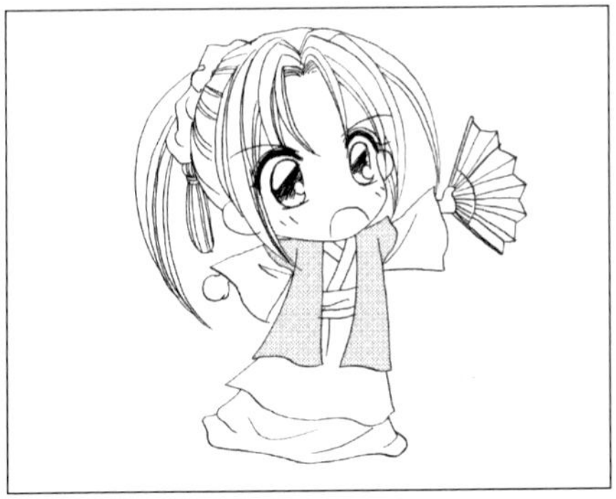

2–2 Regular dot patterns, or layered dot patterns, are good for lighter clothes, such as shirts or summer clothes. They make the clothes look light and airy.

Think About It

Replicating the looks of real fabrics is quite difficult in black and white. You have to make special efforts to draw your lines to indicate how soft or stiff the fabric is. The contours of a silk shirt would be drawn very differently from those of a wool sweater.

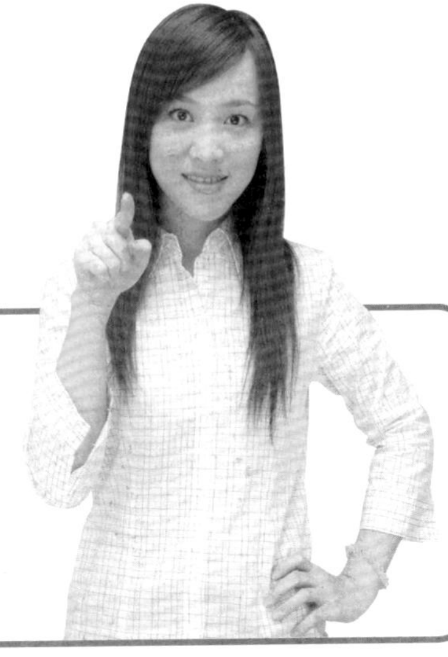

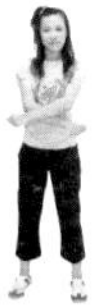

Facial Expressions

Facial expressions are very important in manga. If you want to express the emotional journey your character is going on, then you'll need to know how to draw a variety of facial expressions.

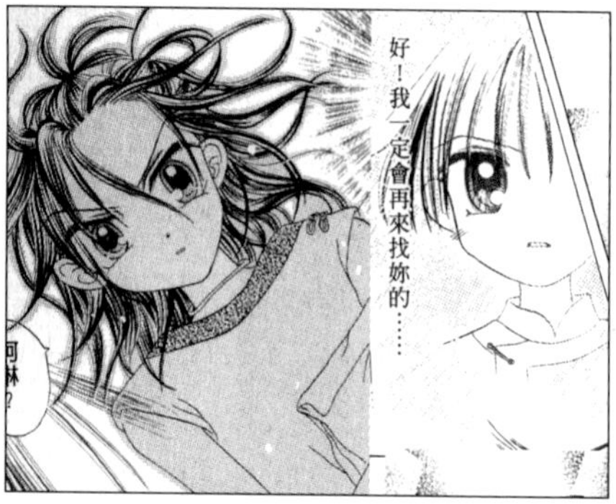
好！我一定會再來找妳的……

1 Every artist develops their own way of illustrating characters' emotions and that's their style. That's why there can be many different ways of drawing the same emotions. But there are some basic rules. If you're trying to make your character look happy, don't put on a long face. Try to be happy yourself and extend that happiness to your character.

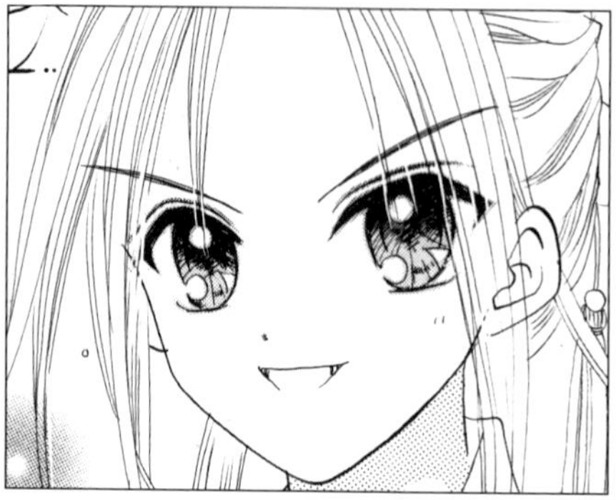

2–1 Happy eyes can be wide open or squinty. A happy mouth can be laughing aloud or making other cute expressions.

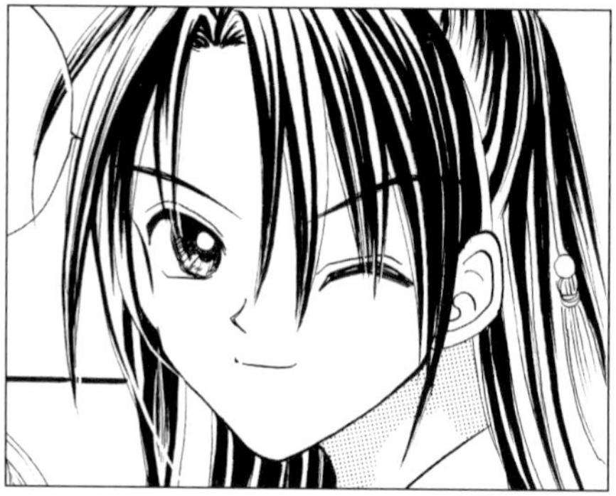

2–2 Doesn't a cute character look even more attractive when winking?

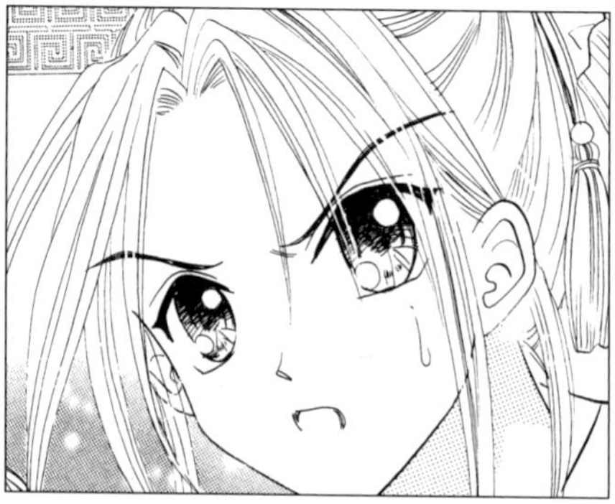

3–1 The eyes, eyebrows and mouth are especially important when trying to make a character look mad.

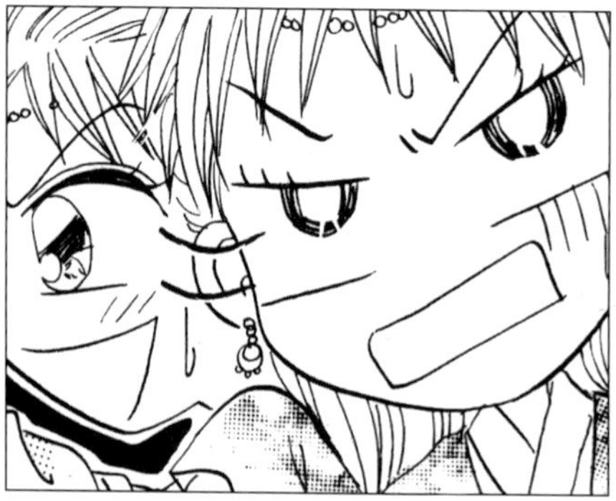

3–2 Angry eyes should look particularly focused and glaring. That way, at least people will take your character seriously.

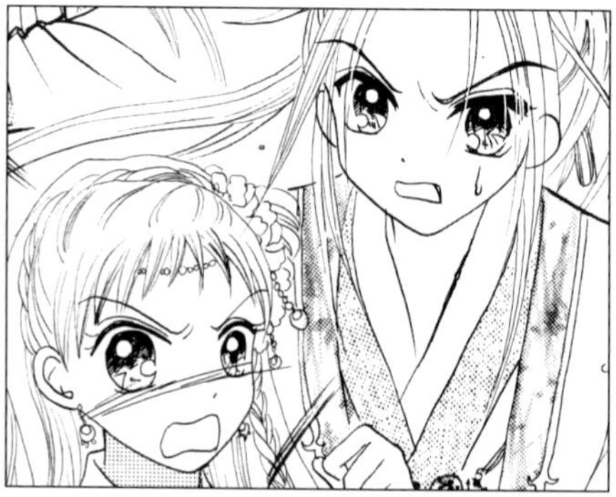

3–3 Manga employs some visual shorthand to tell the reader about the character's emotions. For example, add some "blush" lines to make a character look flushed.

4-1 A sad expression is the opposite of an angry one. Instead of making the eyebrows go up, make them go down. The eyes should look innocent or unfocused. Of course, the mouth has to look sad as well; the character can perhaps wear a bitter or forced smile. Anyhow, no happy faces allowed!

4-2 Sadness, like any emotion, can also be enhanced by gestures.

4-3 To get your point across, combine gestures, facial expressions and an animated mouth (such as one in the shape of a scream).

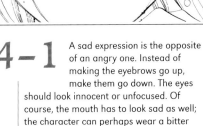

5-1 A happy character makes a happy reader. Don't hesitate to make the character look as happy as possible if you want to make your readers feel the same.

5-2 Chibi versions are great for expressing joy and happiness because the character's features are so exaggerated. If ecstatic joy is what you're aiming for, try drawing a chibi version.

5-3 Some forms of happiness are a bit silly and shy, but they can still make your readers smile!

5-4 You can laugh with your mouth closed. This indicates an effort to hold in the laugh (which often results in "happy pangs").

5-5 You can also laugh with your mouth wide open. This indicates an uninhibited burst of joy. Choose the effect you want to achieve depending on your character's personality.

Friendly Reminder ★ ★ ★ ★ ★

I think the best part about drawing manga is getting to create different expressions for your characters. When you're trying to make your character look a certain way, you'll end up looking that way, too. For example, when you're drawing a happy character, you'll notice that you have a smile on your face as well. It's a very fascinating process. That's why I sometimes end up spending lots of my time creating expressions. Try it and see if it's the same for you!

Manga Character Proportions

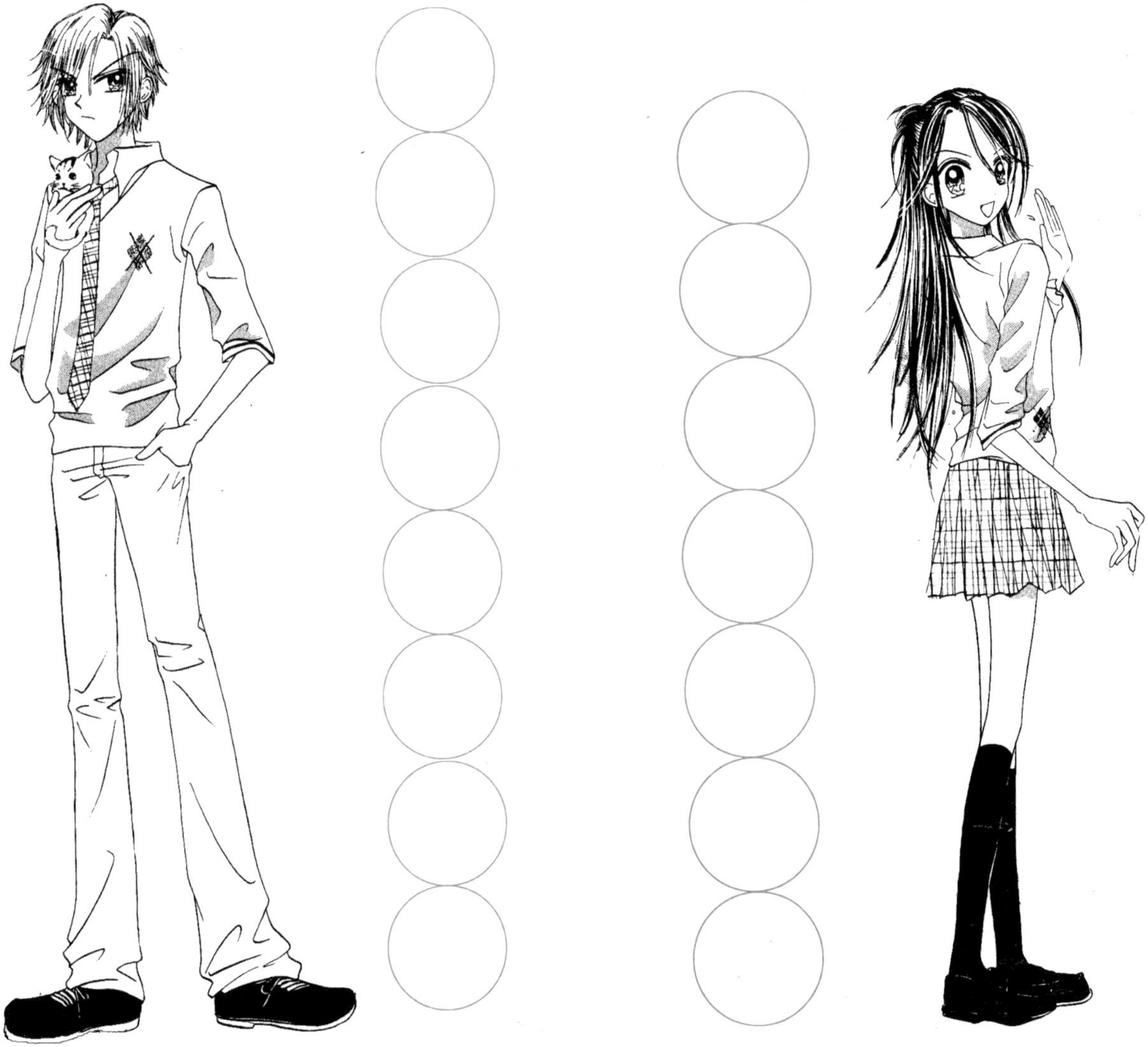

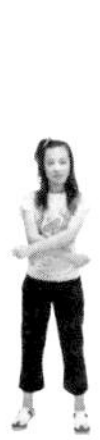

1 Guys: the 8-head principle (1:7). Girls: the 7-head principle (1:6).
Don't worry if you're not familiar with human proportions. Use the general principle of making your characters 7 or 8 heads tall, and your character will have the right proportions for shojo manga.

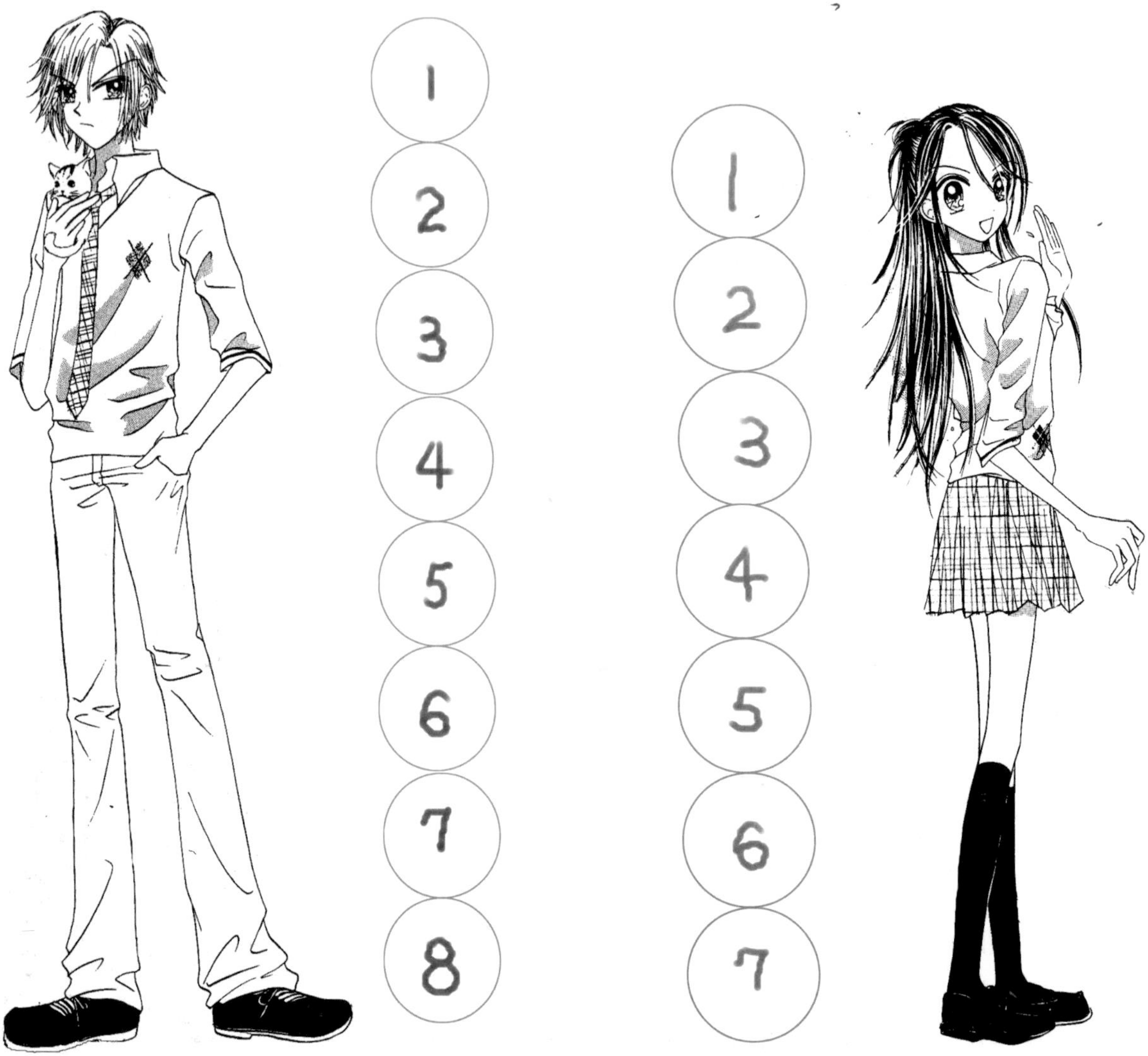
1
2
3
4
5
6
7
8
1
2
3
4
5
6
7

2 Use the head of the character as a unit of measurement. If you stacked 7of her heads on top of each other, you'd get the height of a girl. If you stacked 8 of his heads, you'd end up with the height of a guy.

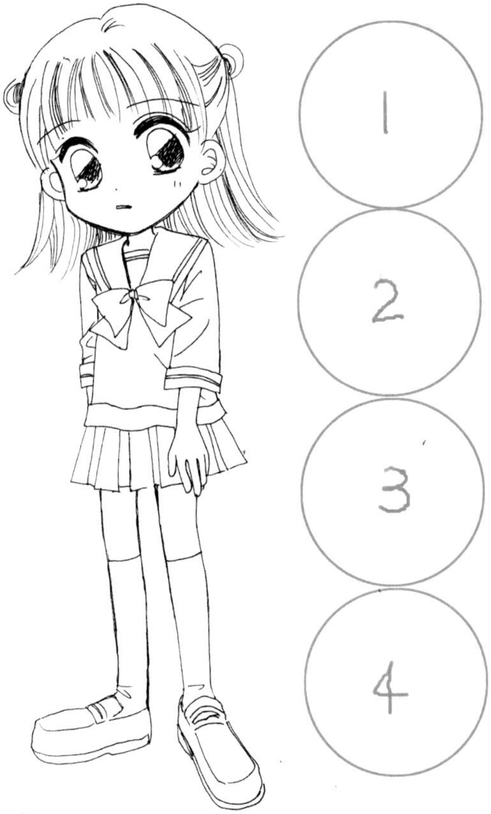
1
2
3
4

3 The proportions of children are different. Because a child's head is usually slightly bigger, they're only about 4-5 heads tall. The exact number depends on the age of the child.

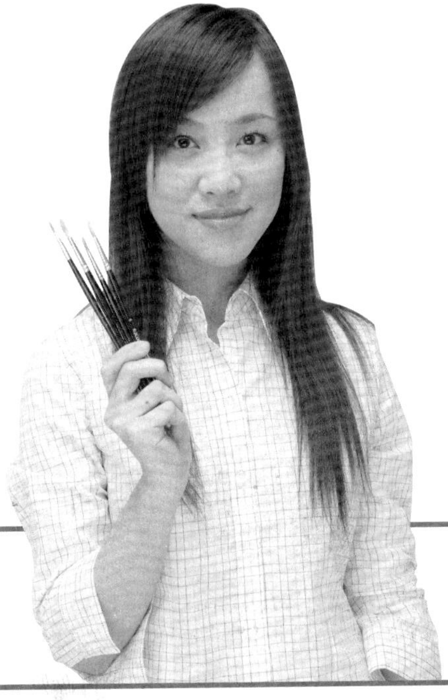

Helpful Hint

You can always sketch out the required number of circles before you draw your character to make sure they're proportional.

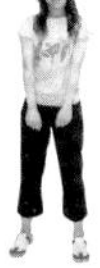

Human Proportions – The Wooden Mannequin

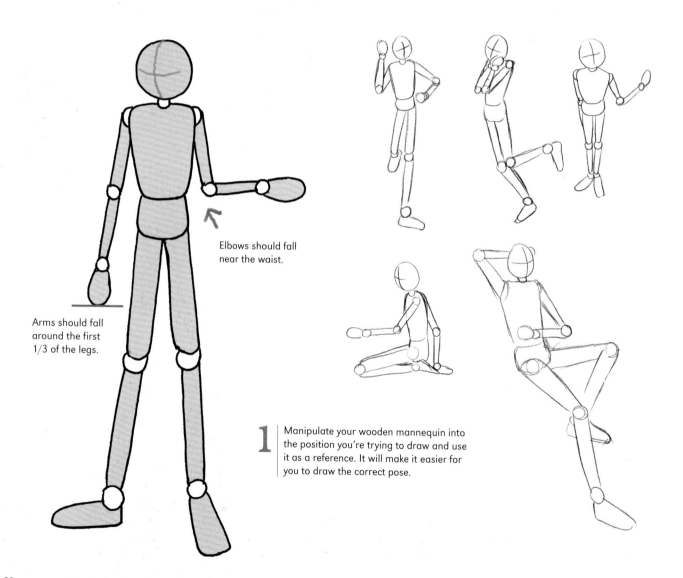

Elbows should fall near the waist.

Arms should fall around the first 1/3 of the legs.

1 | Manipulate your wooden mannequin into the position you're trying to draw and use it as a reference. It will make it easier for you to draw the correct pose.

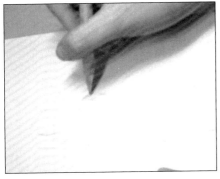

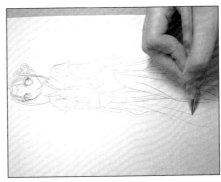

2 | Obeying human proportions, use circles or ovals to sketch the pose you want.

3 | Add contours and details onto the rough sketch.

4 | After all the details are added, erase the circles or ovals you used to outline the proportions.

Remember to practice your proportions!

Friendly Reminder ✳ ✳ ✳ ✳ ✳

Observe the gestures and postures of people around you. Train yourself to simplify complicated movements into proportional sketches. This will help improve your accuracy when it comes to drawing the right proportions.

Chibi Versions

Chibi versions usually follow the 2-head or 3-head principle. But as long as you think it looks cute, you can use any size you want.

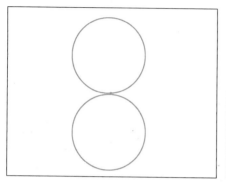

1 Use circles to indicate the proportions you want.

2 Draw the details. And since you're reducing normal proportions from 7-8 heads to 1-2 heads, I suggest that you draw stubby versions of the limbs, too. The characters will look even cuter that way.

3 This is an example of an extremely fun and distorted character: super big head, super tiny body.

4 If you'd like even more exaggeration, you can try drawing proportions of 1:0.5 or something even more dramatic.

Chibi Expressions Mix 'n' Match

Now that we've gone over the proportions of a chibi, we can have a lot of fun mixing and matching different chibi expressions. But how does this mix 'n' match game work? Let's give it a try.

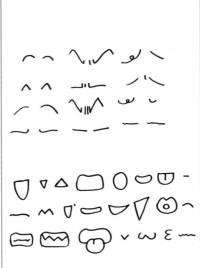

1 Draw a bunch of different chibi expressions: happy, sad, angry, you name it. Here I've drawn all sorts of chibi eyes.

2 Next, try drawing all kinds of eyebrows and mouths. The key to drawing chibi versions is exaggeration. Don't try to be realistic. Who knows? You might come up with something that's one-of-a-kind!

3 Last, draw all kinds of chibi versions of items and effects. Every artist has their own chibi style. For example, I don't draw the nose when I do chibi versions. That's why you don't see any here.

4–1 Now that we have our different categories of chibi expressions to choose from, we can start putting them on our chibi character.

4–2 Choose a pair of eyes, a mouth and an emotional effect, and you'll be able to create many different funny expressions.

4–3 If we choose a pair of smiley McDonald's eyes and a mouth with a tip of the tongue sticking out, doesn't our character look like she saw something yummy to eat?

4–4 Add some simple effects near the eyes, mouth and in the background. They'll add a whole new dimension to the picture.

4–5 Even crying looks livelier when you can mix 'n' match. So experiment as often as you can. You might never be able to stop!

Helpful Hint

Seriously, try out different combinations of expressions. There's no limit to what you can do in manga. If you have fun drawing, your drawings will look fun, too. So give it a try!

Composition

You don't necessarily need to show the whole face when you want to communicate a certain emotional effect. Sometimes just showing parts of the face is even more effective. The following four examples illustrate the different ways to express tension.

…?

1 A frontal shot directly communicates the character's emotions.

我已經說得夠明白了。

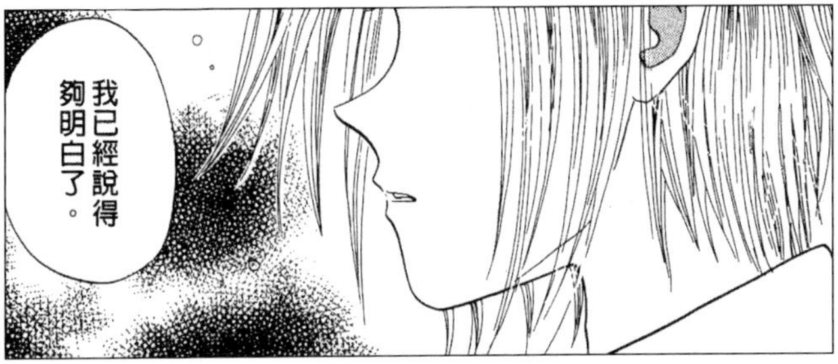

2 Though you can only see part of the face, you can still feel the tension.

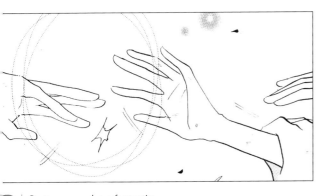

3 Gestures are also a fantastic way to express emotions.

哼

4 Emotions can be expressed by a gaze, too. There's a lot of emotions to observe, and it helps to know how one emotion changes into another. Watch what happens in real life and observe how other artists express emotions and you'll have your footing when it comes to bringing your characters' emotional lives to life!

Where the Characters Are Looking

READ R TO L

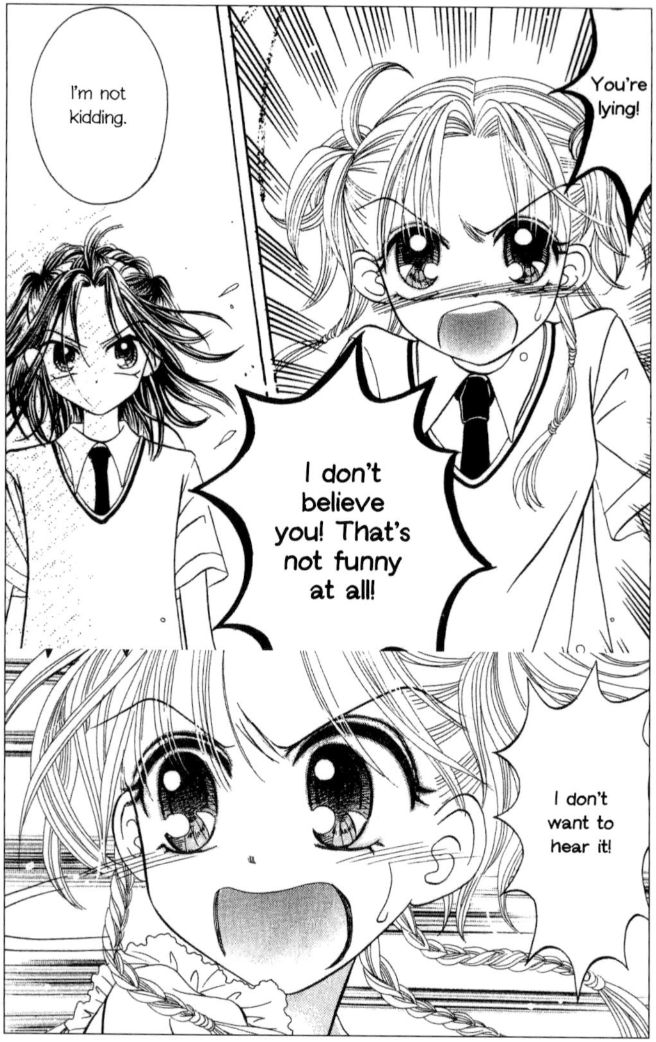
You're lying!
I don't believe you! That's not funny at all!
I'm not kidding.
I don't want to hear it!

1 When you read a manga, do you feel yourself feeling sad when the character's sad and happy when the character's happy? This is what we call empathy. As manga artists, fostering this is our goal; we want our readers to feel what our characters are feeling.

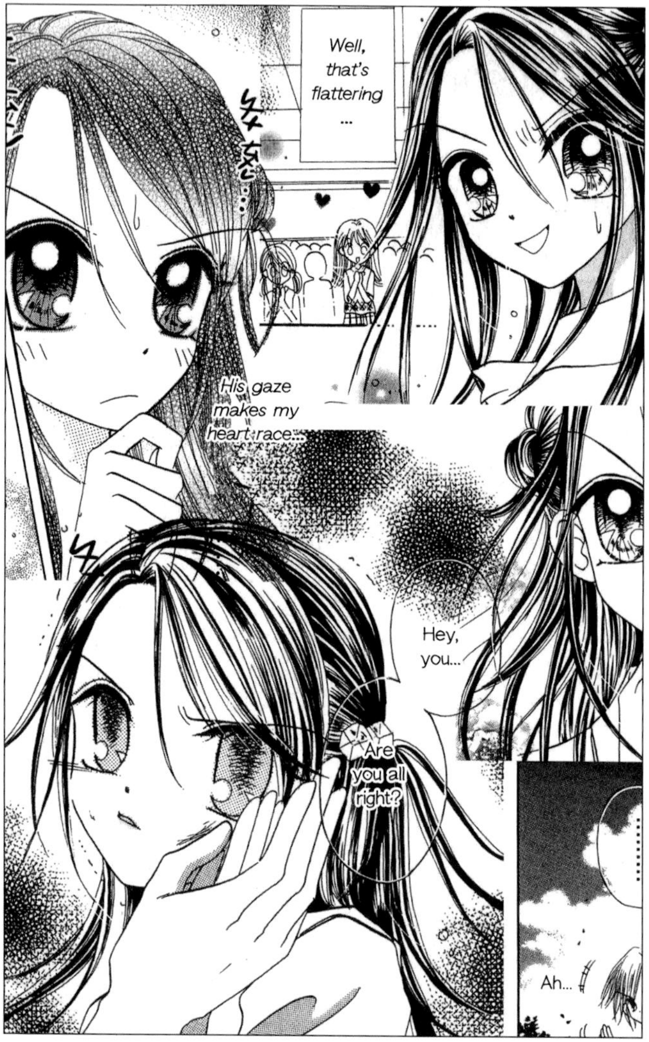
Well, that's flattering ...
His gaze makes my heart race...
Hey, you...
Ah...
Are you all right?

2 Where the characters are looking and the nature of their gaze defines the mood of the story.

Compare these two examples. The drawings are almost the same, except the character is looking in different directions. One of them is looking at the reader. This makes all the difference.

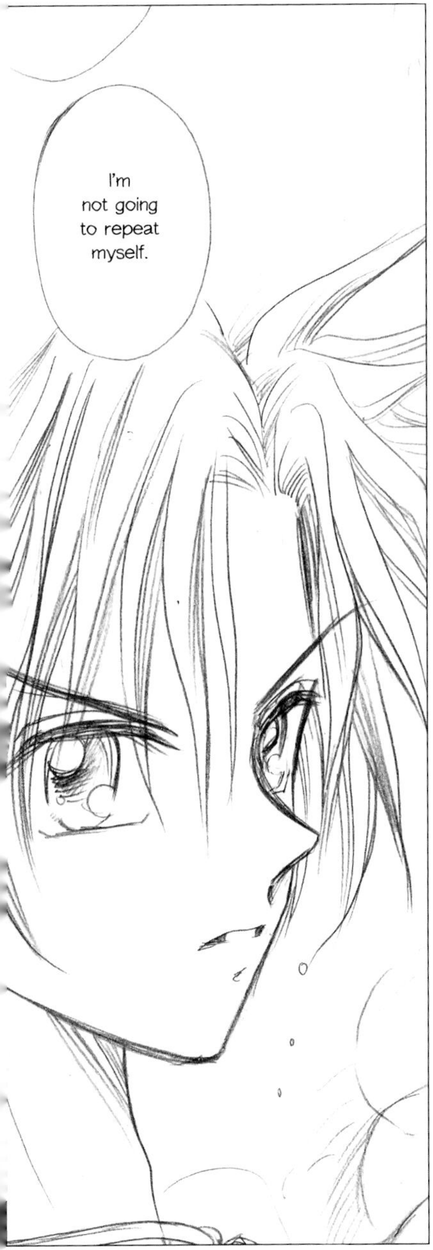
I'm not going to repeat myself.

3 | Looking directly at the reader.

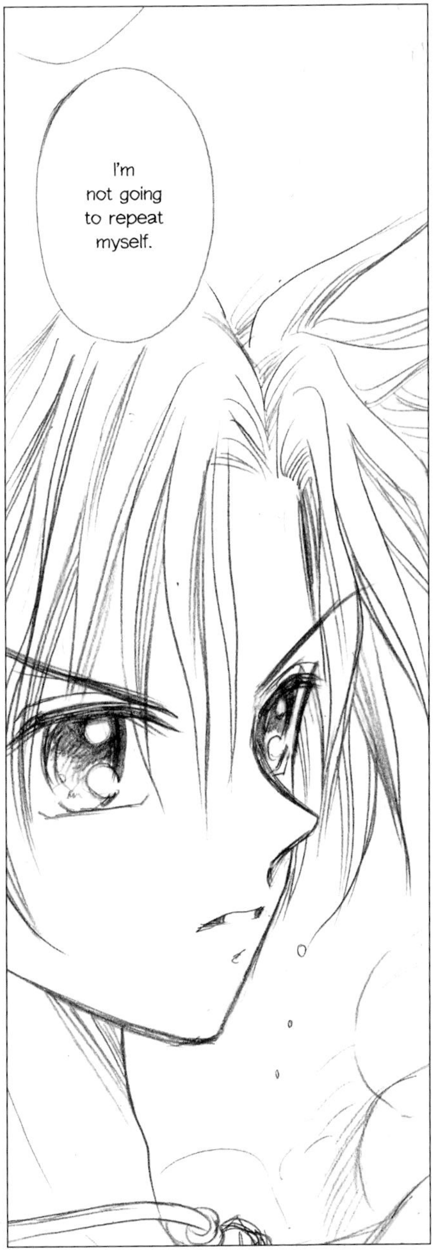
I'm not going to repeat myself.

4 | Looking somewhere else.

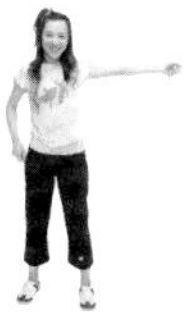

Drawing Backgrounds

We've finished inking and shading the drawing with tones. The image is nearly complete. But sometimes it isn't enough to fill a background with screentone. Sometimes you need a real setting. Let's look at how to do that.

1 Perspective, simply speaking, is a method used to recreate a three-dimensional image on paper.

2 If the lines of a building were to continue into space, you'd notice how they'd converge at a single point. You can try this out by looking at a photograph.

3 The point at which all the lines converge is called the vanishing point.

4 You already know that things look smaller the farther away they get from you, right? Well, then you won't be surprised to learn they vanish at the vanishing point.

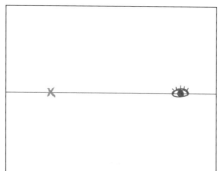

5 These are the basic rules for perspective drawing. Draw an eye on a piece of blank paper. Draw a horizontal line traveling through the eye. Choose a point on the line to be the vanishing point. Now we're going to do a little exercise.

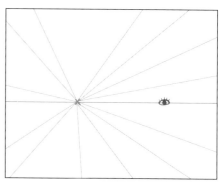

6–1 Draw some trajectory lines radiating from the vanishing point. Think of what you would like to place along those lines. Notice the sense of depth.

This looks a bit difficult...

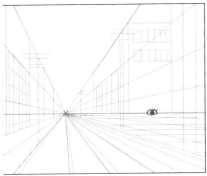

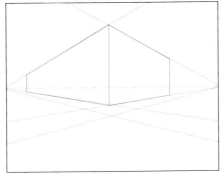

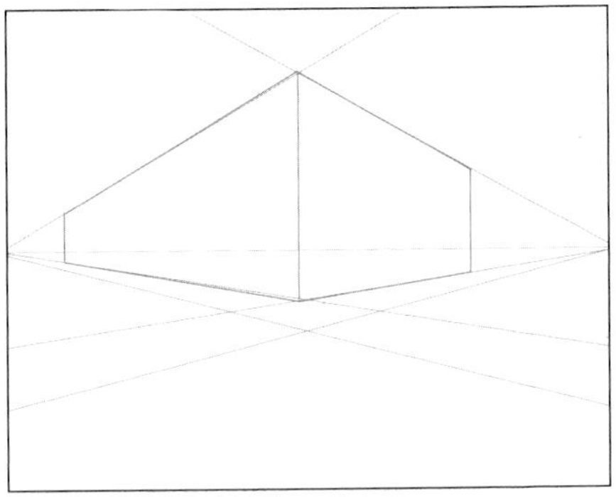

6–2 Draw some vertical lines against the horizontal ones. Now you can accurately render the distance of objects when drawing. Just keep in mind that objects become smaller and more crowded as they recede into the vanishing point; they become bigger and more spaced out as they come closer to you. You can use this principle to construct even more complicated perspective drawings.

7–1 2-point and 3-point perspective drawings follow the same principle. Besides creating your own background by following the perspective principle, you can also draw your background from a real photo or picture.

7–2 3-point perspective drawings are often used for buildings or to emphasize the authority of a character. This technique will not only make your image more powerful, but also more realistic.

Friendly Reminder

Background settings seem to be so difficult to draw and complicated to understand. We just draw manga. We're not architects or landscapers. How can we learn to draw backgrounds better? Well, even though we're not experts, we can still do our best to observe and gather information.

Drawing Backgrounds from Photos

1 Use a copy machine to make A4 or B4 copies of the photo you want to use for the background. You'll want this image to be as large as possible, that way it will look better when the size is reduced. Make copies that are clear and well-defined. No smudged or dark copies!

2 Take the copy and use a dark pen to retrace any lines that didn't come out clearly.

3 Just like with inking, put the copy on the light table and use a 0.05-0.3 fine point pen to trace the photo.

4 After you're finished, you'll be able to use this background over and over again.

Helpful Hint ★ ★ ★ ★ ★

When trying to draw a complicated building or setting, use a fine tip pen, such as a round-nib pen. If you're not used to drawing with a dip pen, you can also use a 0.05 felt tip pen. Remember to be patient! Pay attention to the angle between the ruler and the pen. If it's not kept at a 45 degree angle, your drawing risks getting very messy. Beware!

Points of Emphasis

READ R TO L

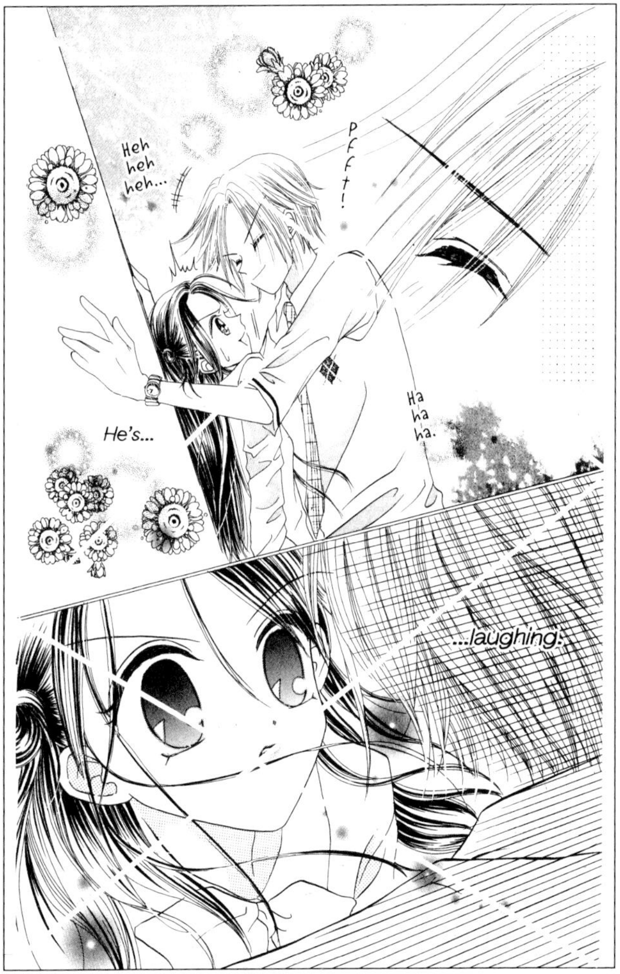
Pffft!
Heh heh heh...
Ha ha ha.
He's...
...laughing.

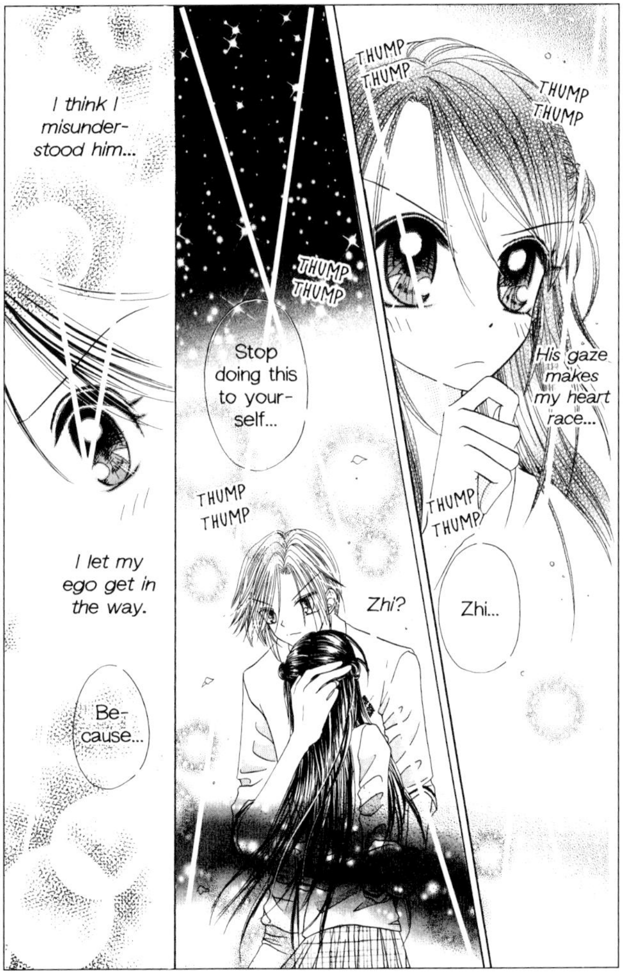
THUMP THUMP
THUMP THUMP
His gaze makes my heart race...
THUMP THUMP
Zhi...
THUMP THUMP
Stop doing this to your-self...
THUMP THUMP
Zhi?
I think I misunder-stood him...
I let my ego get in the way.
Be-cause...

1 The point of emphasis is not a difficult concept to grasp. Pick up any manga and turn to any page. Draw two diagonal lines originating from the corners of a panel. The point where the two lines intersect is the point of emphasis. That area is where you're trying to draw your reader's attention to.

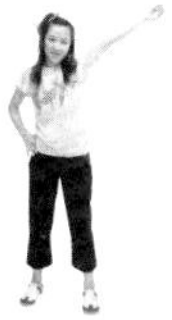

READ R TO L

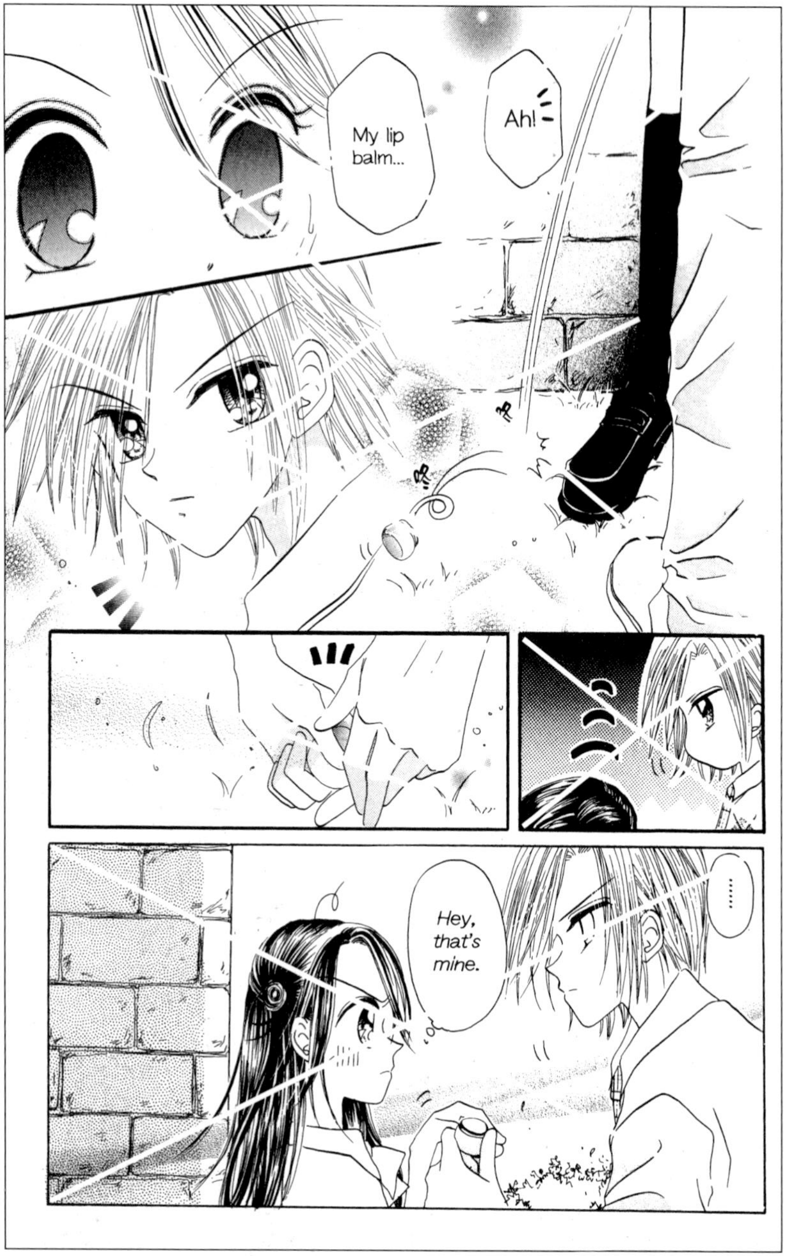
Ah!
My lip balm...
……
Hey, that's mine.

2 Take a look at the example on the left. The point of emphasis might not be a character or their eyes. It could be an object, a gaze or even dialogue.

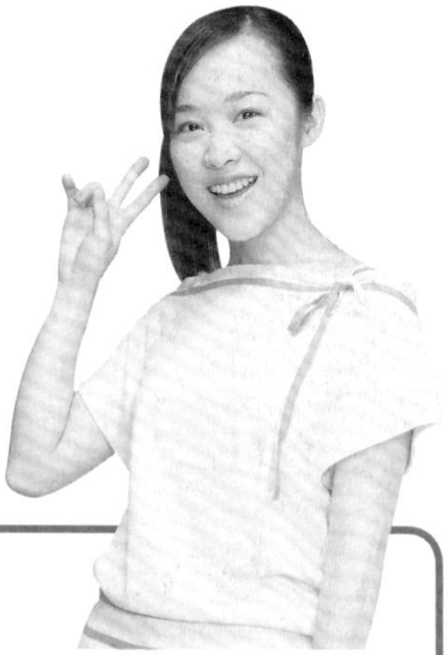

Helpful Hint

Anything can be your point of emphasis. It's whatever the artist wants to emphasize in a particular panel. It's what sets the mood of the panel and what readers see first when they come to the panel. Strung together, they form a complete manga story. So it's essential to plan how your story will progress through the points of emphasis.

Hand-Drawn Text Effects

Most dialogue and sound effect text in manga are typed. But sometimes you can use hand-drawn text effects to express emotions, too.

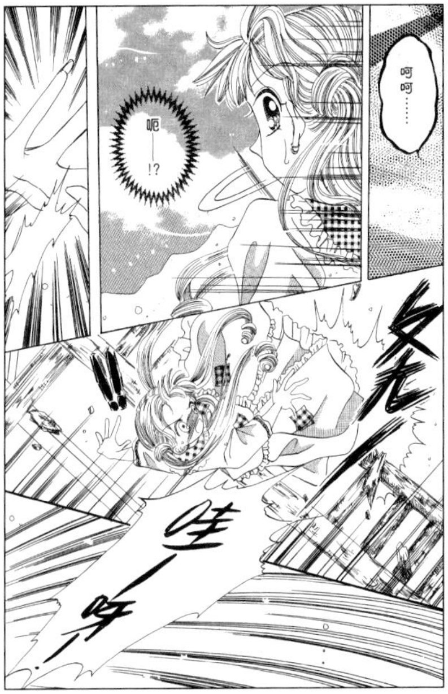
呵呵……
呃——!?

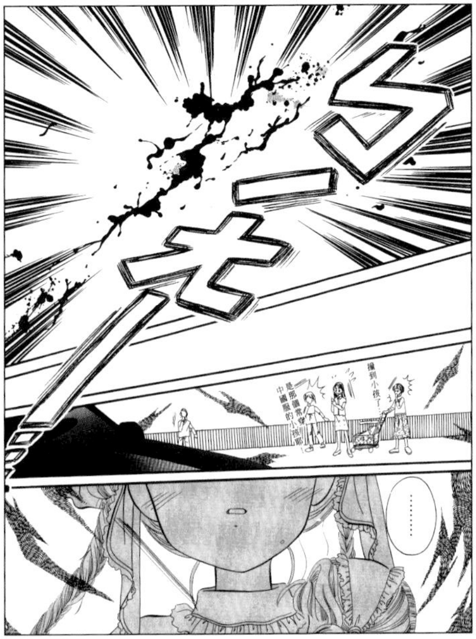
……

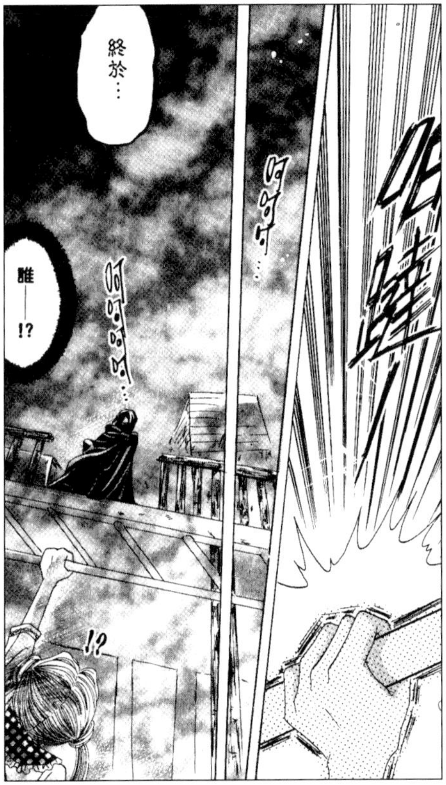
終於……
呵呵呵……
呵呵呵呵……
誰——!?
!?

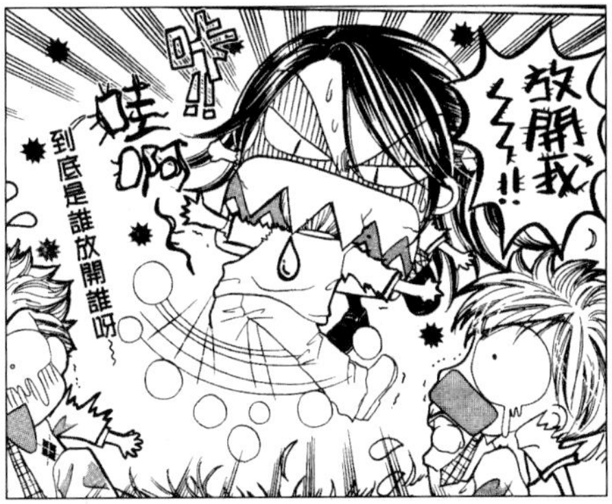
放開我~~!!
哇啊
到底是誰放開誰呀~~

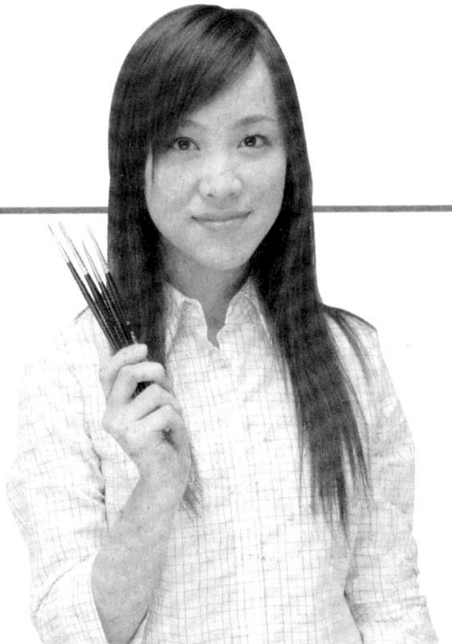

Helpful Hint

I'm sure you've noticed while reading manga that the line between text and art is a thin one. Sometimes typed text can't express the kind of emotions expressed by artistic hand-drawn text effects. So in some instances, you can consider using hand-drawn effects to best describe a sound or emphasize the mood behind a sentence. Compare the difference between hand-drawn text and typed text in these example pages. What effect do each have on the reader? Consider which one best achieves the effect you want for a particular scene.

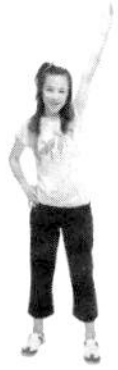

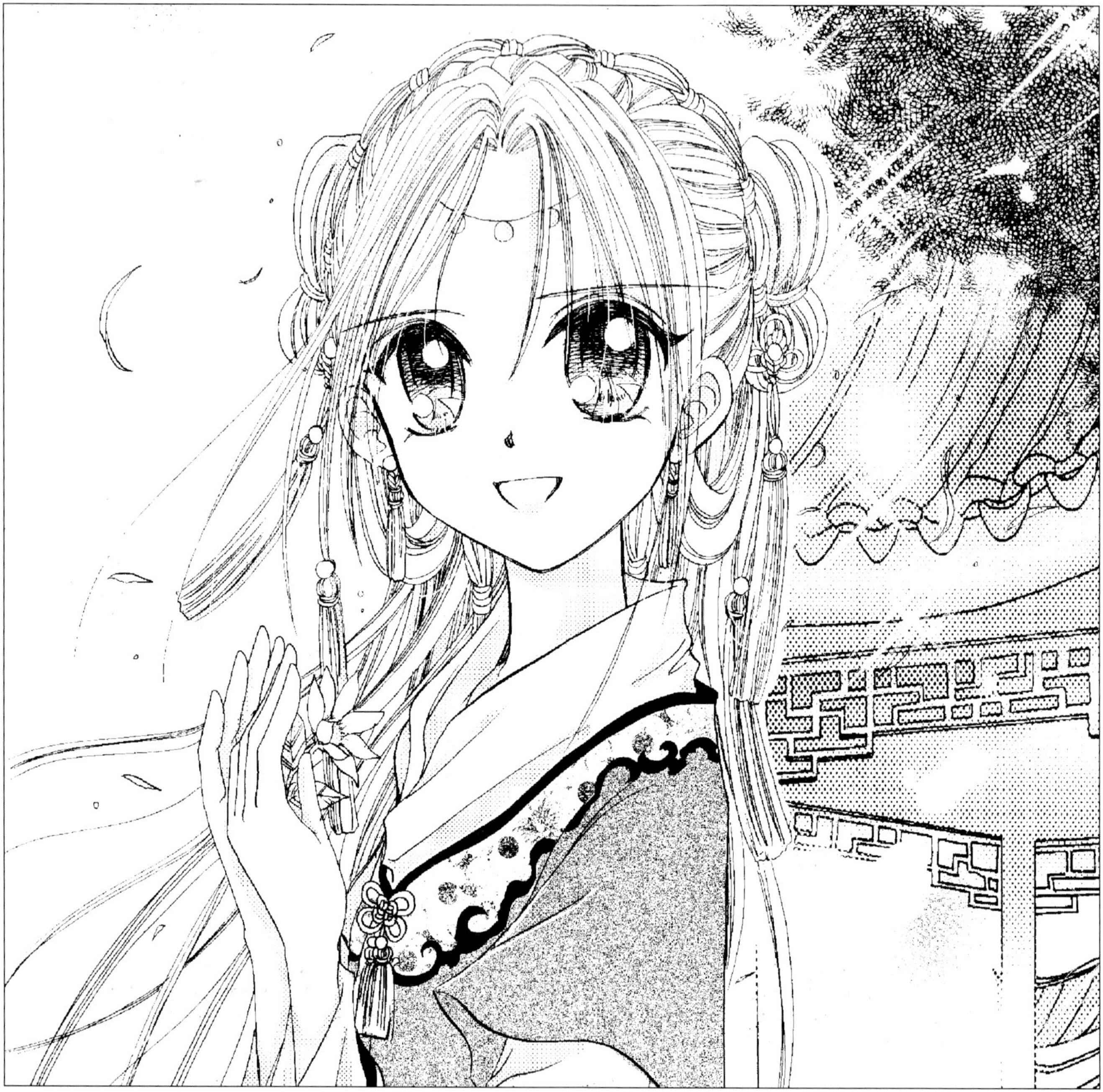

Lesson Five

Coloring

We're going to enter the world of color now. Who doesn't want to see their manga come to life in color? But how do we color our drawings? Actually, coloring your characters is very much like putting make-up on them. Just like with putting on make-up, experimentation and practice is key. Looks like you'll learn both the principles of make-up and how to brush on color at the same time. Convenient, isn't it? Now let me show you how.

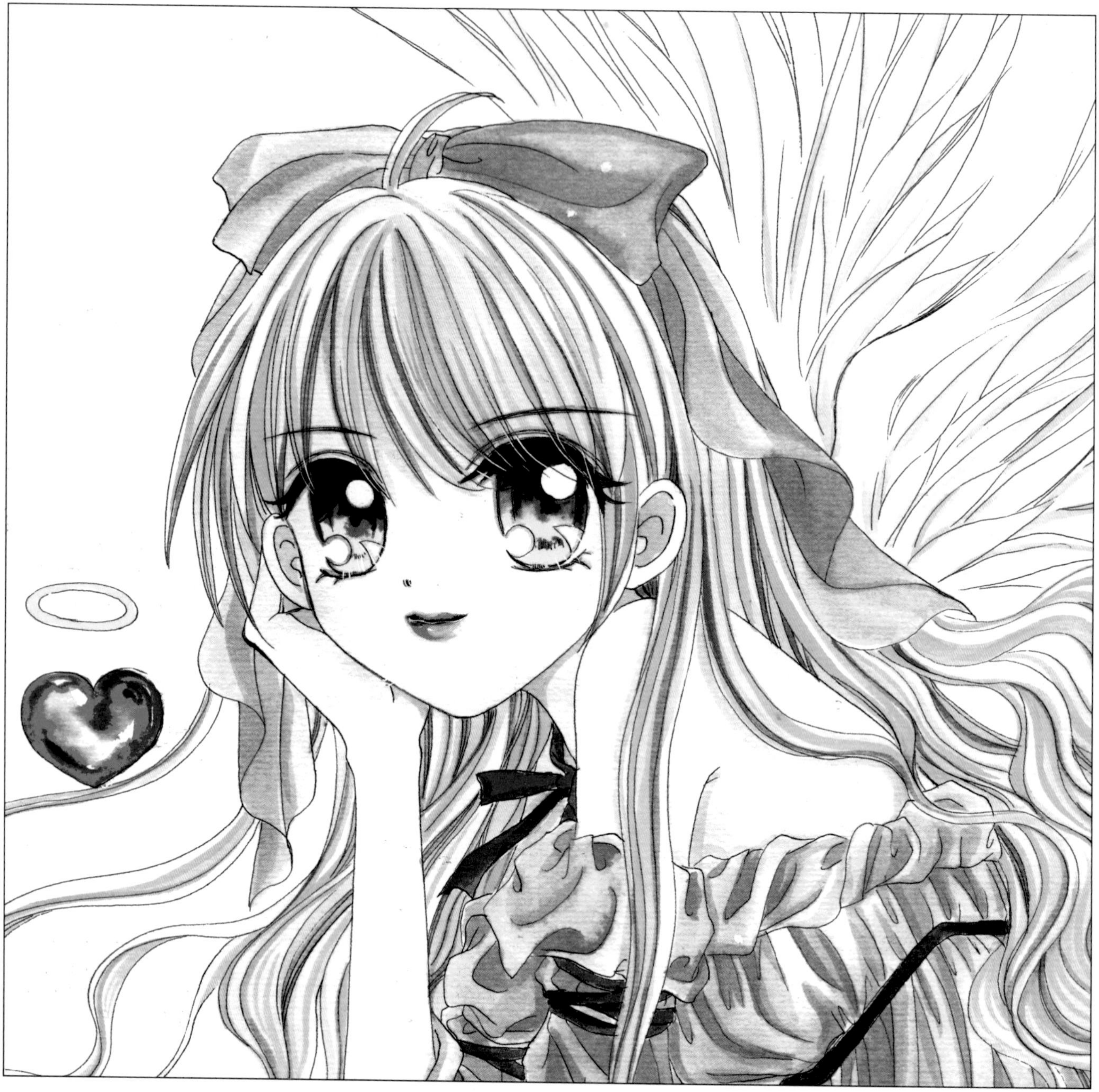

Preparation

Take a look at the colored picture on the left. In the following pages, I'll show you the steps I took to complete it.

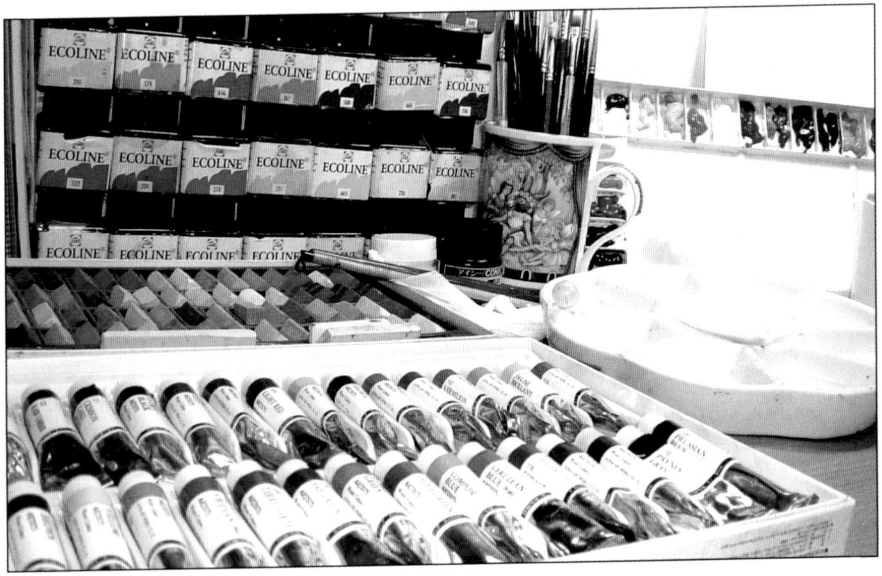
ECOLINE

(1) Assorted brushes (2) Transparent watercolor (3) Colored ink (4) Black water-resistant ink (5) Dip pen, round-nib (6) Palette (7) Container for rinsing brushes (8) Eye dropper (9) White correction fluid (10) Watercolor paper (11) Paper towels or a cloth

Make sure that the kind of paint you choose to color with is somewhat transparent, like watercolor ink, otherwise it will cover up your inked lines. Once you have all the tools and materials ready, you can start coloring your manga.

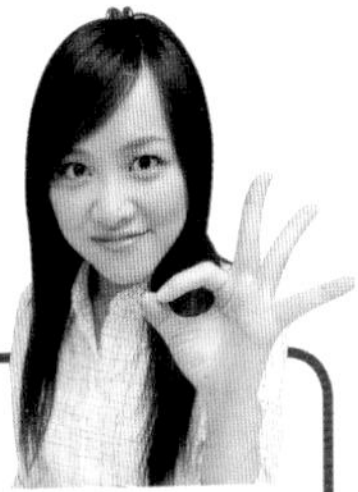

Helpful Hint

Remember to choose ink that is water-resistant. If you're not familiar with what kind of ink to buy, ask someone at an art supply store. The black or colored ink you use for inking has to be water-resistant. If not, your inked lines will probably dissolve as soon as you apply watercolor over them.

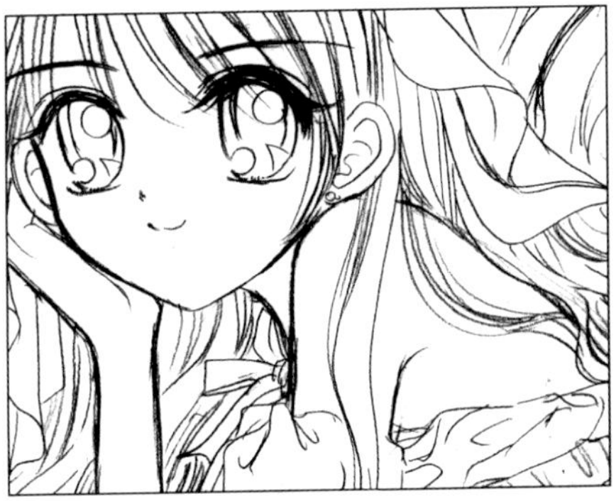

1 Using a light table, trace a drawing from manga paper onto watercolor paper. Use a round-nib pen and water-resistant superfine pigmented black ink.

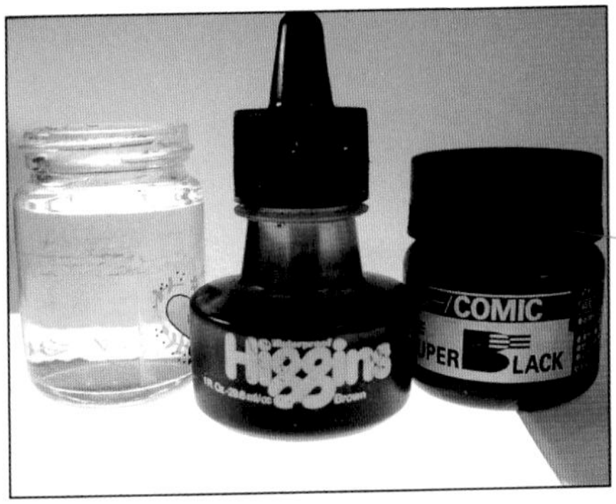
Higgins
COMIC

2 If you don't want your colored drawing to have lines that are black, you can go to an art supply store and get any color of water-resistant ink you like.

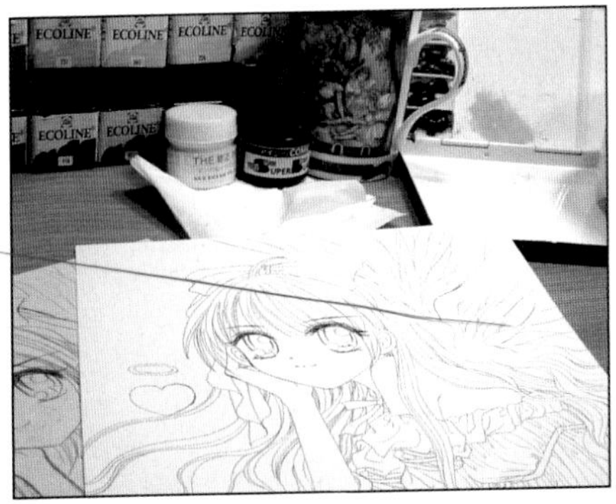
ECOLINE

3 After you've finished inking the drawing, remove the manga paper from behind it. Now you can begin coloring.

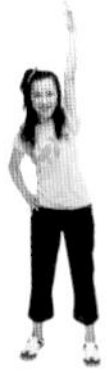

Preparing Your Tools

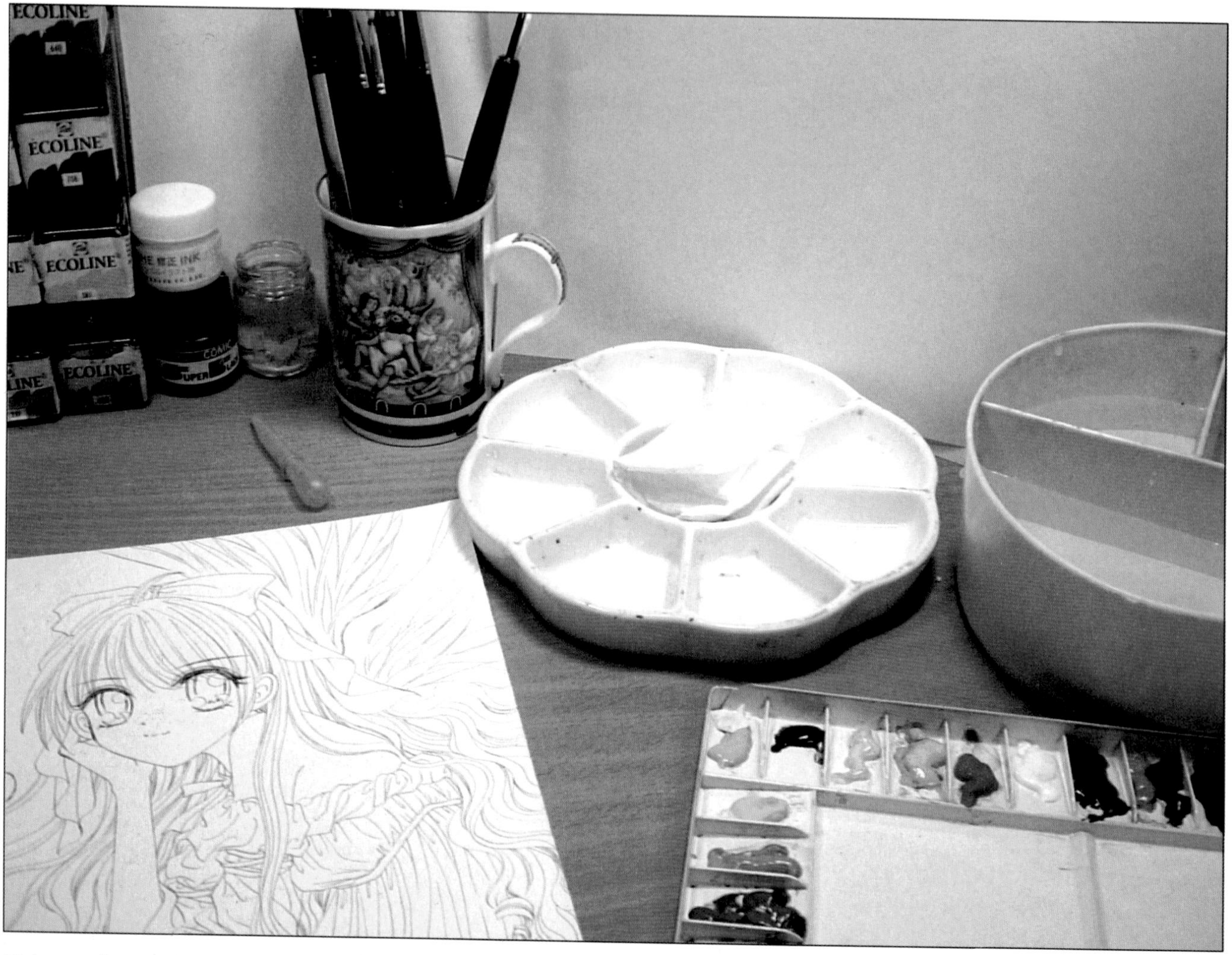
ECOLINE
ECOLINE
ECOLINE
ECOLINE
COMIC

Make sure that your brushes, palette and rinsing container are clean and dry. Fill up your rinsing container with water, and prepare a piece of dry cloth or paper towels. Lay out your tools in the way that is the most convenient for you. The locations of the rinsing container, palette and cloth/towels are especially important. Make sure that you don't get the drawing wet when you're rinsing your brush or mixing your colors! I suggest putting these tools on the right side of the drawing if you're right-handed. If you're ready, we can start coloring.

Skin and Facial Tones

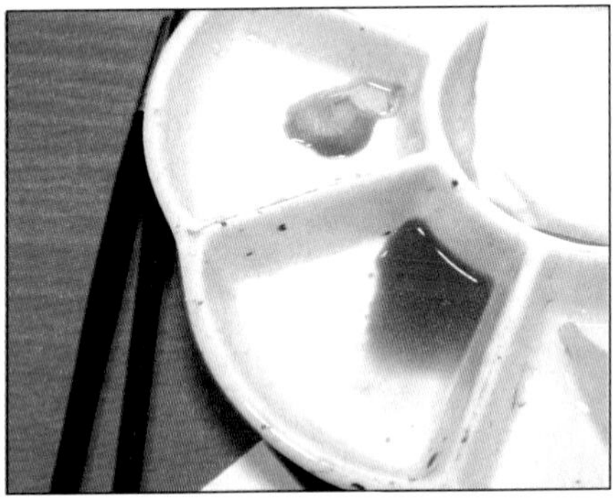

1 There's a rule about coloring: start light. In this case, that means we'll start with the skin color. Mix pink and light yellow (slightly less yellow than pink). Because we want to have the same skin color over all the drawing, make sure you mix enough to use for the entire skin area.

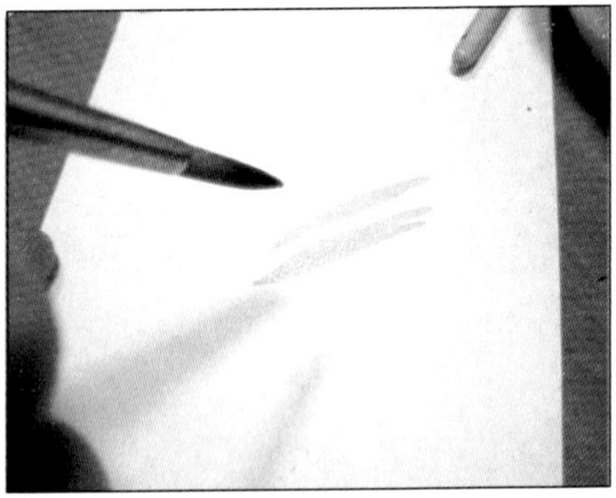

1–2 Test out your color on another piece of the watercolor paper. Mix in light red to create a blush color. Make sure you mix enough now, otherwise it will be very difficult to get the same shade later.

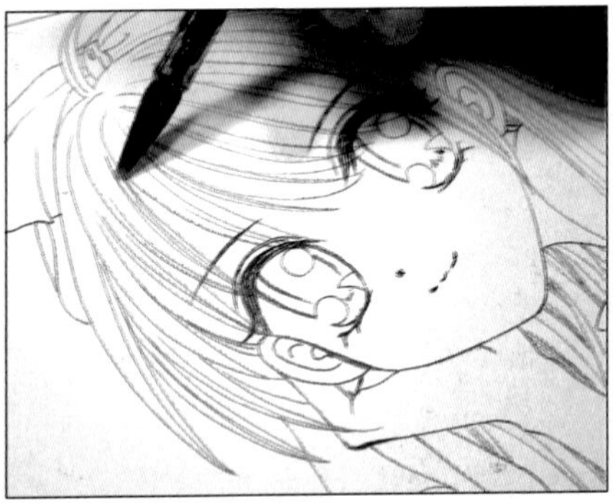

2–1 Rinse your brush clean. Brush a small amount of clear water on to the facial area you're about to color. The water should be just enough to wet the paper. Don't leave the paper too dry or dripping wet.

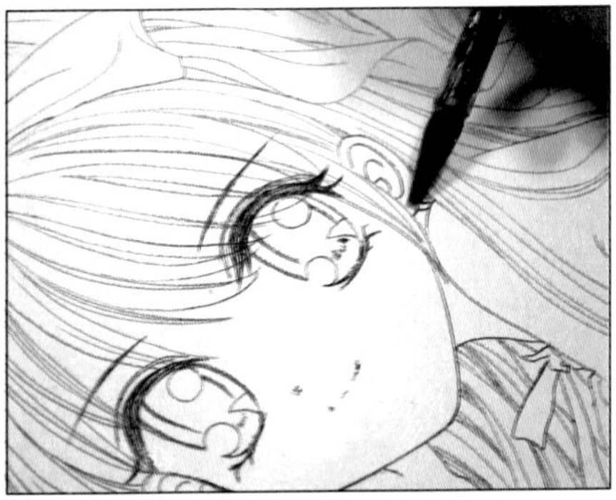

2–2 It's best to wet all the areas you're about to color if they are the same color and connected to each other. For example, when you're wetting the face, wet the ears, too. The color will turn out more even that way.

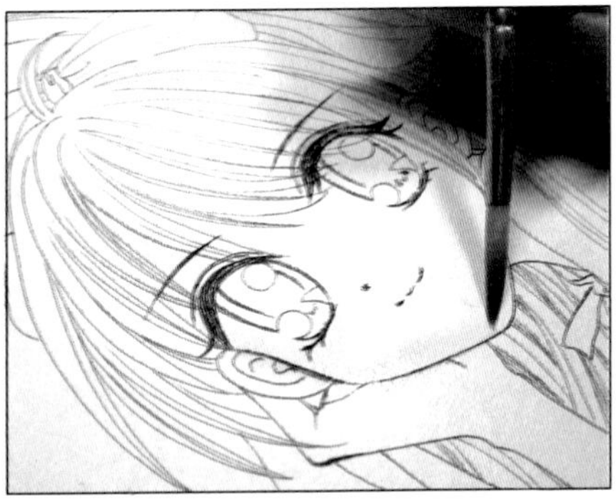

3–1 Apply the color before the water dries on the paper. Start from the sides. Spread the color from the lines outward.

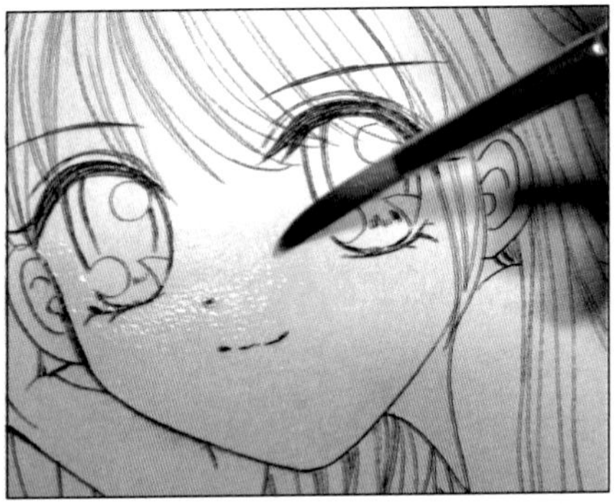

3–2 Now we want to gradually spread the color towards the middle and achieve a natural blending effect. The water that's already on the paper will help you achieve a smooth application.

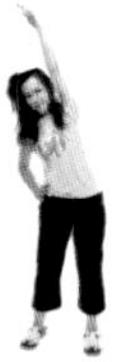

4 Now we can apply the second layer. Since adding a second layer increases the intensity of the color, we apply a second layer to the parts of the face where we want more shade and dimension. Shoot for the amount of intensity that seems right to you.

5-1 Brush on a thin layer of blush before the skin color dries. This will give the character a healthy glow.

5-2 Remember to apply only a small amount of blush color. Try applying it when the face is still around 40% damp for best results.

5-3 After you've applied the blush, remember to blend it into the page with a moist brush that has been rinsed clean.

6-1 Apply lip color when the paper is almost dry. Dab on a red or pink lip color. Because the paper is still somewhat wet, the lip color will naturally diffuse into the surrounding uncolored areas, creating the desired blending effect.

6-2 If you want your lip color to look brighter or the lips to look fuller, apply another layer of color when the paper is about 80%-90% dry.

7-1 After you're done coloring the face, don't forget that there are other skin surfaces to color. Apply the water and color in the same method to all those other areas.

7-2 Wait until all the skin surfaces have dried. Now you're done with coloring the skin. Remember, knowing when to apply color on a wet surface makes all the difference!

Great!
I learned that knowing when to apply color to a wet surface is the key!

Friendly Reminder Before Coloring

In order to create a sense of romance and beauty, most colored drawings in shojo manga are done using the wet-on-wet technique. This allows the colors to diffuse into soft, smooth washes. The later stages of layering, where your brush is fairly dry, are mostly used for embellishment and emphasis only.

ECOLINE
ECOLINE
COLINE
ECOLINE

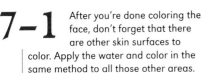

Hair

Once the skin surfaces have dried, we can start coloring the hair.

1 First determine what the character's hair color will be. Using this color as your starting point, create lighter and darker shades. These colors will be the ones you use for coloring the hair.

2 Find out what shades you like. For example, if you choose grass green as your main color, adding water will make it fresh green, and adding a darker green will make it forest green. Now you have your main, light and dark shades.

3 As in the previous example, wet the area you want to color using a clean brush. If you're not sure whether or not you can finish applying all the shades to the whole area before it dries out, proceed in segments.

4–1 Quickly apply the lightest shade over the hair, avoiding areas you want to highlight. Stroke a fully saturated brush onto the parts you want darker, such as both sides of the neck, and then proceed to blend the color out from that point.

4–2 It's very important to brush on the color when the paper is still moist. The hair usually covers a larger surface area. Remember, if you're not sure you can finish applying the first layer of color before the paper dries out, paint it in segments.

4–3 Start by applying the first layer of color to the hair on top of the head. Then proceed to the right, and then the left. Carefully color these areas with a light green.

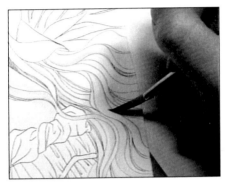

5 While the paper is still half wet, brush on your main color. Apply a second layer to the places where you want to increase the intensity of color and shade.

6 When the paper gets even drier, apply the main color again using a thinner brush to define hair strands and blocks of color. This is similar to the layering technique, but the effects are more pronounced. You will see a more prominent division between the main color and the lighter color.

7 Keep on using this method for further definition. By the time you're finished, the paper should be close to dry. Now we can start applying the darkest shade.

8-1 Use the layering technique to brush on the darkest shade. When you've applied this shade, you will have created an even sharper contrast.

8-2 Because the areas we are now shading with dark paint are rather limited, you can switch to an even thinner brush.

9 Now your character's hair is complete! It has dark and light shades, giving it body and dimension.

Clothes

Not all fabrics have the same textures, and each reflect light differently, so they're not all colored the same way. Nevertheless, the main principle regarding the wet-on-wet watercolor technique remains the same. Here I'll show you how to color a light gauze fabric.

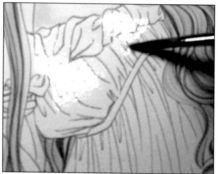

1 The main color used here is plum purple. Adding water will make it a light purple, and adding grape purple will make it a darker, bluish purple. The character's dress covers a large surface area, so remember to mix enough of each shade to begin with. It's very challenging to mix a new supply before the paper dries out.

2 As before, the lighter shade will be the first layer, the main color will be the second layer, and the darkest shade will be used for emphasis. After we've mixed our different shades, use a clean brush to wet the area to be colored. Again, because the area of the dress is so large, we'll color it in segments.

3–1 First quickly apply the lighter shade, coloring in the areas you want to be darker. Our first strokes usually fall where the folds are because this is where we want to have a darker base for contrast.

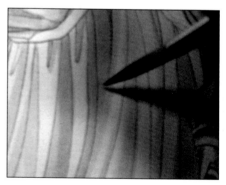

3–2 We'll use the ribbon at the waist as a separating point. After coloring the top part of the dress, we'll now proceed to color the waist down.

3–3 The dress covers a fairly large area, so try to finish applying the first layer when the paper is still around 70%-100% wet, otherwise the water and color will not blend naturally, and you'll get watermarks.

4 Then apply a second layer of contrast furthering shading the folds using your main color. The paper should be about 50%-70% wet when this is done.

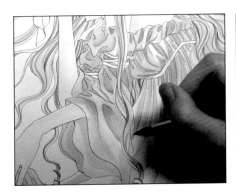

5 The paper is now even drier. When the second layer is almost dry, make some parts even darker using the blending layering technique we've used a lot of.

6 The paper should be almost completely dry now. Wait until the paper is dry before you apply the last (darkest) shade. This will keep the colors distinct.

7-1 When the paper is pretty much dry, use the dark, bluish purple to push the contrast where needed. Now we've finished coloring most of the character.

7-2 Of course, an outfit doesn't just consist of one color. As you add the additional colors you need to other parts of the outfit, use the same techniques we've just covered, and you'll be able to color just about anything without a problem.

Friendly Reminder

Clothes usually cover a very large area and take time to color, so it's important to plan ahead so that your layers are applied when the paper is still moist enough.

Eyes

1 Before you begin coloring the eyes, you need to choose the color of the eyes and where the reflections are going to be. The usual coloring scheme for eyes is: upper part dark, middle part gradually lighter and bottom part bright. The bright part is the character's "eye color." Tweak this format as you need for your style.

2 As before, we'll mix a variation of 3-4 shades from light to dark. Because I've chosen golden yellow to be the eye color of this character, I'll use a shade of orange as my lightest dark shade, brown as my middle dark shade and dark brown as my darkest shade.

3–1 We want the colors of the eyes to blend as well, so we'll still start by wetting the eyes with water.

4 Remember, start light. We'll first apply our lightest shade to the bottom part of the eye. Since strokes are usually applied from top down, we can turn the drawing upside down.

5–1 Next we'll apply the lightest dark shade. This shade will be where the light and dark colors merge. Remember that the paper needs to be wet enough to let the color diffuse naturally.

5–2 Eyes are where the personality of a character shines through. They need to be bright and telling. Therefore, when coloring the eyes, avoid colors that are too light.

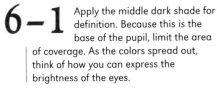

6—1 Apply the middle dark shade for definition. Because this is the base of the pupil, limit the area of coverage. As the colors spread out, think of how you can express the brightness of the eyes.

6—2 Now apply the dark brown. Also fully define the pupil. Then apply a darker shade of black to the top of the eye to bring out contrast.

7 Now color the lids/lashes. I suggest that you choose a color that is a darker shade of the eye color. The colors will look more consistent and the eyes will look livelier.

8 Use the same method of color application for the other eye. Make sure that the colors in both eyes follow the same pattern so they match each other.

9 Your character's eyes are all done now! If you like, you can add some highlights to the eyes or even brush on some eye shadow.

We saved the eyes for last, but they're the finishing touch that makes all the difference!

I hope you found some practical techniques for drawing manga in this book. Drawing your own manga doesn't seem so hard now, does it? There's no limit to what you can do in the world of manga. Experiment, practice and take an interest in the world around you. You're bound to make new discoveries each day.

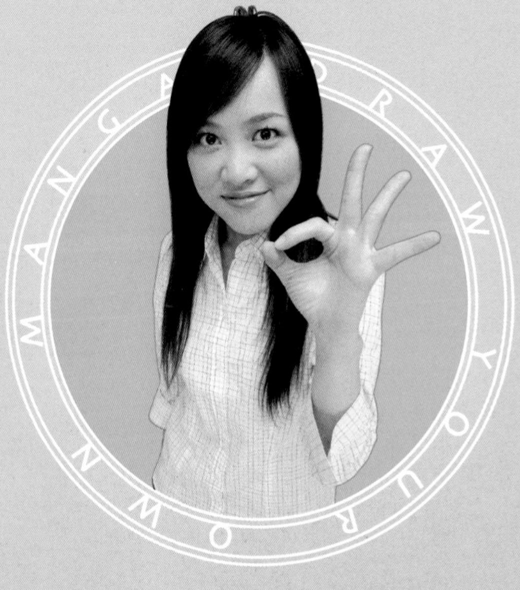
DRAW YOUR OWN MANGA

Selena's Gallery

Hidden

(Included in this book, 1997)

Hidden flutters of you
Hidden longings for you
Yearning, hidden no longer,
Because of you

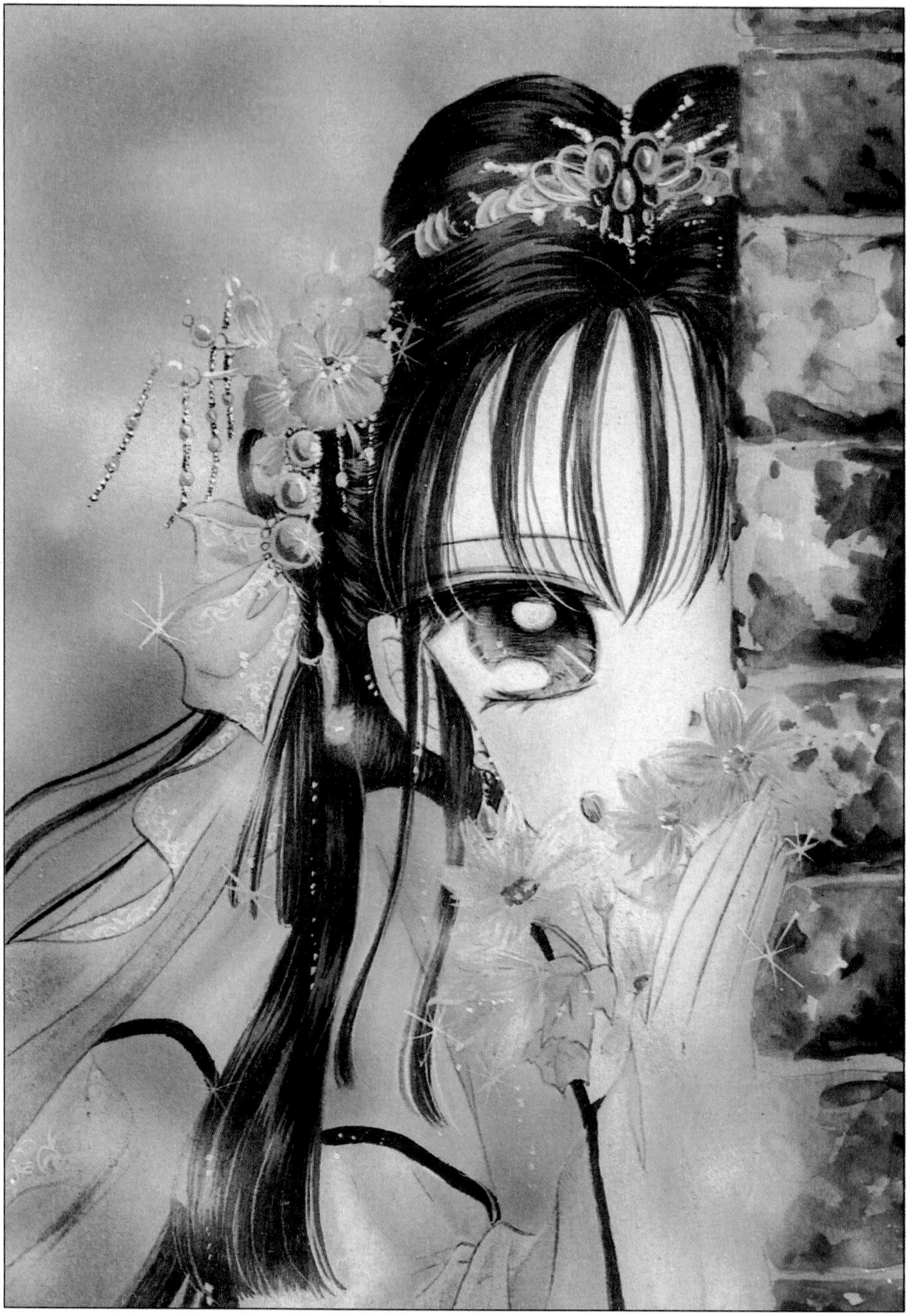

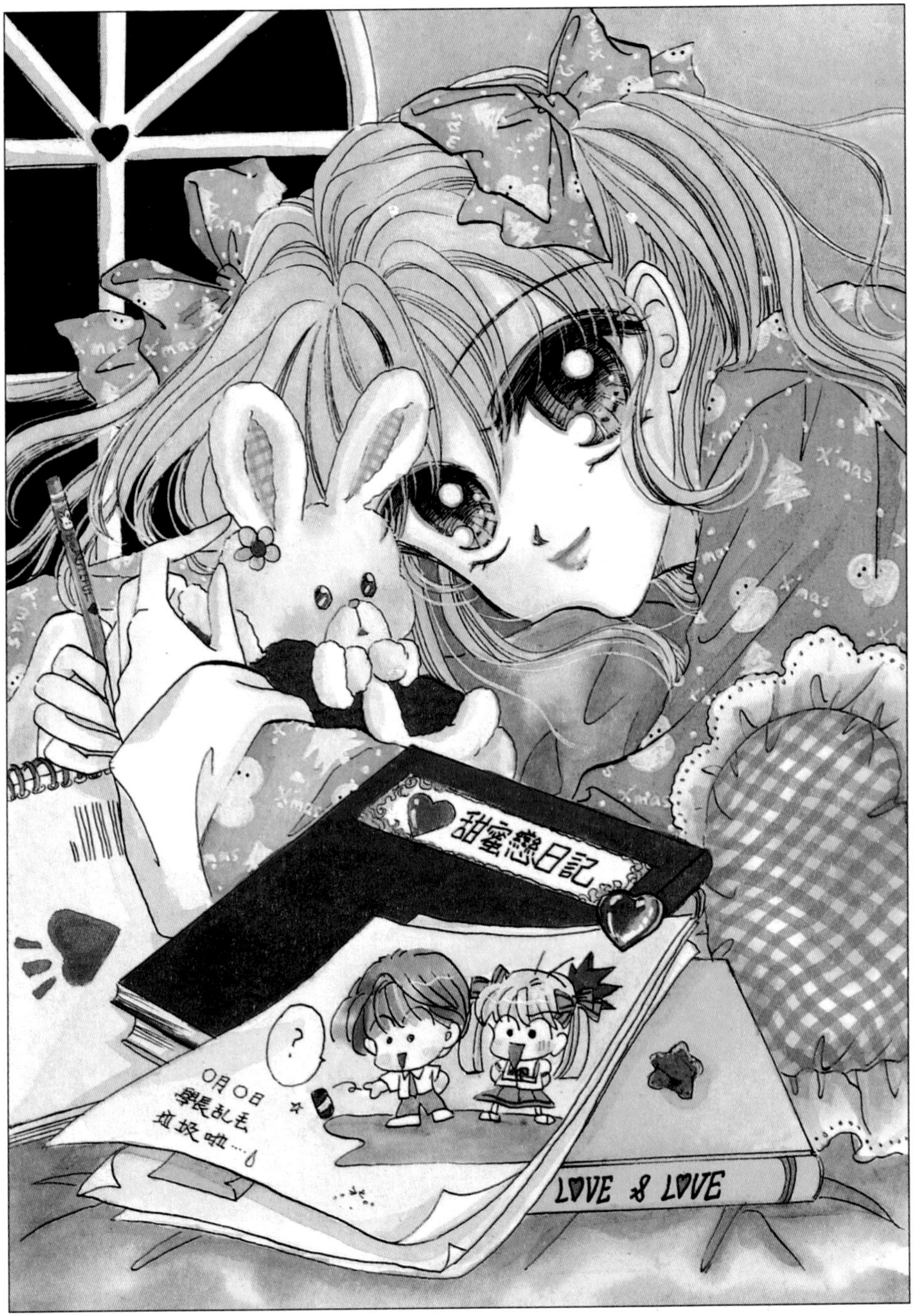
甜蜜戀日記
LOVE & LOVE

Love in a Diary

("Sweet Love in a Diary," *Angel Magazine*, 1999)

I end my diary with "I miss you"
I put down the time I miss you
I put down the date I want to see you
I put down everything in my sweet diary

Missing You

("Sweet Love in a Diary," *Angel Magazine* preview page, 1999)

The colors go wild when I miss you
I radiate with joy when I think of you
Because of you, the world is filled
with sweet, sweet fragrance

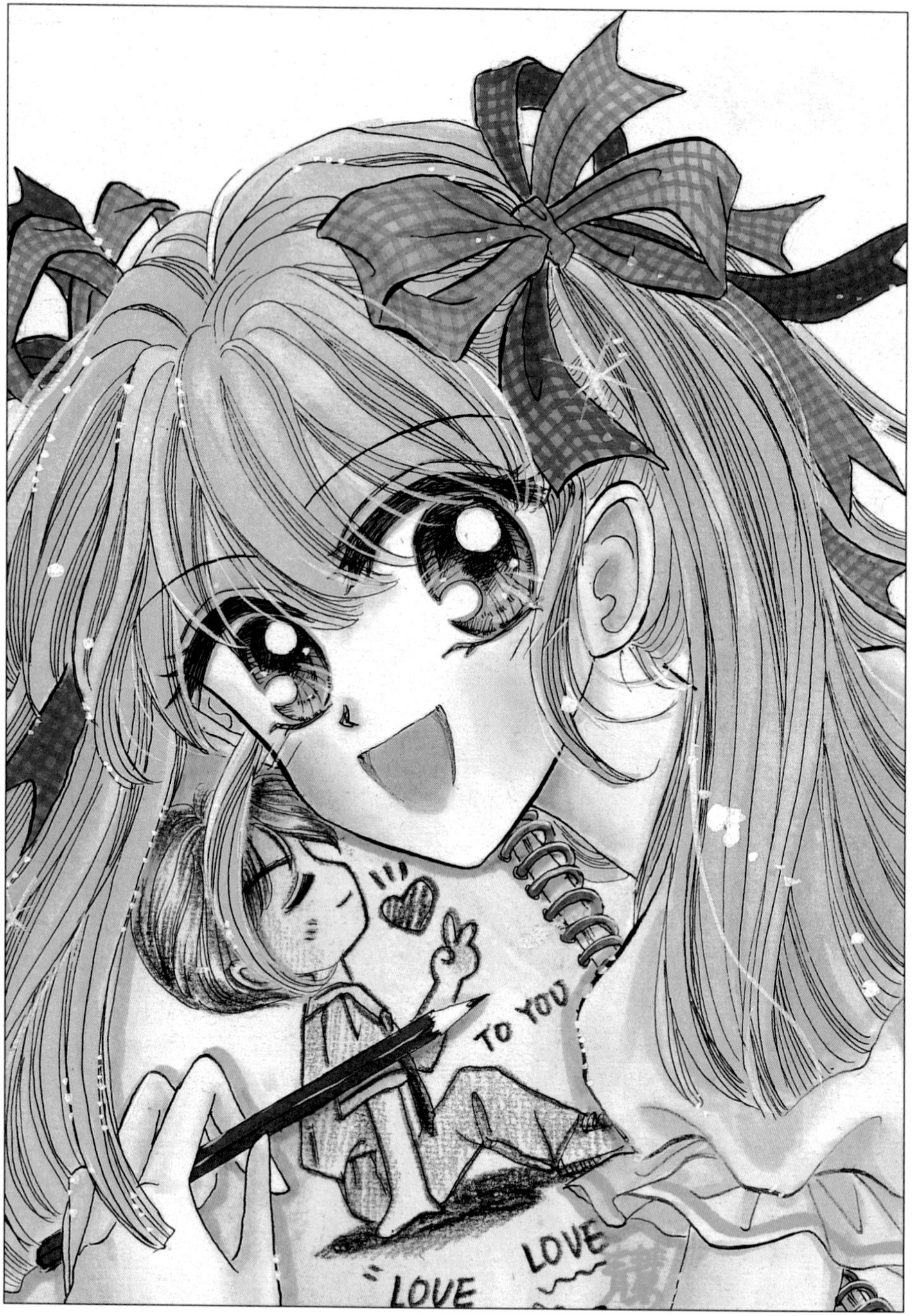
TO YOU
LOVE
LOVE

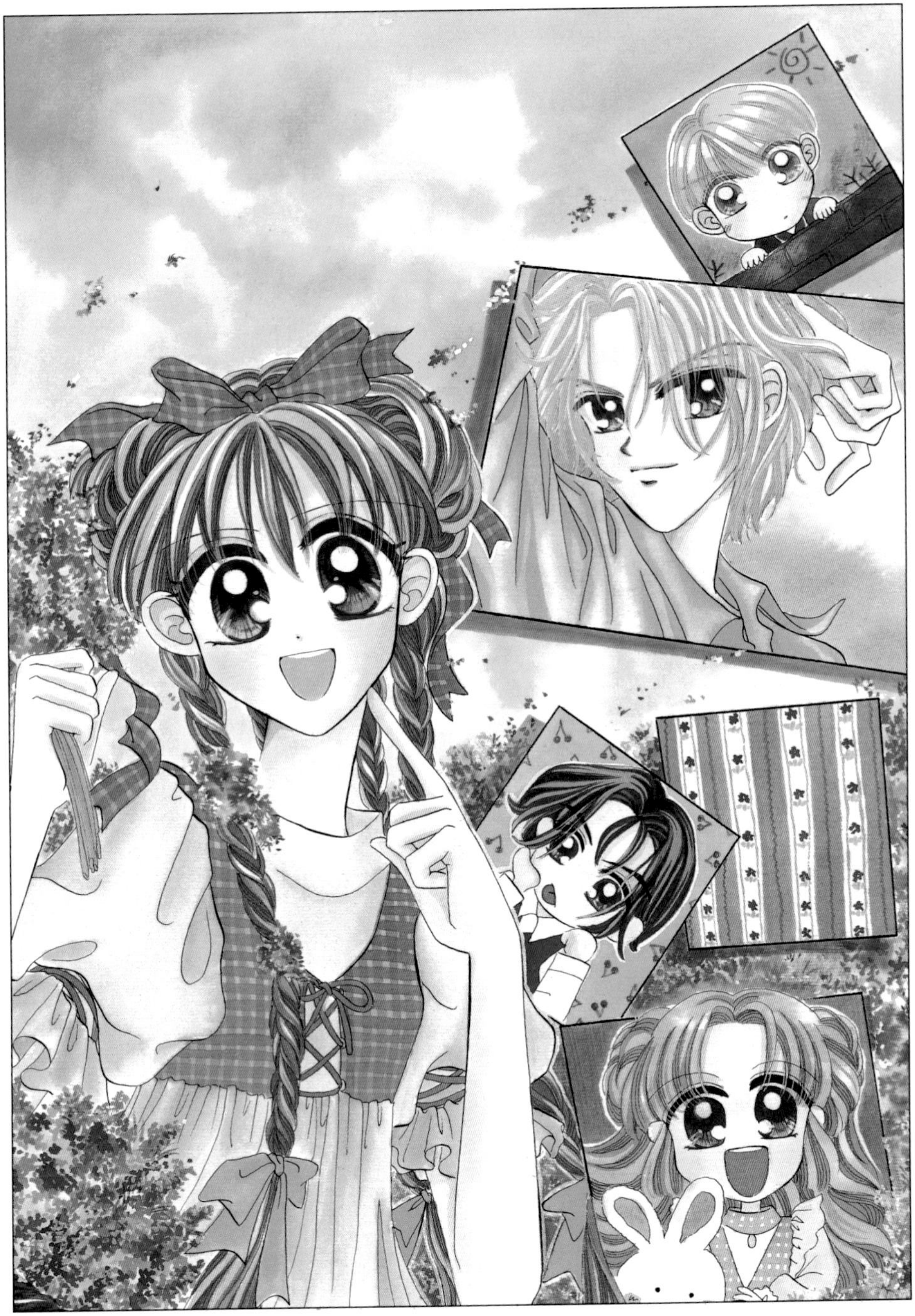

Lavender Memories

("The Glass Slipper," *Angel Magazine* extra, 2000)

Lavender colors, lavender scent
With a basket of lightly scented lavender flowers
who are you thinking of now?

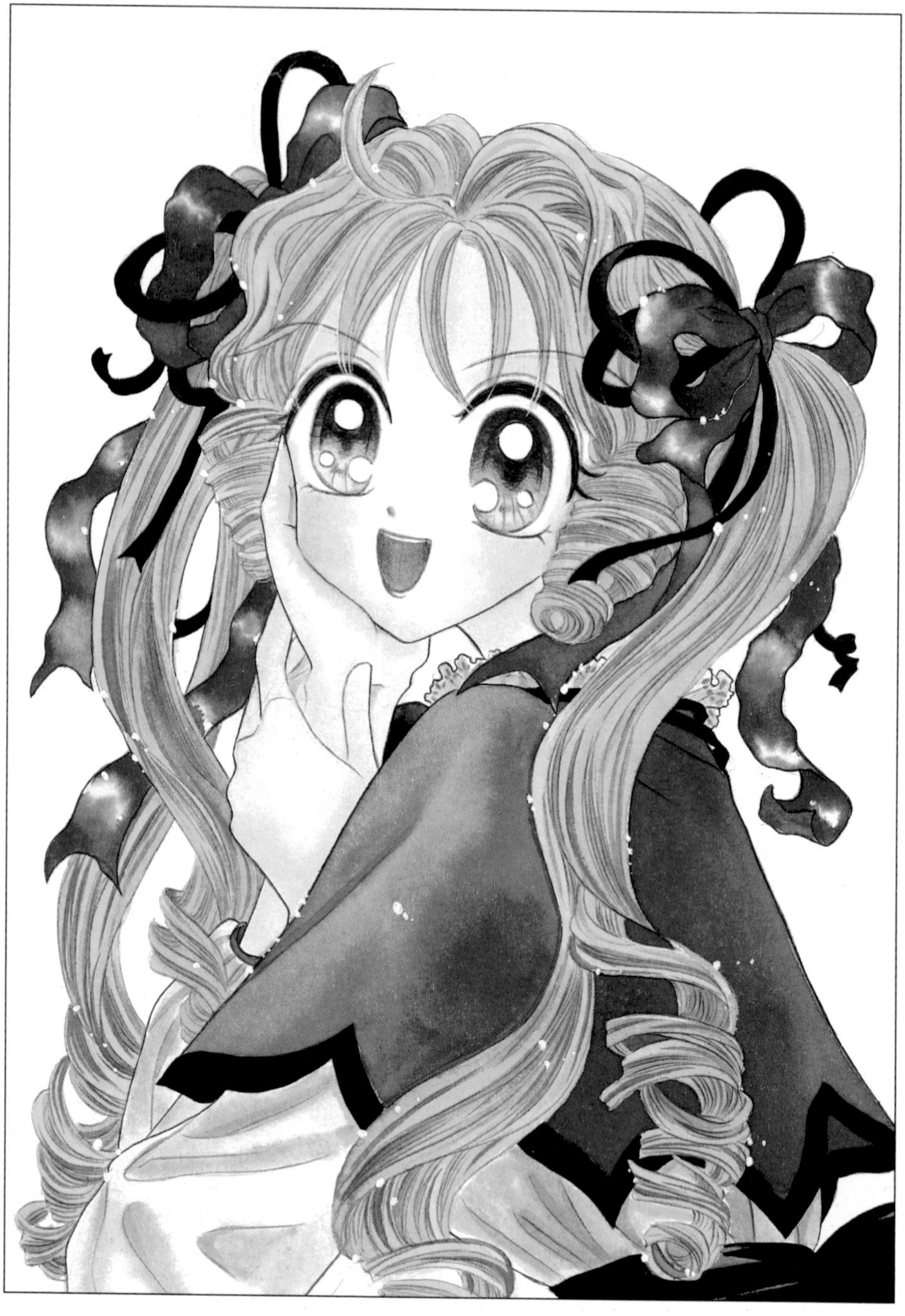

Orange

("White Night Melody," *Angel Magazine*, 2001)

Orange tones, bright smiles
It seems that the air is filled with
the sweet sensation of love

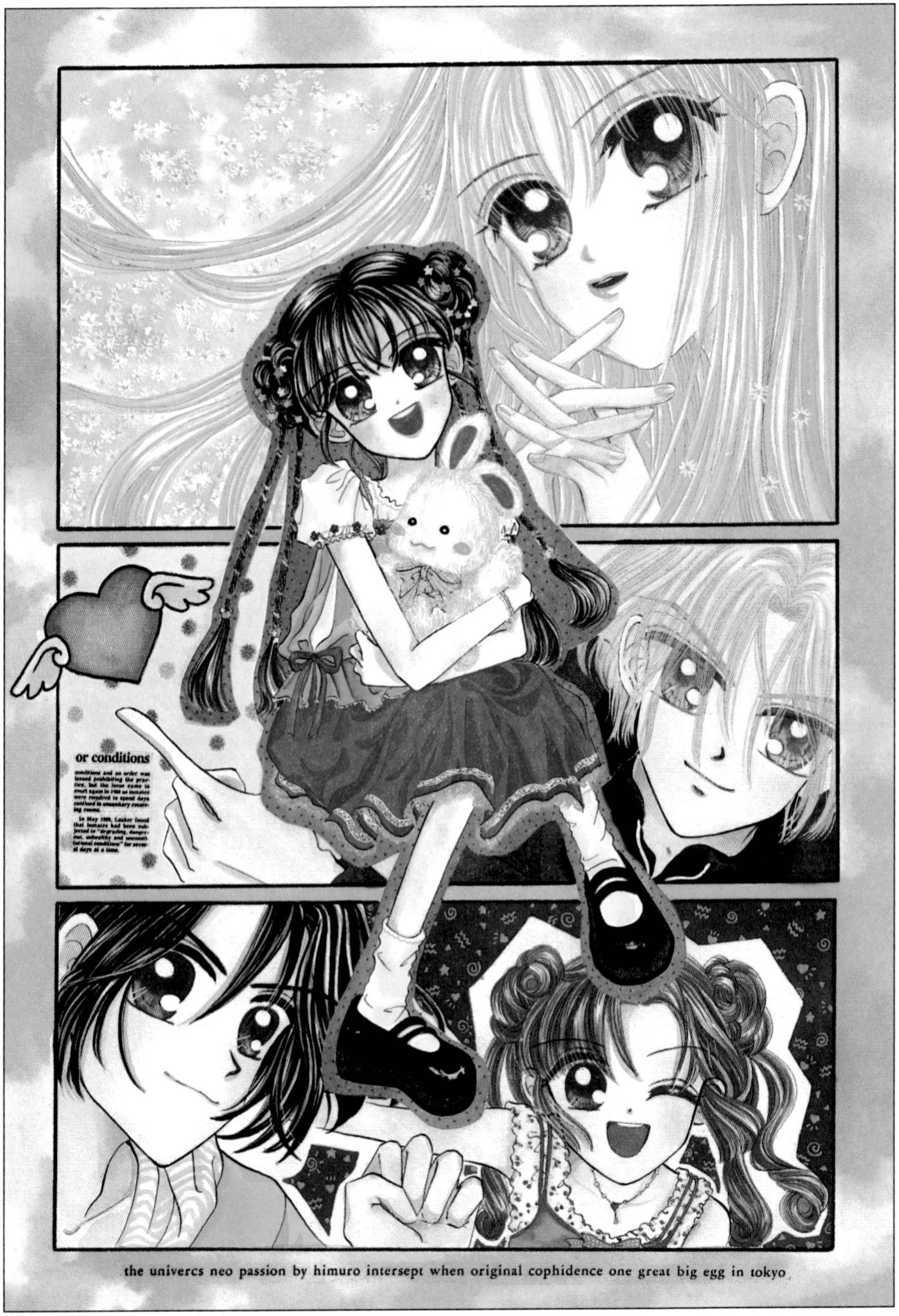
or conditions
the univercs neo passion by himuro intersept when original cophidence one great big egg in tokyo

Party

("The Glass Slipper," *Angel Magazine*, 2001)

All the happy faces are here for you to see
Don't you feel the wings of happiness
beckoning?

Sakura Fairy

("White Night Melody," *Angel Magazine*, 2001)

I cup a handful of sakura water and pray
That in the season of the sakura blossom
Everyone will see happiness

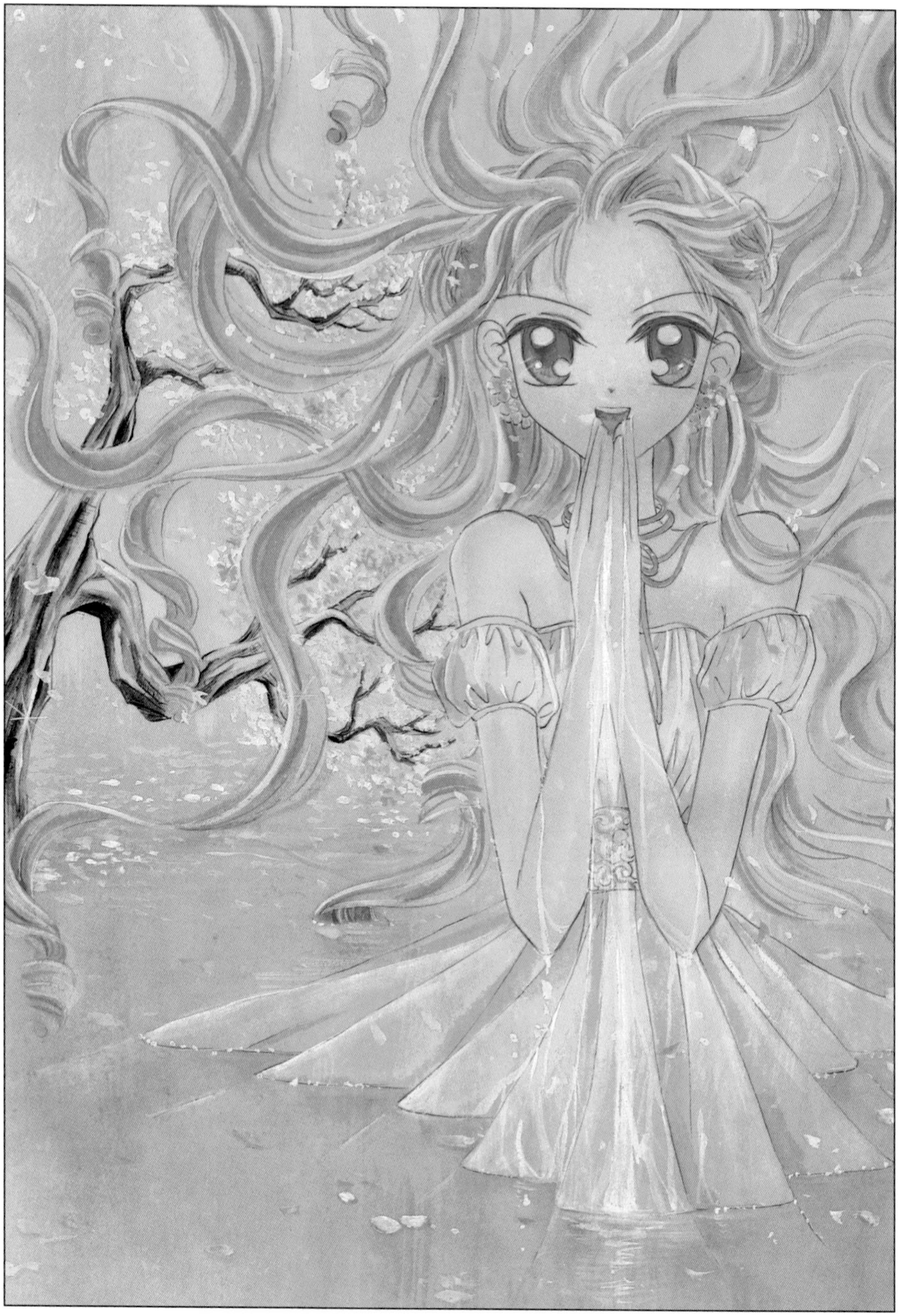

Dance of the World

(*Angel Magazine* bonus poster, 2001)

The sky is not one kind of blue
Happiness is not one kind of smile
Times can meet
Fantasies can become reality
Because you are with me

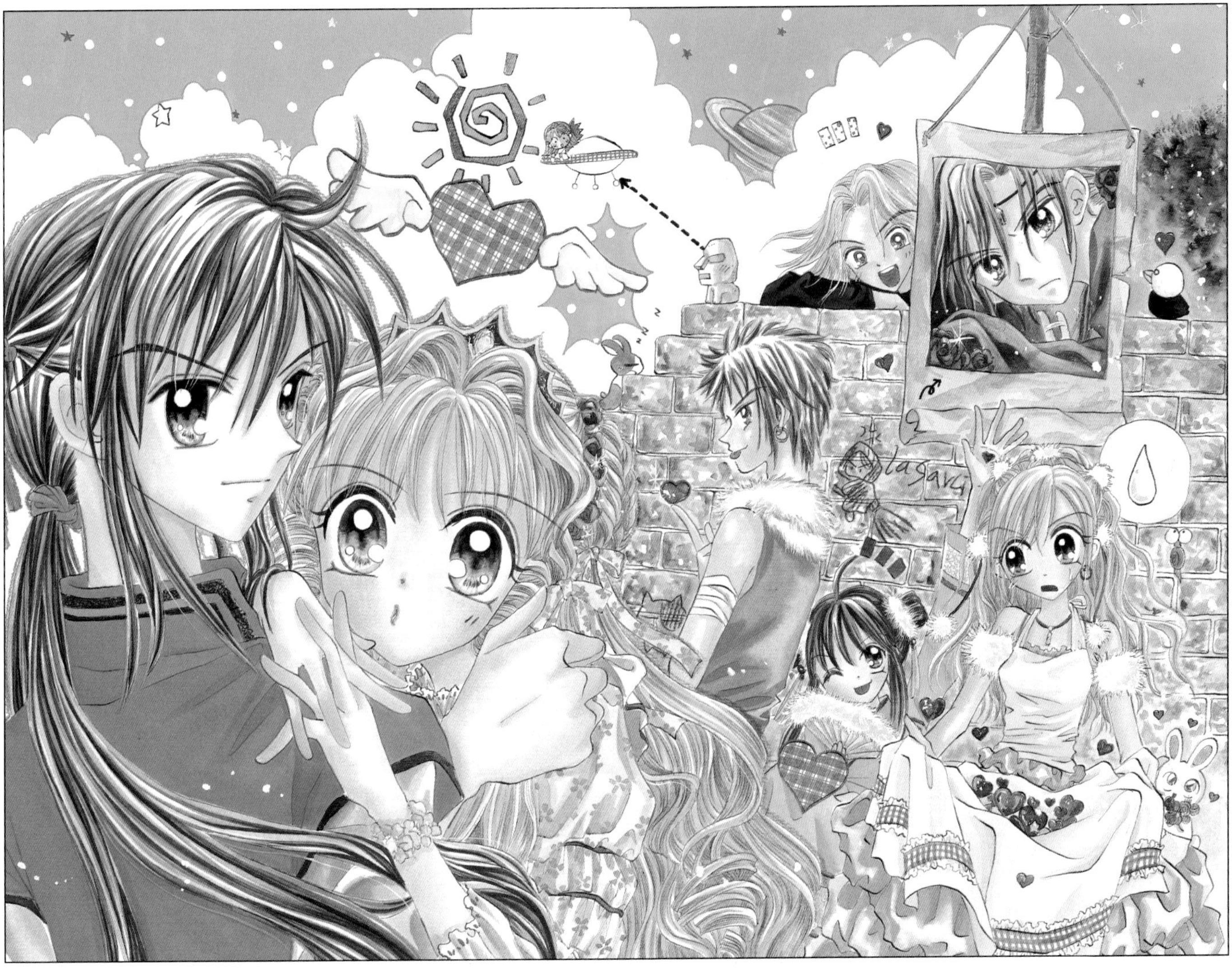

Reflections
("White Night Melody," *Angel Magazine*, 2001)

Under the willow...a time in memory
Far, far away
A piece of my memory...
Reveals...your reflection

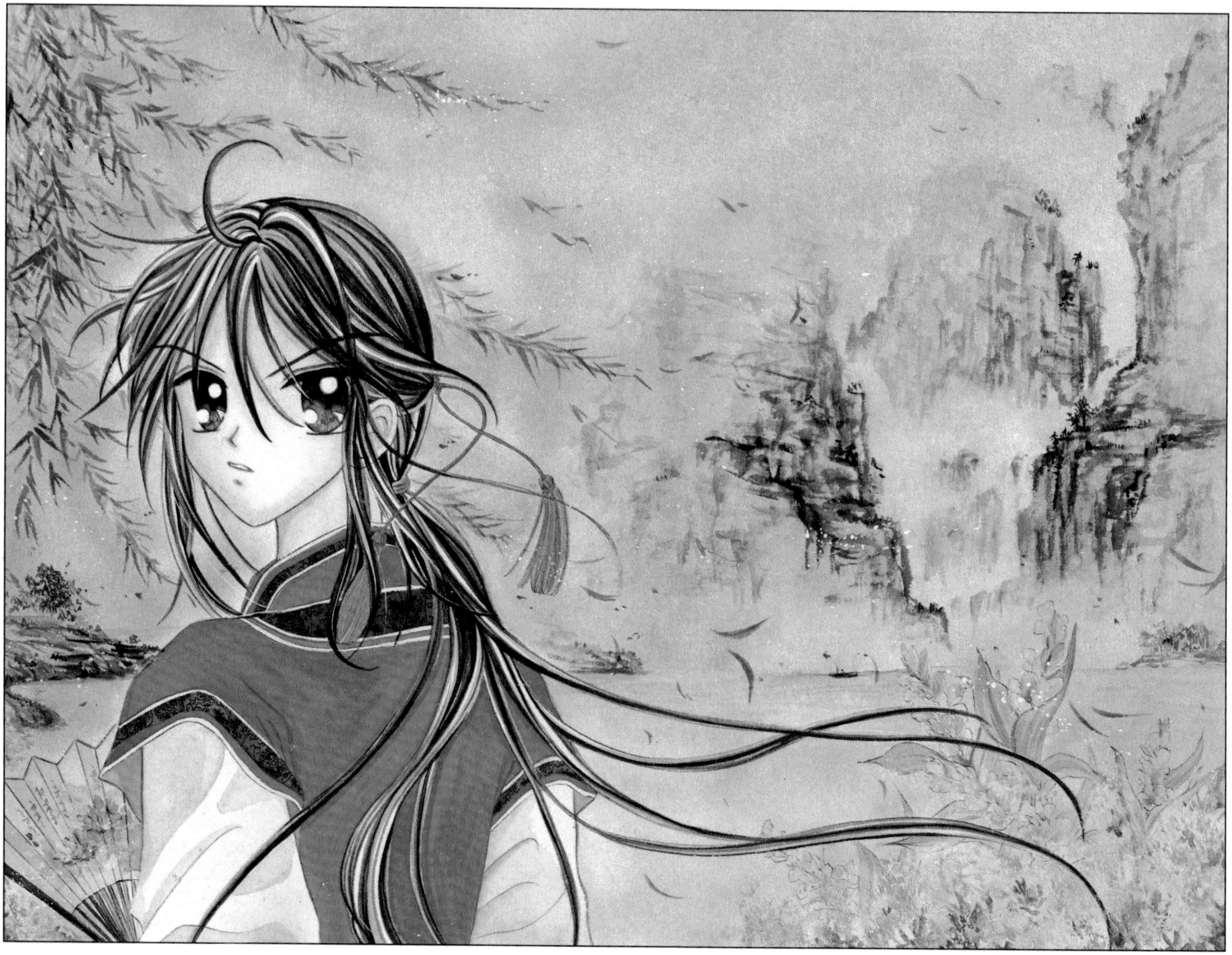

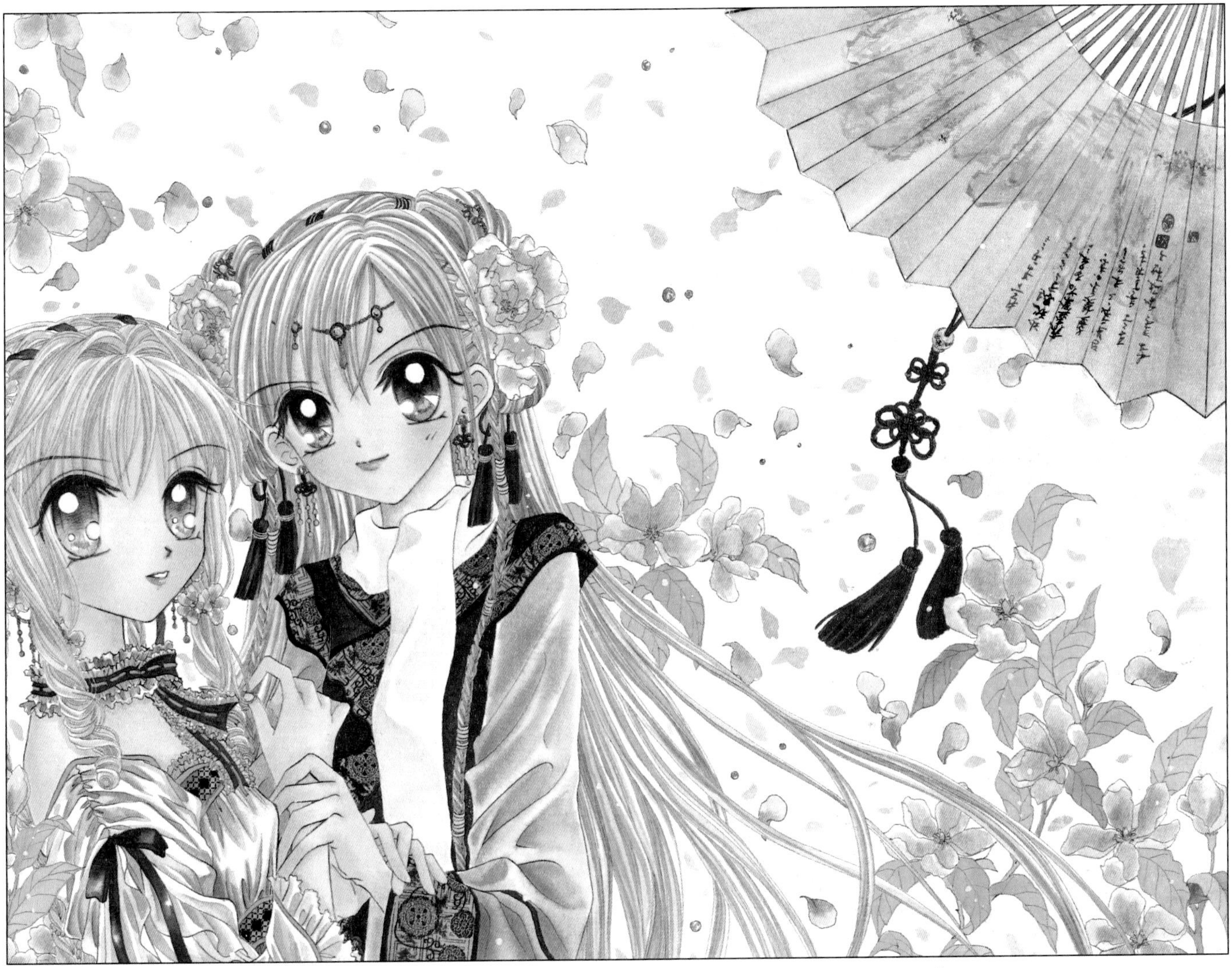

Together in Admiration
("White Night Melody," *Angel Magazine*, 2001)

Young faces in the sun...We once held hands
And gazed at the sky in admiration
But it must have been in another time, another life...

An Angel's Christmas Eve

("Sweet as Candy," *Angel Magazine*, 2002)

A star studded night
A list of endless wishes
The light ringing of Christmas bells
Carrying the blessings of angels
I just want to fill the sky
With my wishes to see you

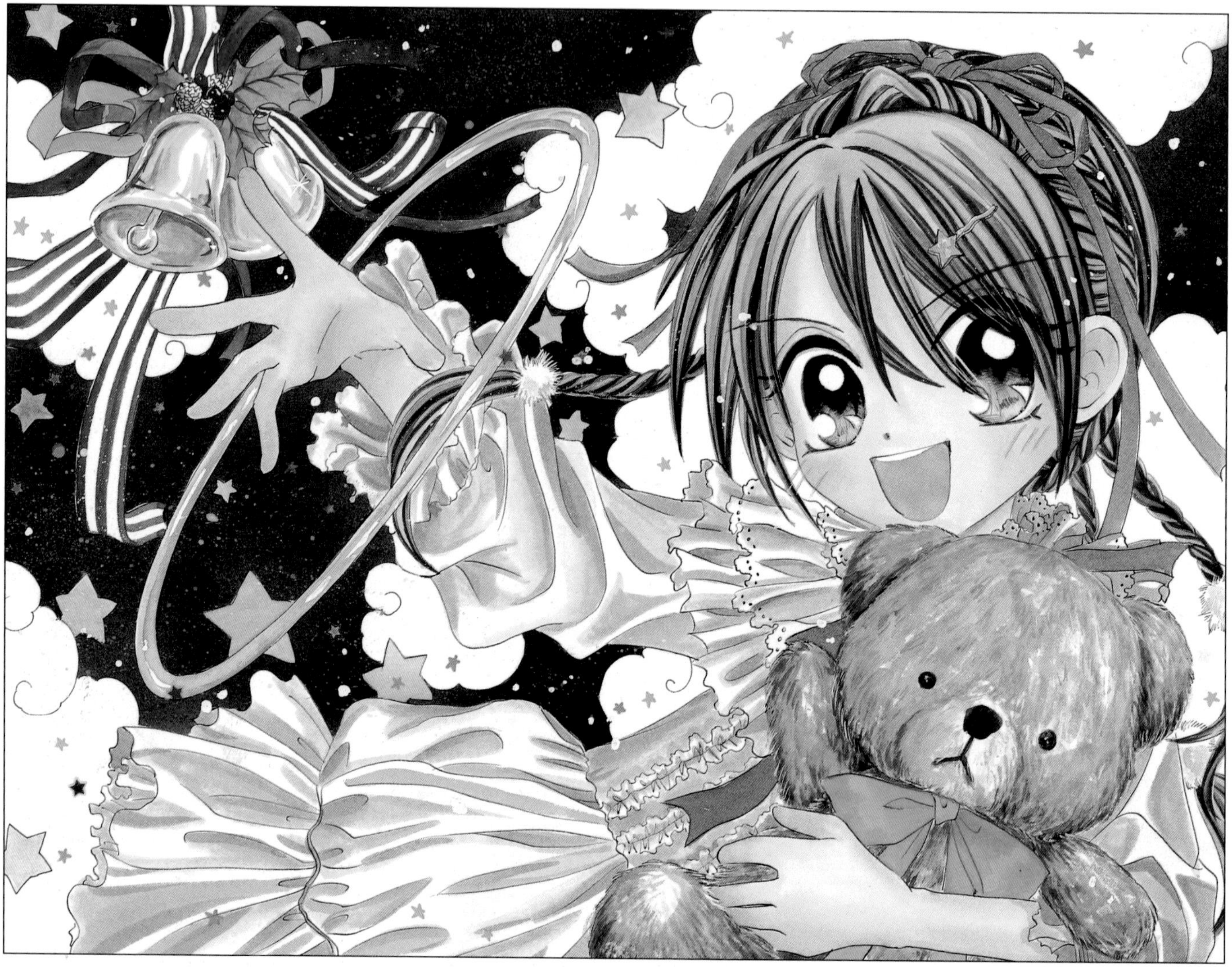

Practice Drawing Your Own Manga

Draw something from what you've learned!

The best advice from the best artists!

Comickers Magazine, a leading Japanese manga and anime authority, brings together the top manga artists to showcase their trademark techniques and specialities. With original advice and detailed step-by-step projects from each artist, the **Comickers Art** series is great for artists who have mastered the basics and want to develop their art into something even greater.

Comickers Art: Tools and Techniques for Drawing Amazing Manga
ISBN: 978-0-06-144153-0

Comickers Art 2: Create Amazing Manga Characters
ISBN: 978-0-06-145254-3

Comickers Art 3: Write Amazing Manga Stories
ISBN: 978-0-06-145207-9

Available August 2008

Comickers Coloring Book
ISBN 13: 978-0-06-124204-5

COLLINS | DESIGN
An Imprint of HarperCollinsPublishers
www.harpercollins.com

MONSTER BOOKS OF MANGA

Learn how to draw even MORE manga with these Monster Books!

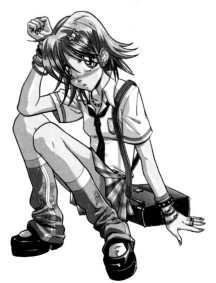

The Monster Book of Manga
ISBN 978-0-06-082993-3

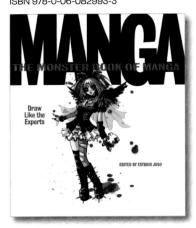

MANGA
THE MONSTER BOOK OF MANGA
Draw Like the Experts
EDITED BY ESTUDIO JOSO

The Monster Book of More Manga
ISBN 978-0-06-115169-9

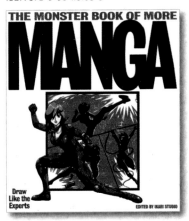

THE MONSTER BOOK OF MORE
MANGA
Draw Like the Experts
EDITED BY IKARI STUDIO

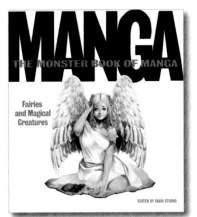

The Monster Books of Manga are the ultimate step-by-step guides to help you become a master mangaka. Follow the six stages of creating manga art, from black and white drawing to final full-color illustration. With 300+ pages of helpful hints and tips, each book covers drawing by hand and on the computer. Unleash your imagination!

The Monster Book of Manga: Fairies and Magical Creatures
ISBN 978-0-06-124203-8

MANGA
THE MONSTER BOOK OF MANGA
Fairies and Magical Creatures
EDITED BY IKARI STUDIO

The Monster Book of Manga: Girls
ISBN 978-0-06-153794-3

Available September 2008

MANGA
THE MONSTER BOOK OF MANGA
Girls
EDITED BY IKARI STUDIO

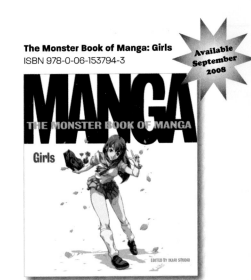

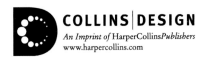

COLLINS | DESIGN
An Imprint of HarperCollins*Publishers*
www.harpercollins.com

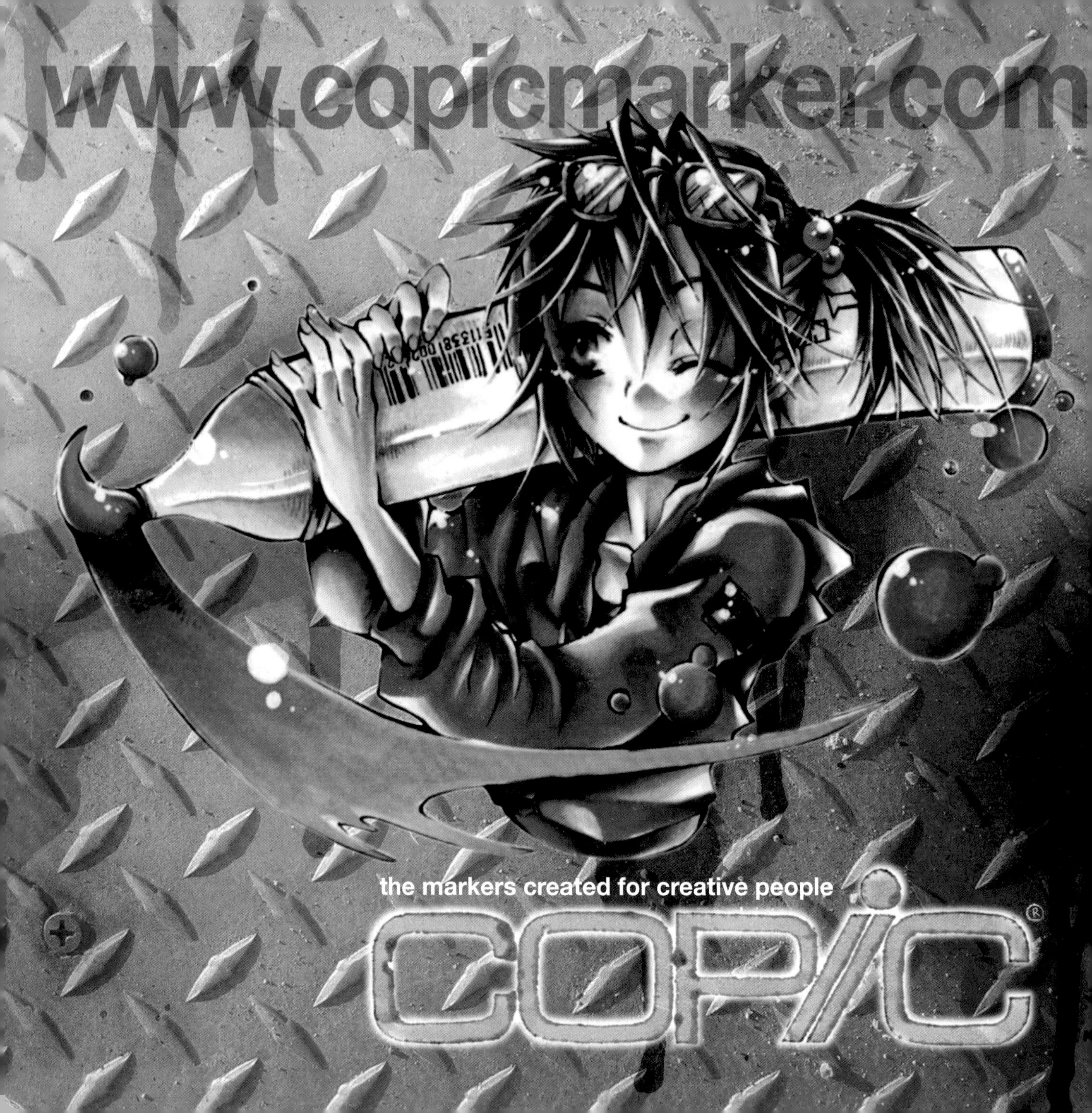
www.copicmarker.com
the markers created for creative people
COPIC®

Manga School with Selena Lin: Draw Your Own Manga

Created by Selena Lin

Lettering - Lucas Rivera
Cover Design - Jennifer Carbajal

Editor - Hope Donovan
Digital Imaging Manager - Chris Buford
Pre-Production Supervisor - Lucas Rivera
Managing Editor - Vy Nguyen
Creative Director - Anne Marie Horne
Editor-in-Chief - Rob Tokar
Publisher - Mike Kiley
President and C.O.O. - John Parker
C.E.O. and Chief Creative Officer - Stu Levy

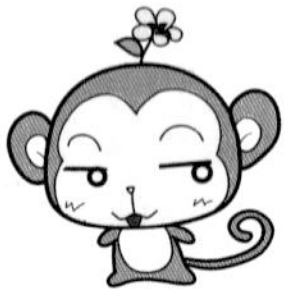

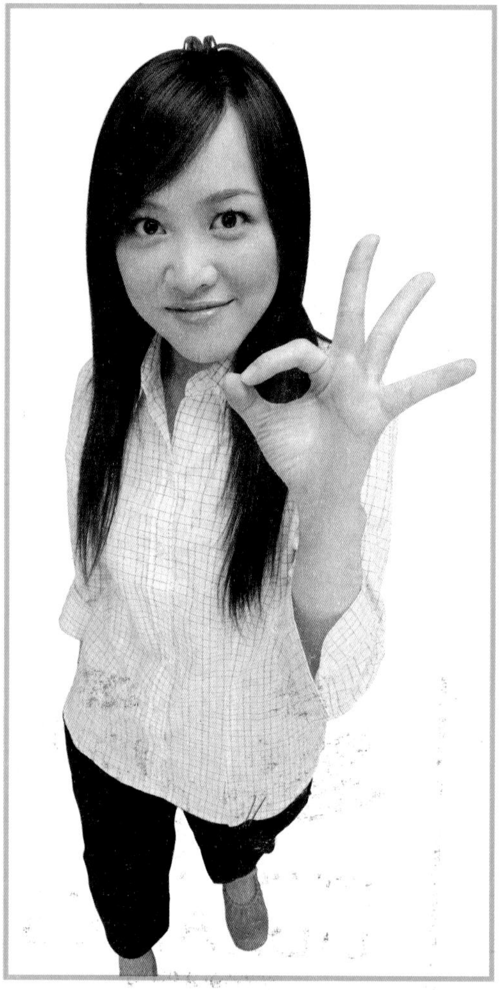

A TOKYOPOP® Manga

TOKYOPOP and are trademarks or registered trademarks of TOKYOPOP Inc.

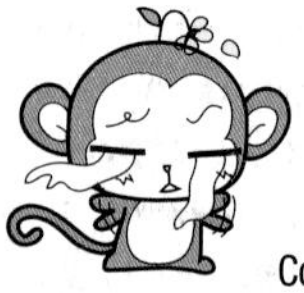

TOKYOPOP Inc.
5900 Wilshire Blvd. Suite 2000
Los Angeles, CA 90036

E-mail: info@TOKYOPOP.com
Come visit us online at www.TOKYOPOP.com

ISBN: 978-1-4278-1023-6

First TOKYOPOP printing: June 2008
10 9 8 7 6 5 4 3 2 1
Printed in the USA

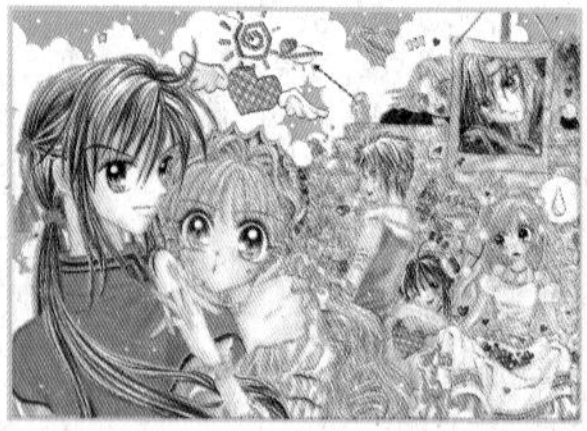

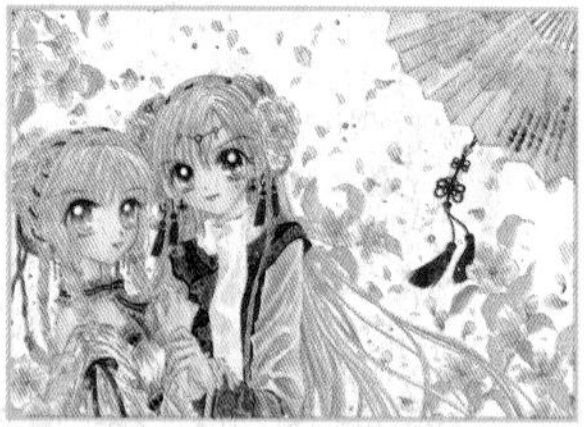

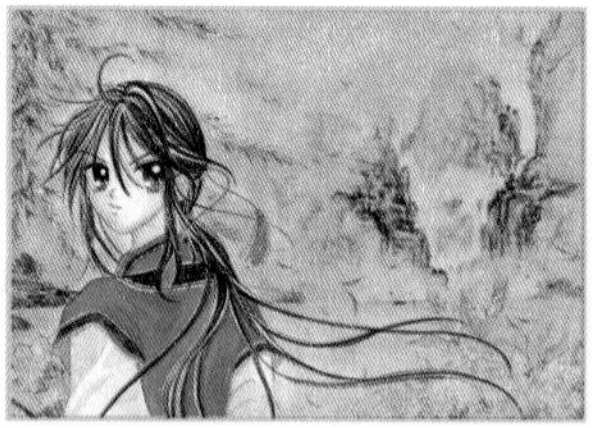

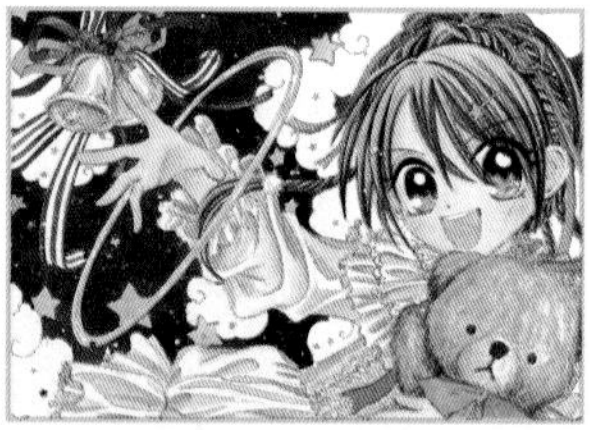

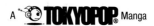

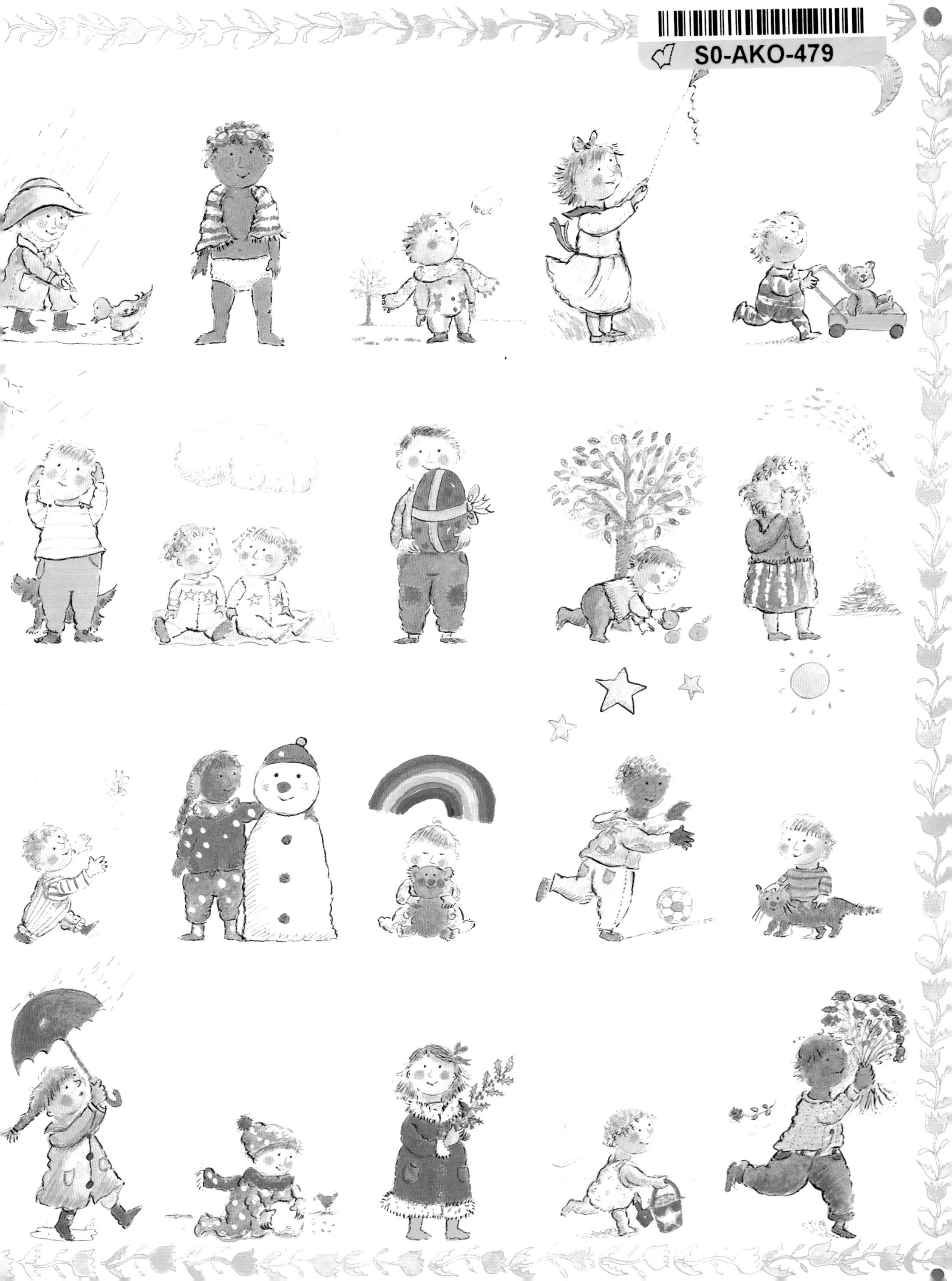

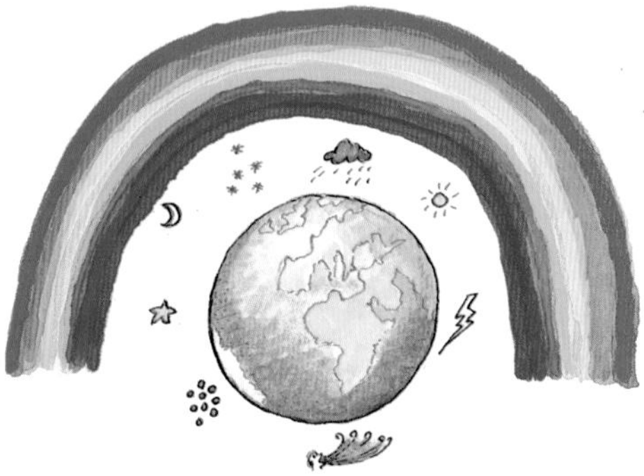

VIKING

Reprinted by permission of VIKING, a division of Penguin Books USA Inc.

Penguin Books USA Inc., 375 Hudson Street, New York, New York 10014, USA
Penguin Books Ltd, 27 Wrights Lane, London W8 5TZ, England
Penguin Books Australia Ltd, Ringwood, Victoria, Australia
Penguin Books Canada Ltd, 10 Alcorn Avenue, Toronto, Ontario, Canada M4V 3B2
Penguin Books (NZ) Ltd, 182-190 Wairau Road, Auckland 10, New Zealand

Penguin Books Ltd, Registered Offices: Harmondsworth, Middlesex, England

First published in Great Britain by William Heinemann Ltd
an imprint of Reed Children's Books, 1995
First published in the United States of America by Viking,
a division of Penguin Books USA Inc., 1995

1 3 5 7 9 10 8 6 4 2

Library of Congress Catalog Card Number: 94-61278
Printed in the U.S.A.
Set in Stemple Garamond

SUN SNOW STARS SKY

Catherine and Laurence Anholt

VIKING

Early in the morning the sun comes up.

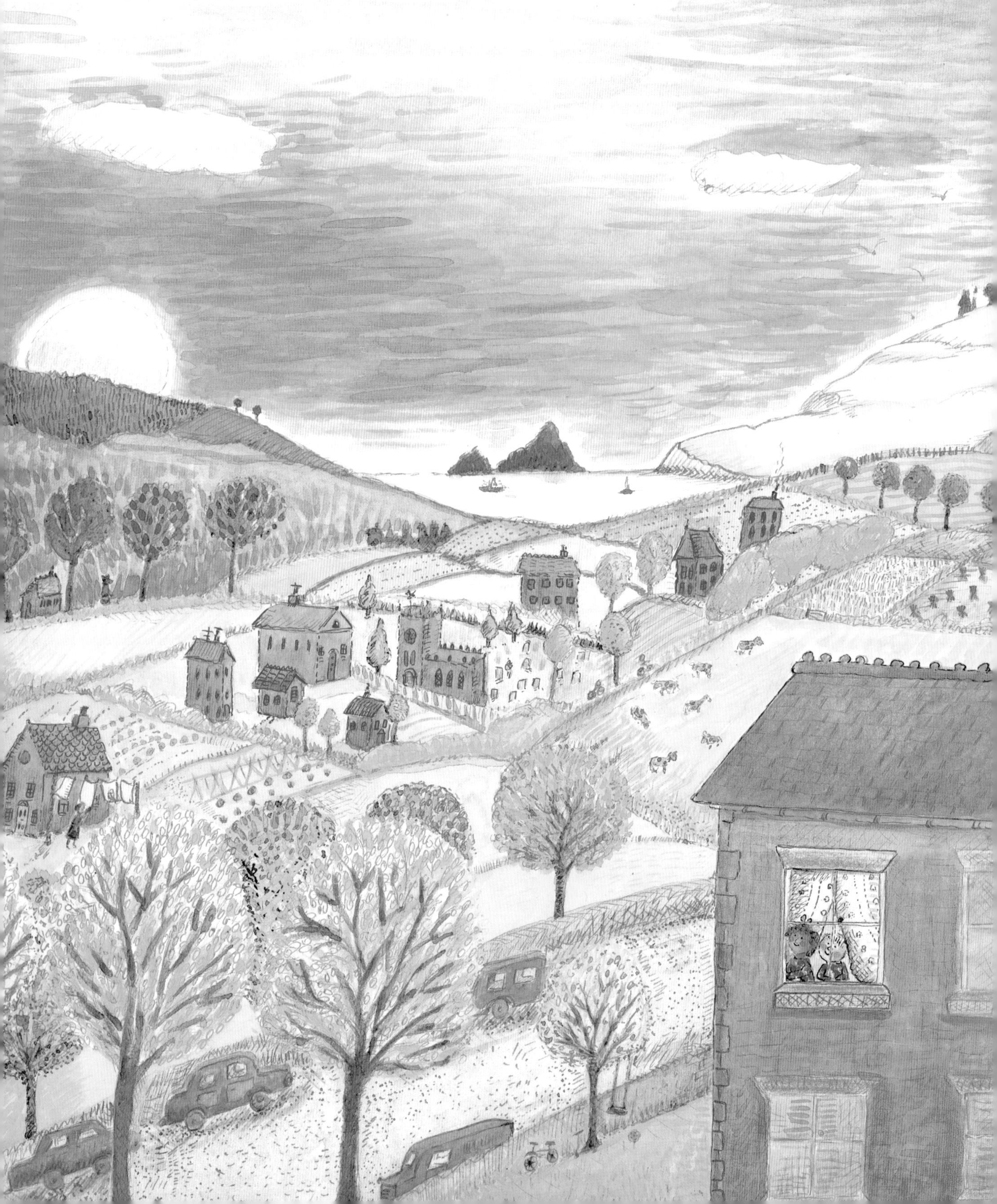

Look out of your window. Is it...

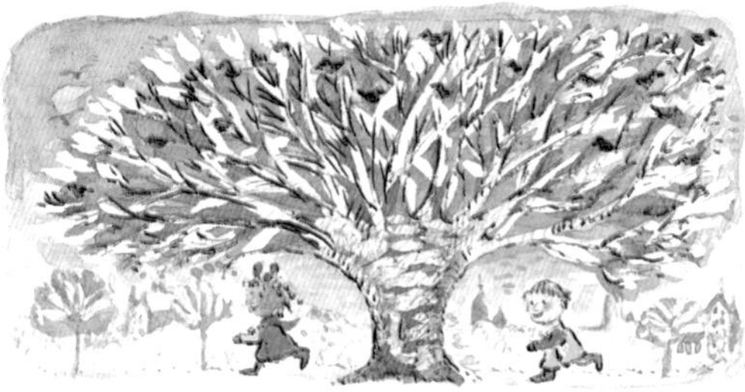

frosty,

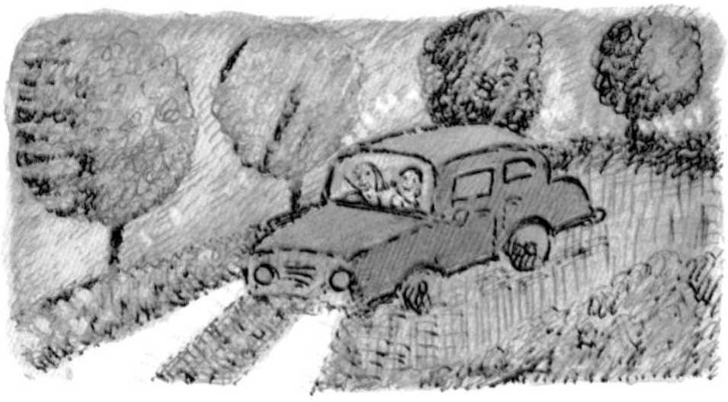

foggy,

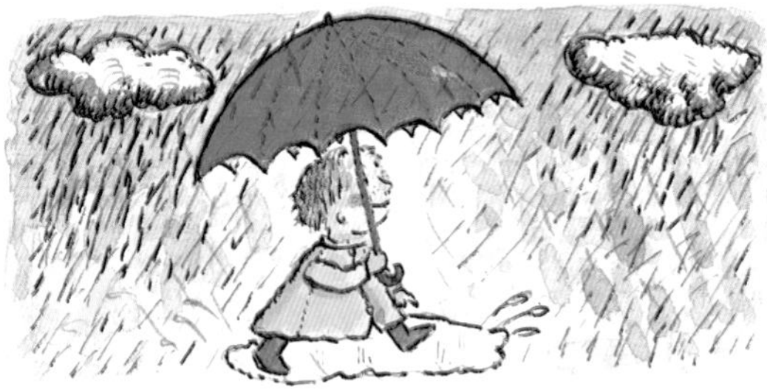

wet,

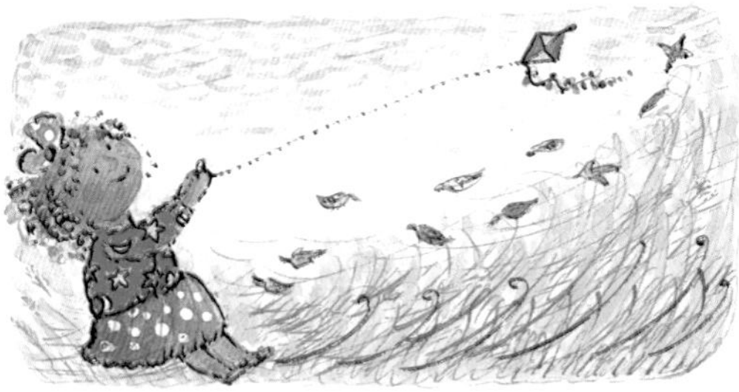

windy,

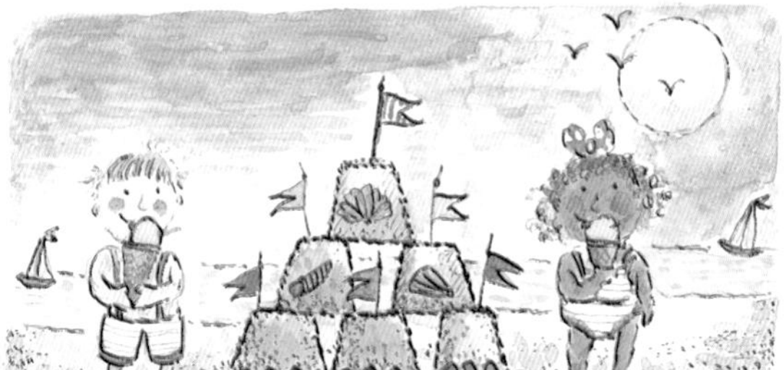

hot,

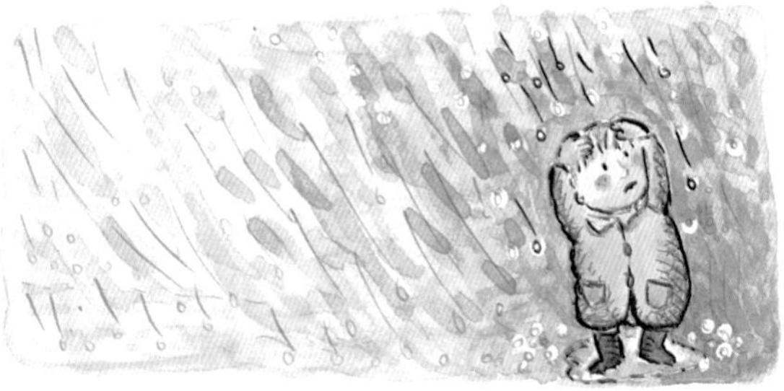

hailing,

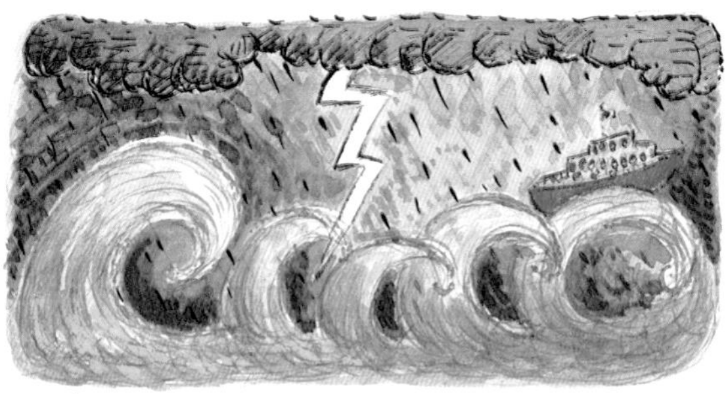

stormy,

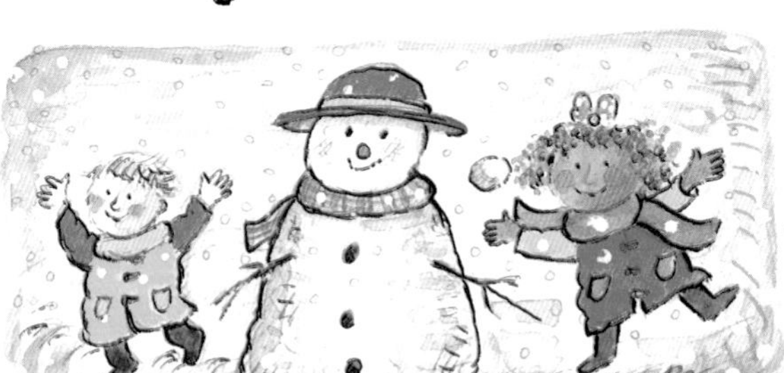

snowing?

What's the weather like today?

On HOT days...

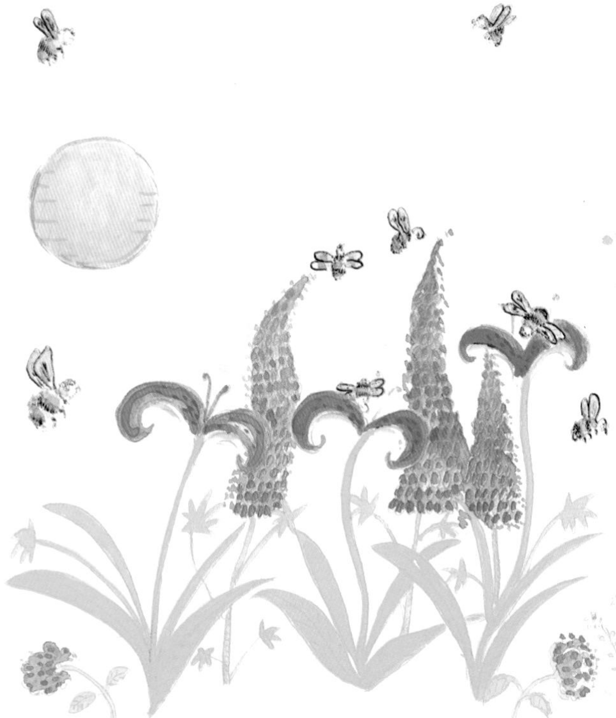

bees buzz,

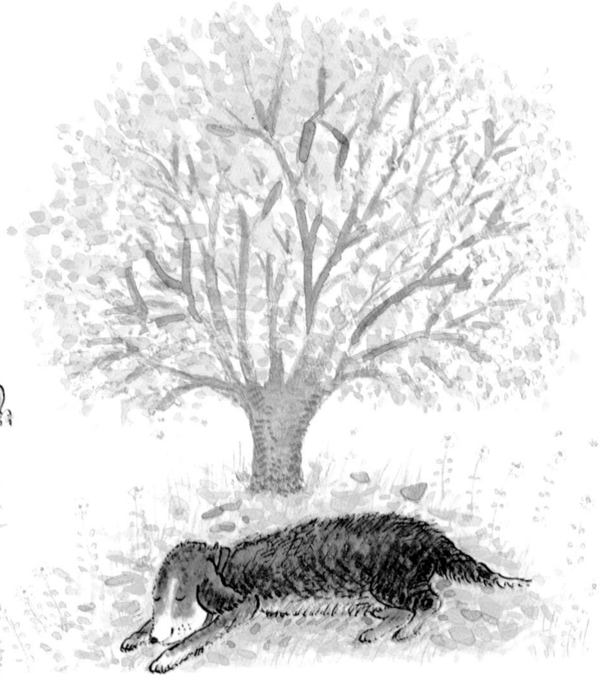

tired dogs search for shade,

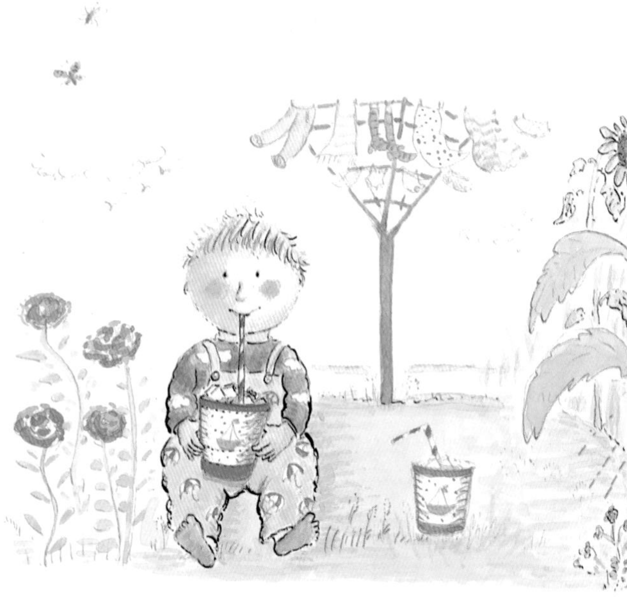

ice tastes nice.

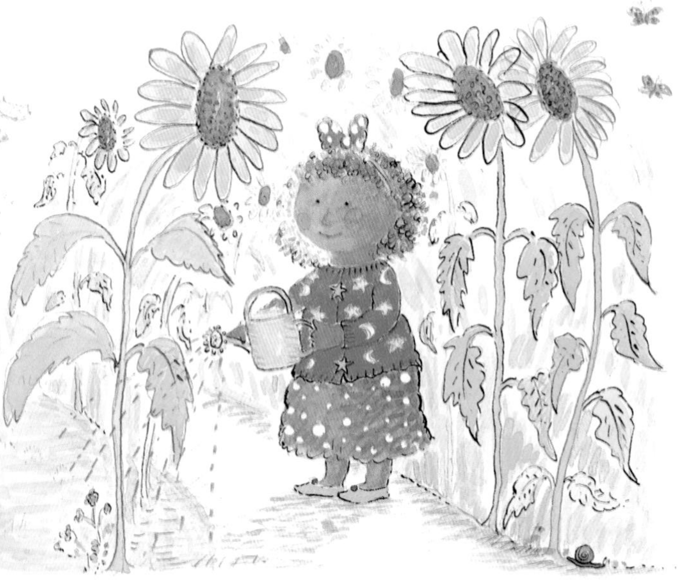

Plants need a drink, too.

We don't wear many clothes,

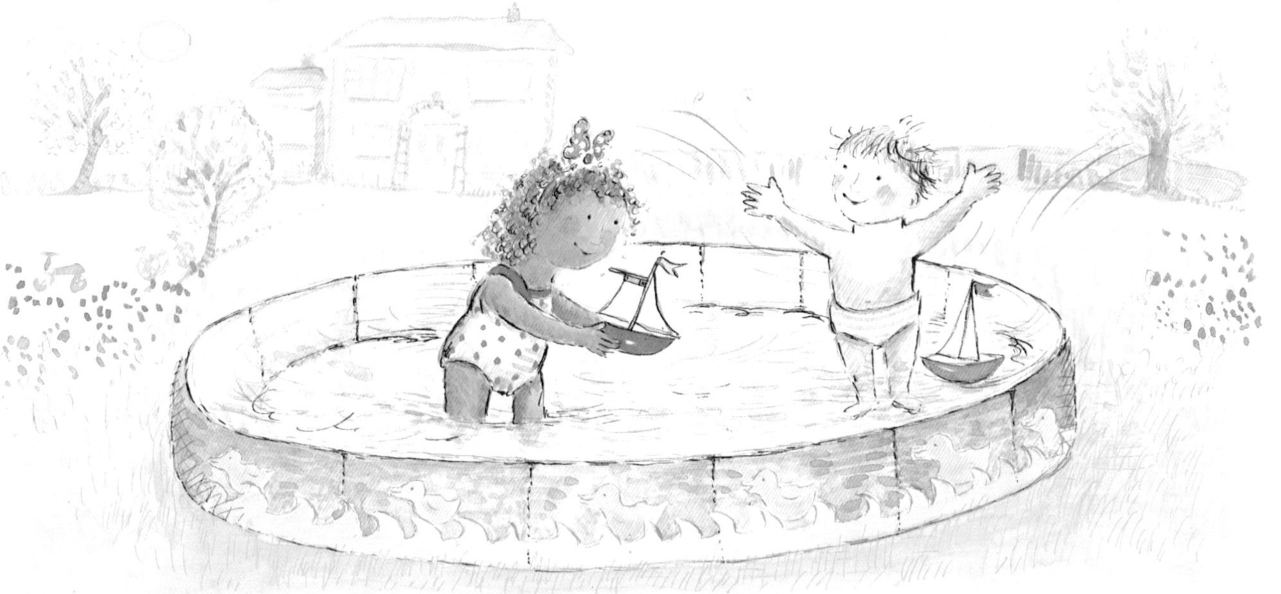

and everyone likes to be outdoors.

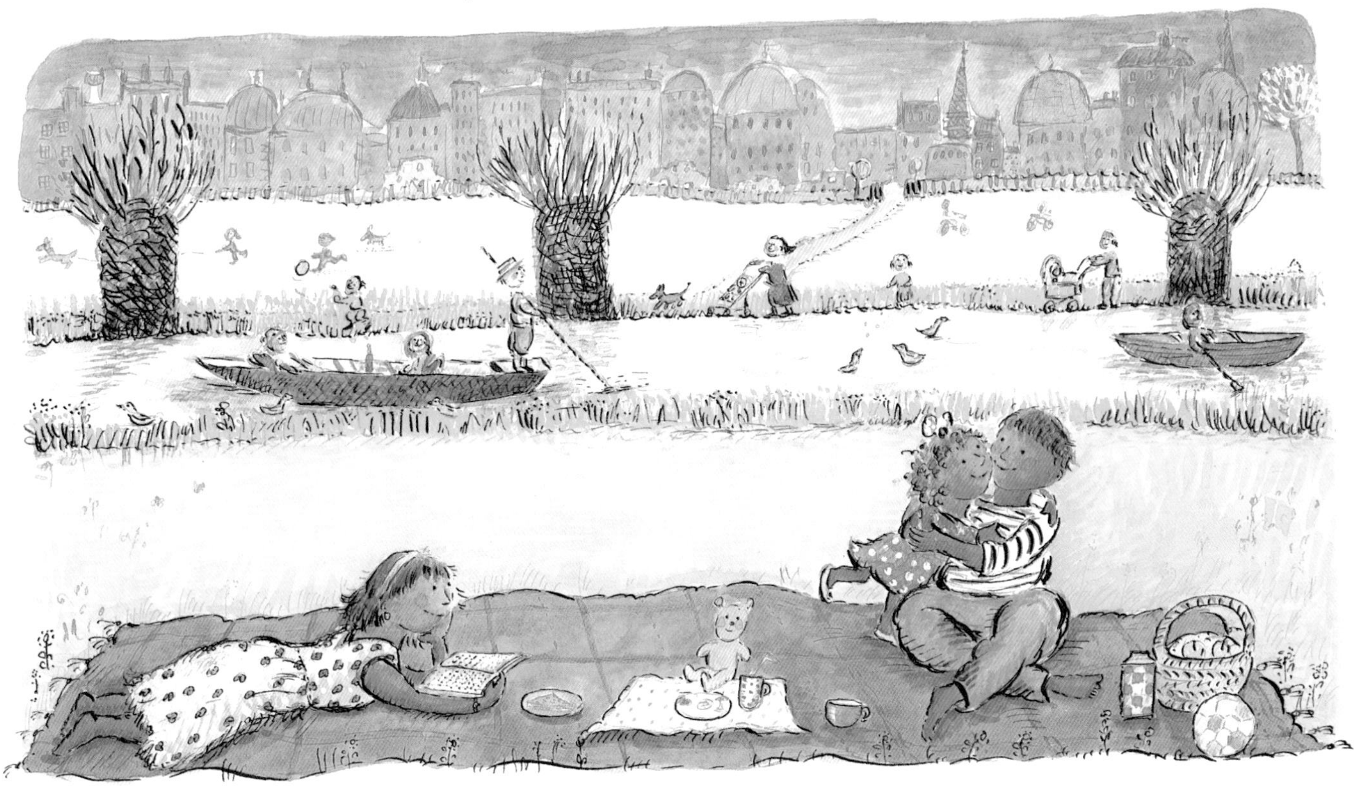

What do you do on HOT days?

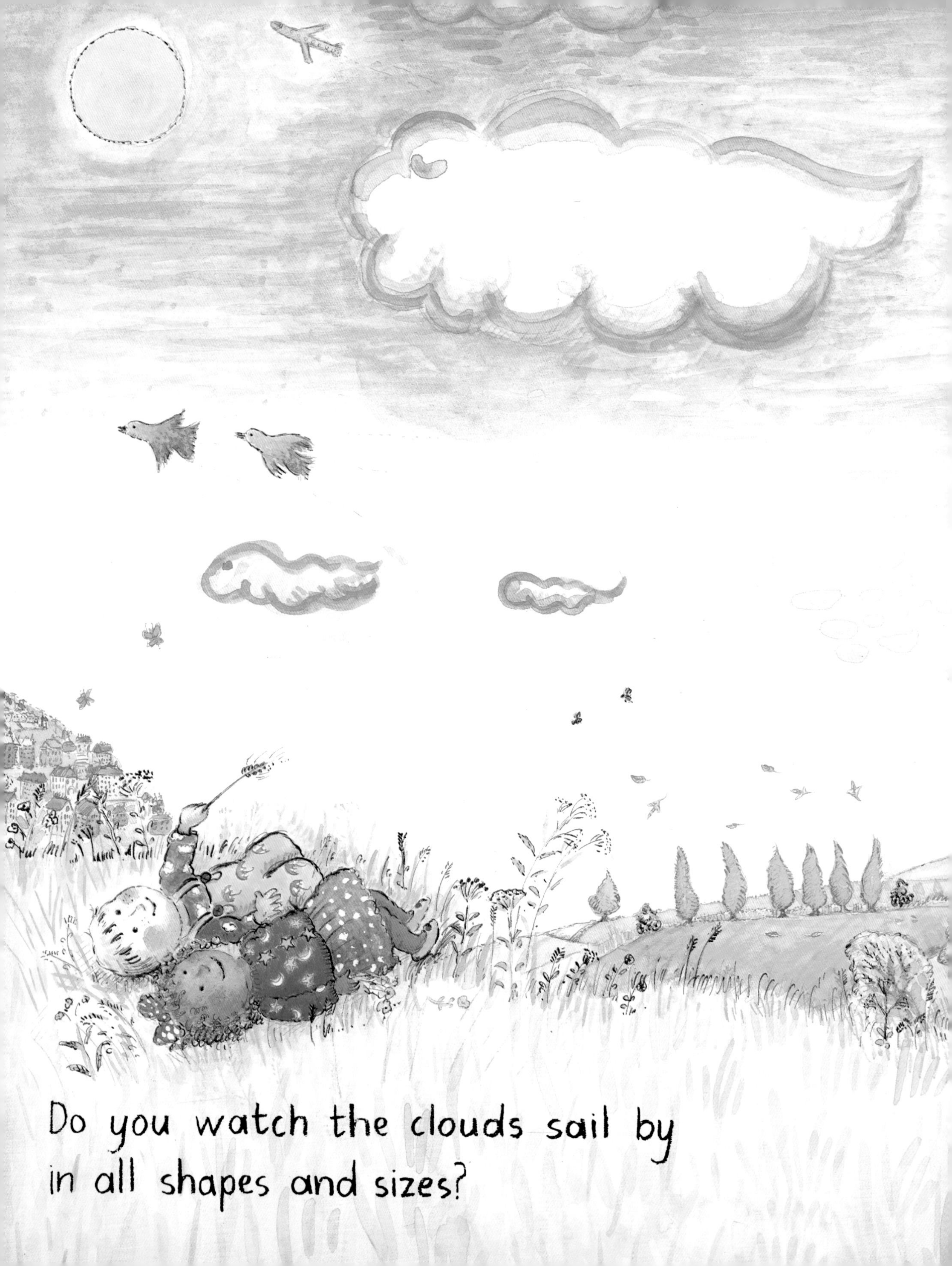

Do you watch the clouds sail by
in all shapes and sizes?

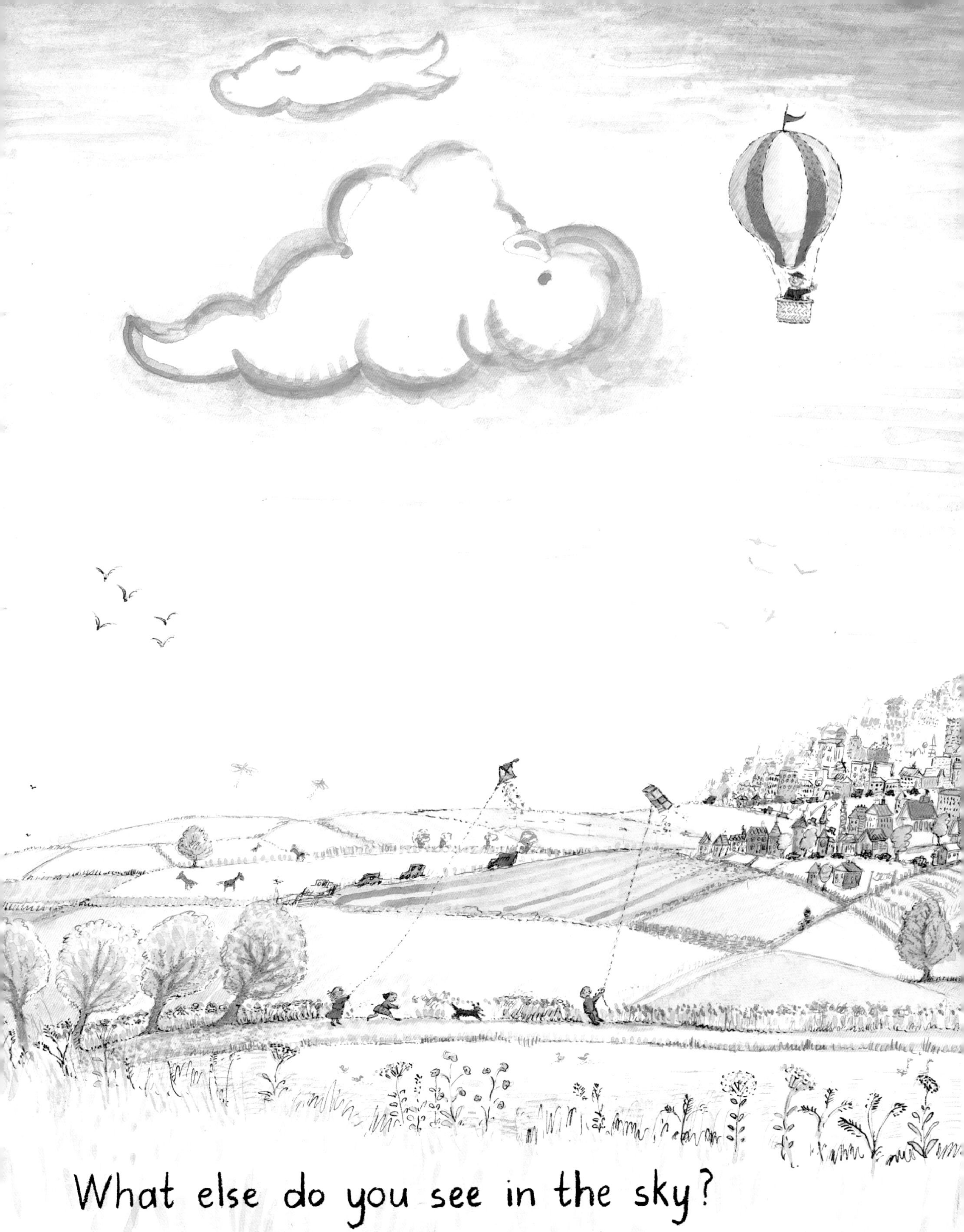

What else do you see in the sky?

On COLD days...

puddles turn
to ice,

cars are hard
to start.

We have
warm drinks

and wear
lots of clothes.

We can see our breath in the air.

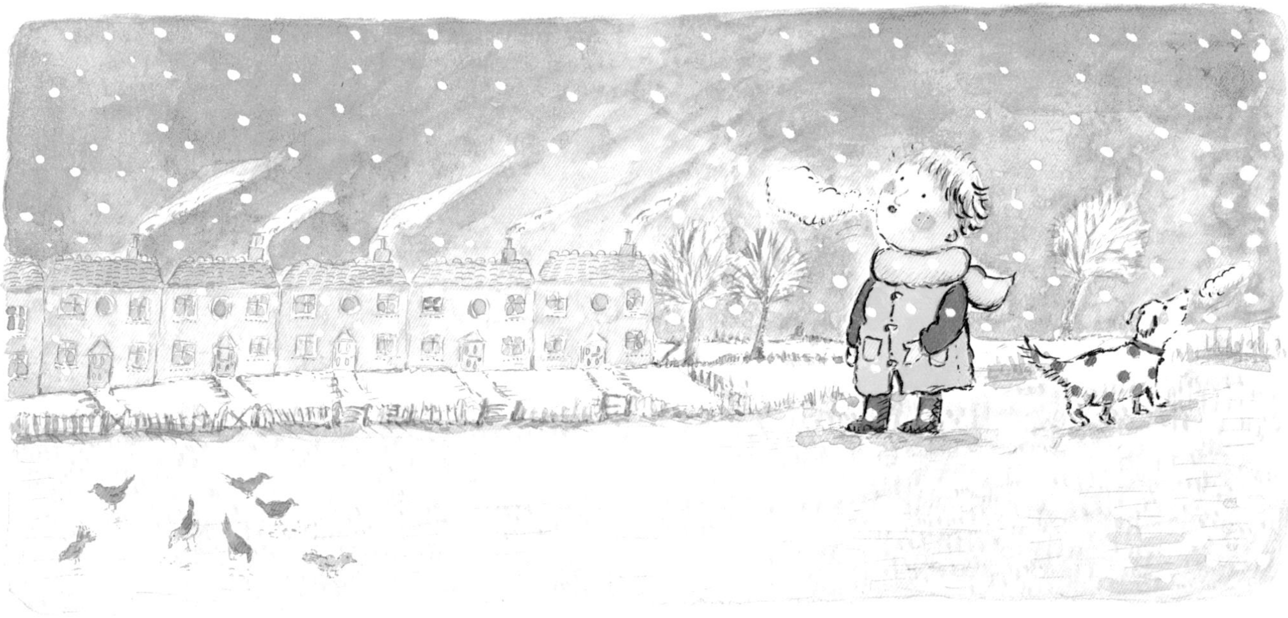

We might find footprints in the snow.

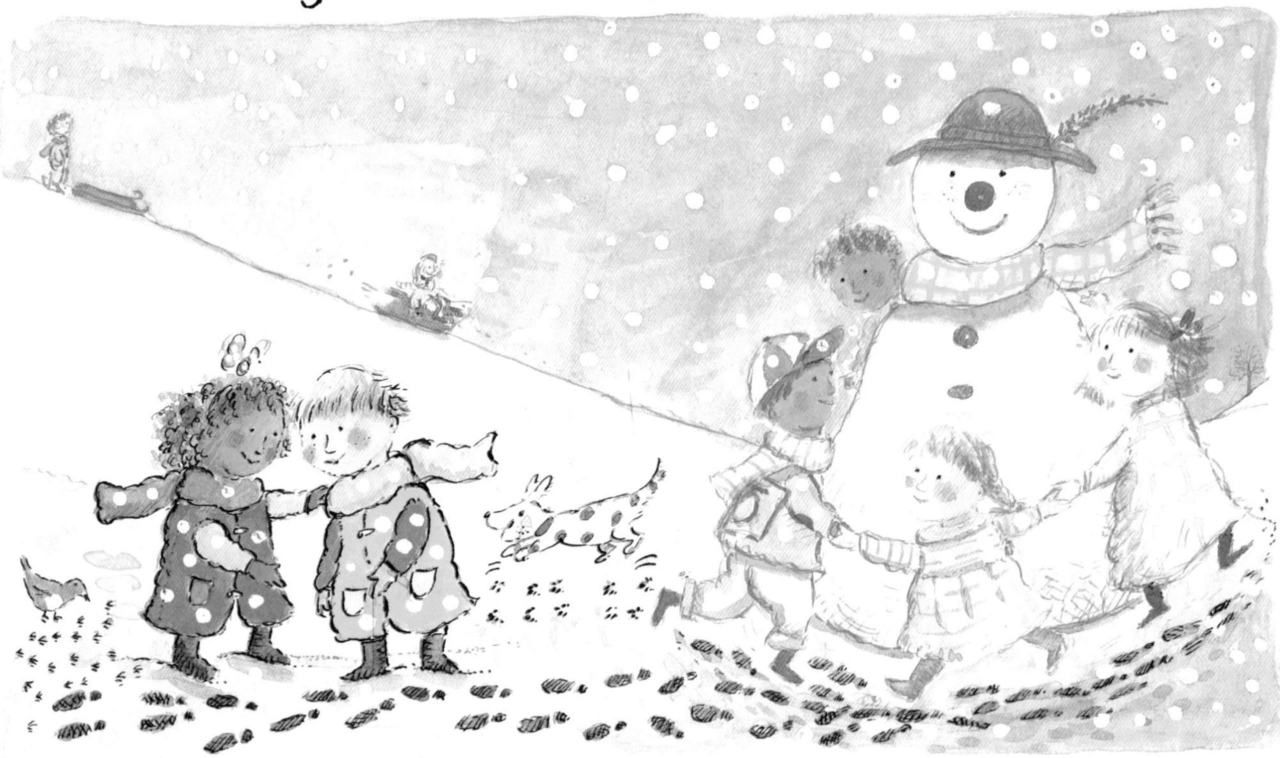

What do you do on COLD days?

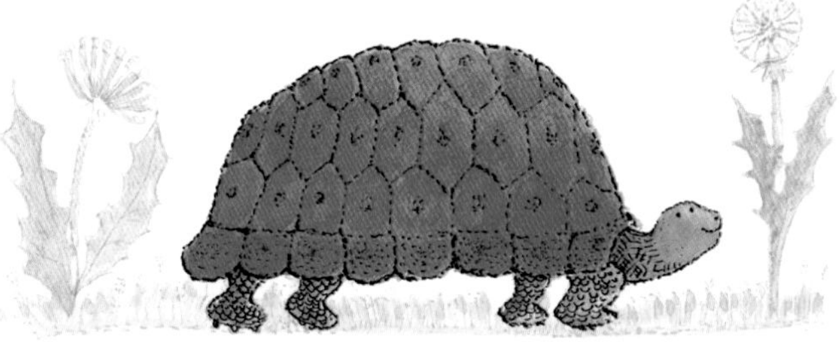
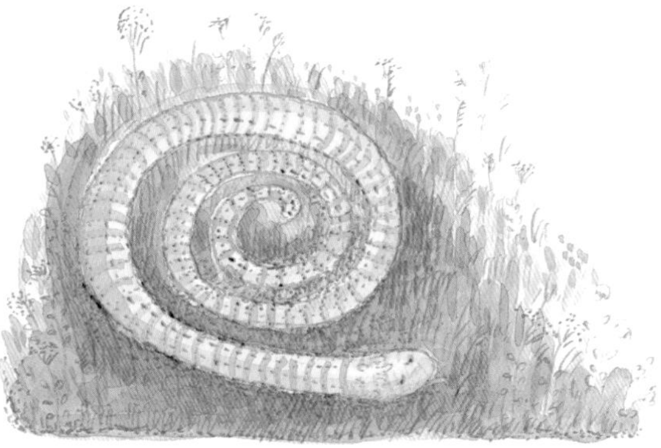
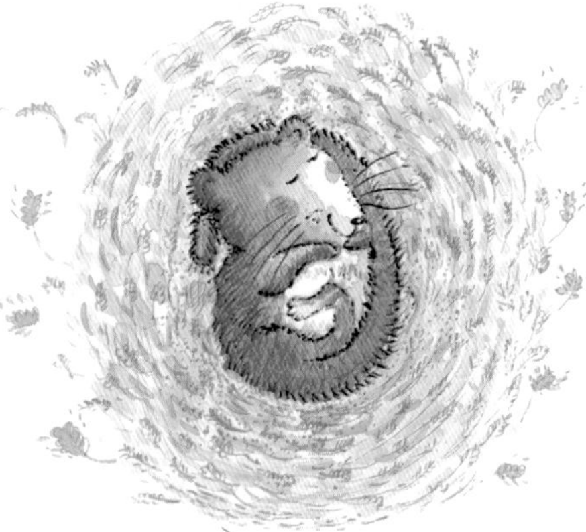
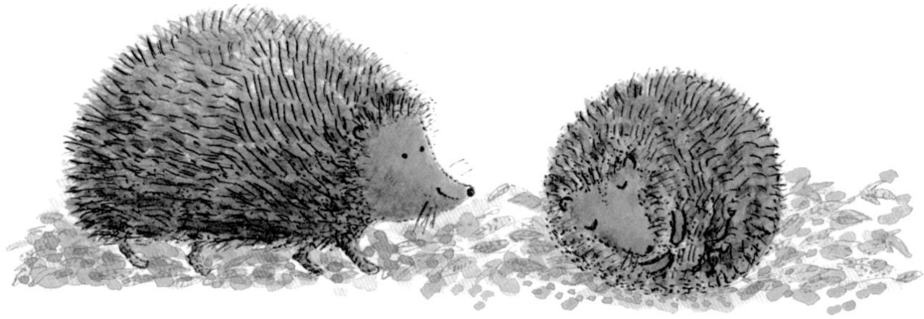

Some animals sleep all winter.
That's called hibernating.

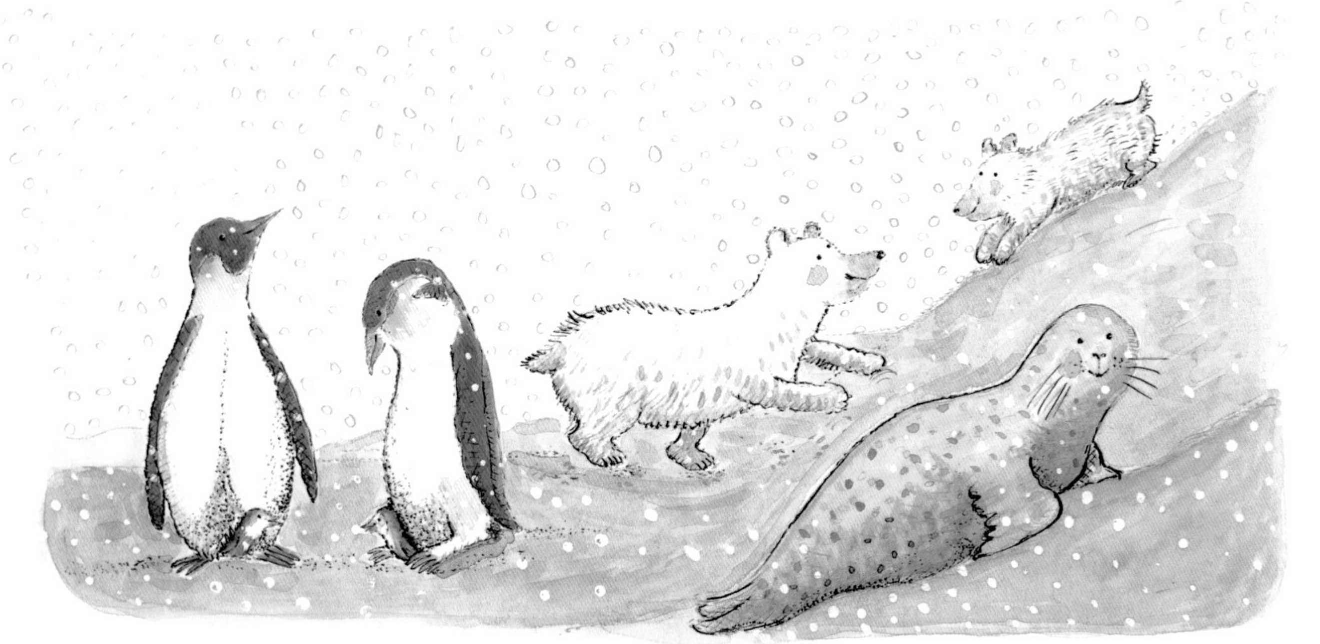

Other animals like the cold.

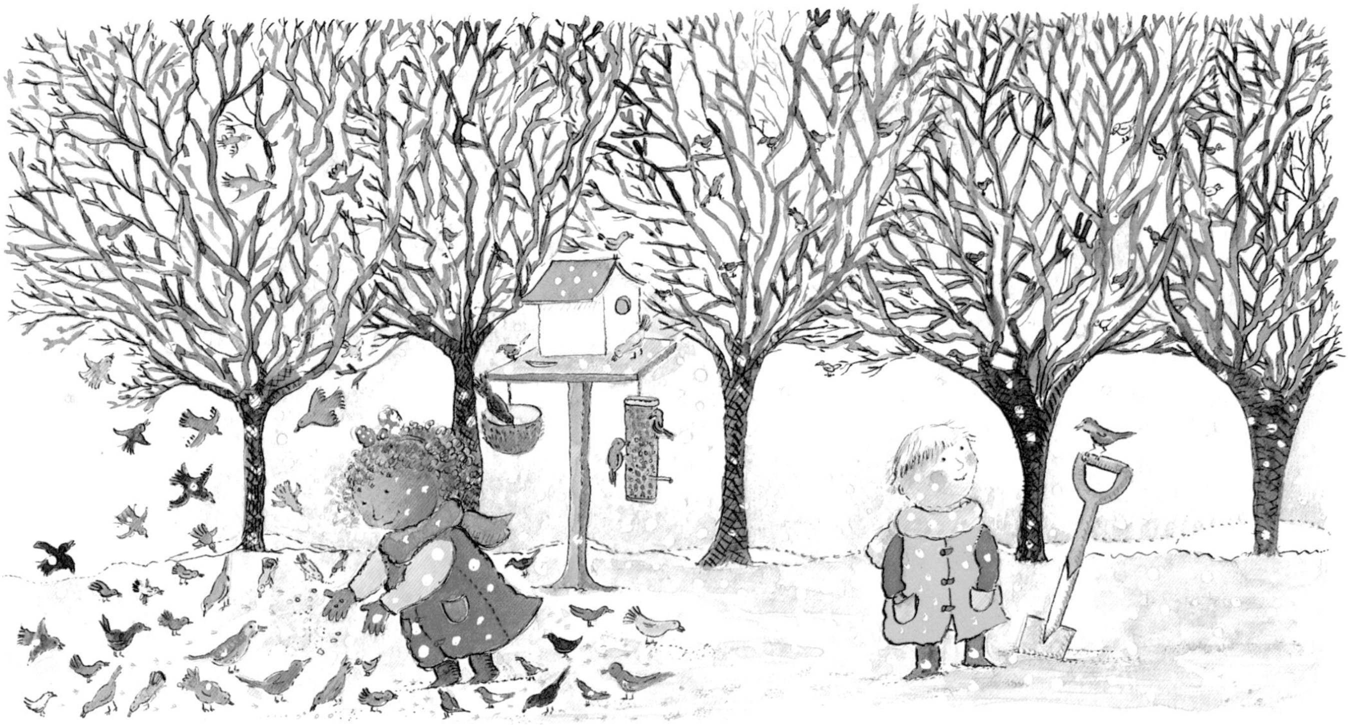

Some birds stay in the garden.

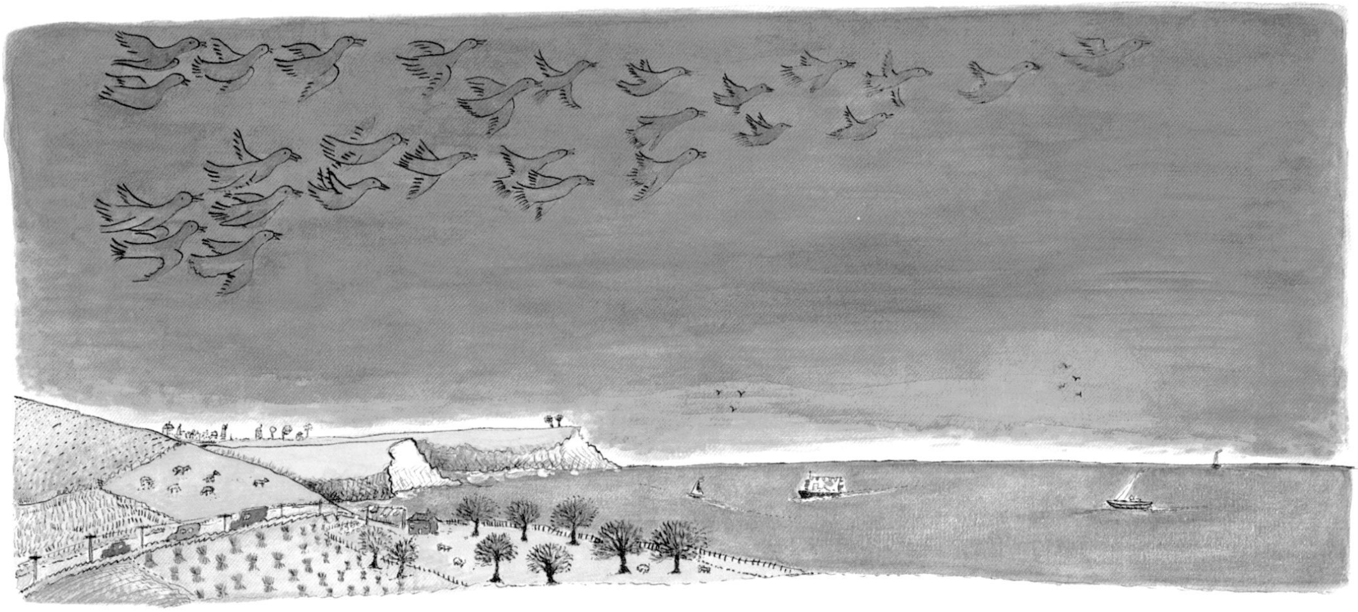

Others fly away to warmer places.

Some countries are very hot.

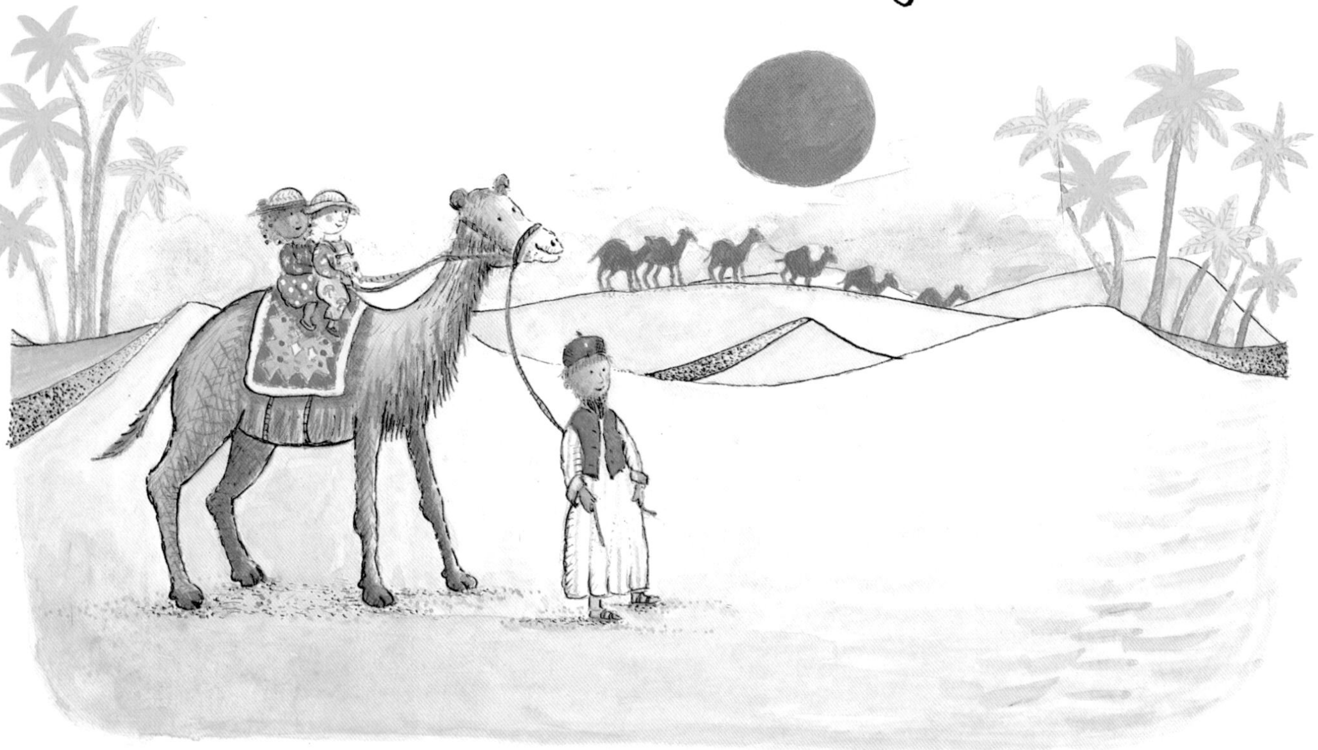

Others are always cold.

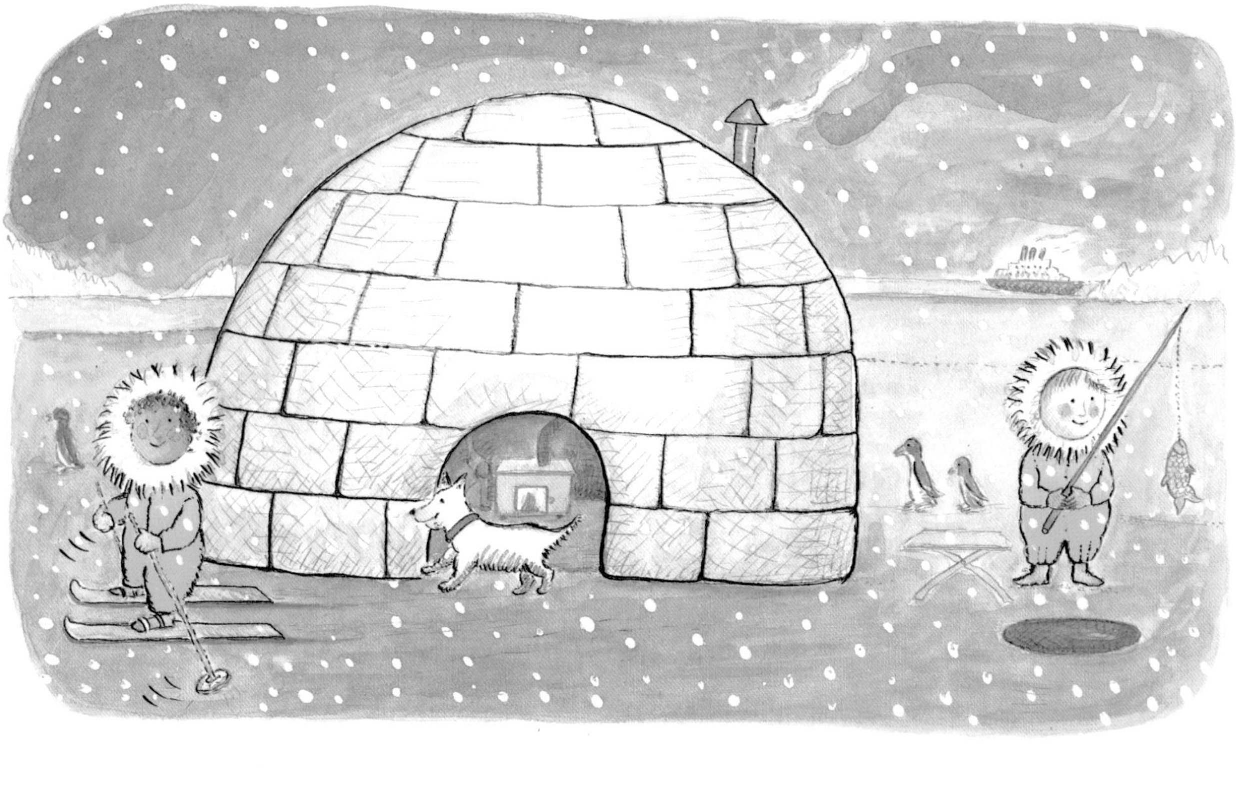

Some animals live only where it's hot.

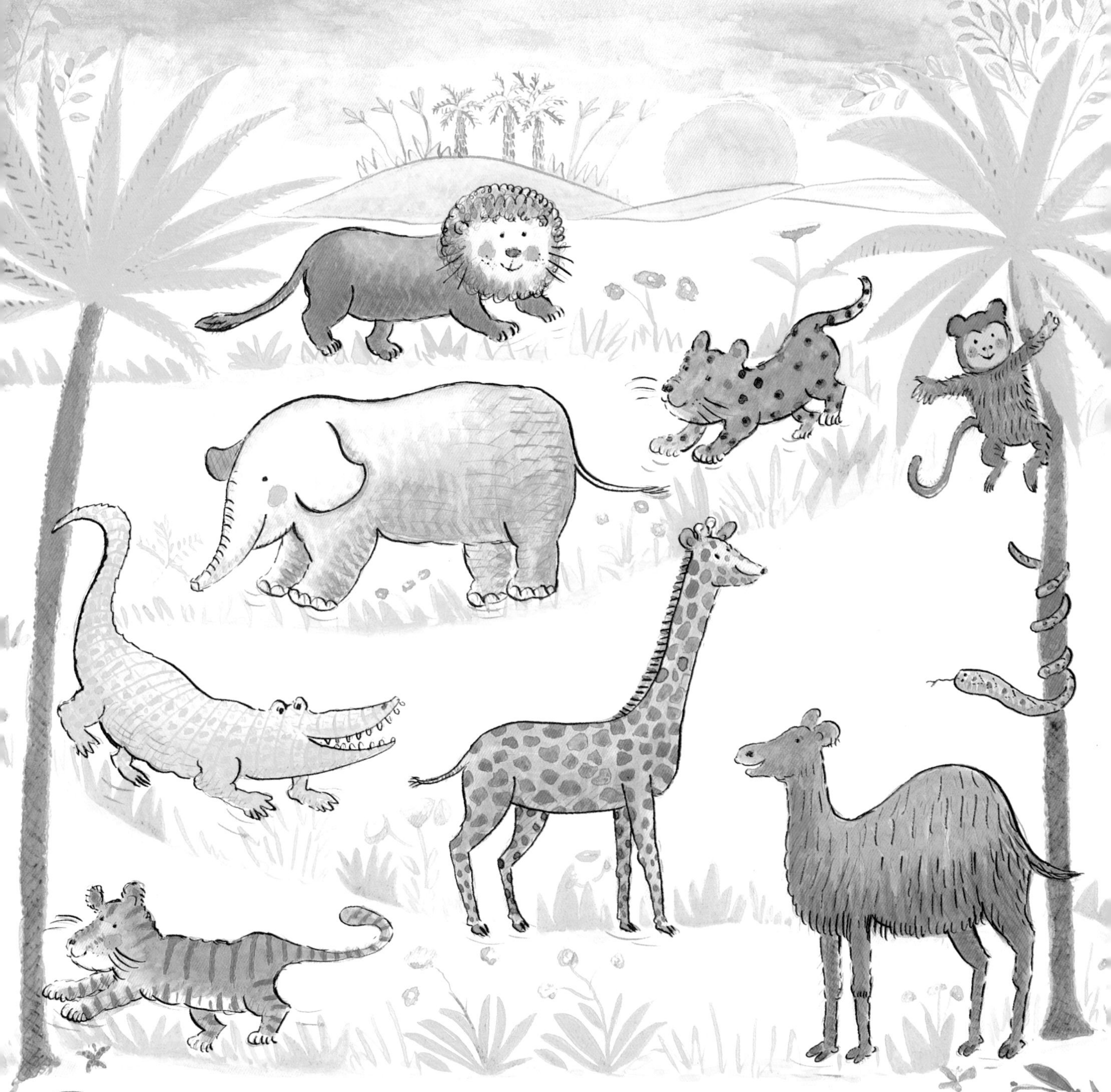

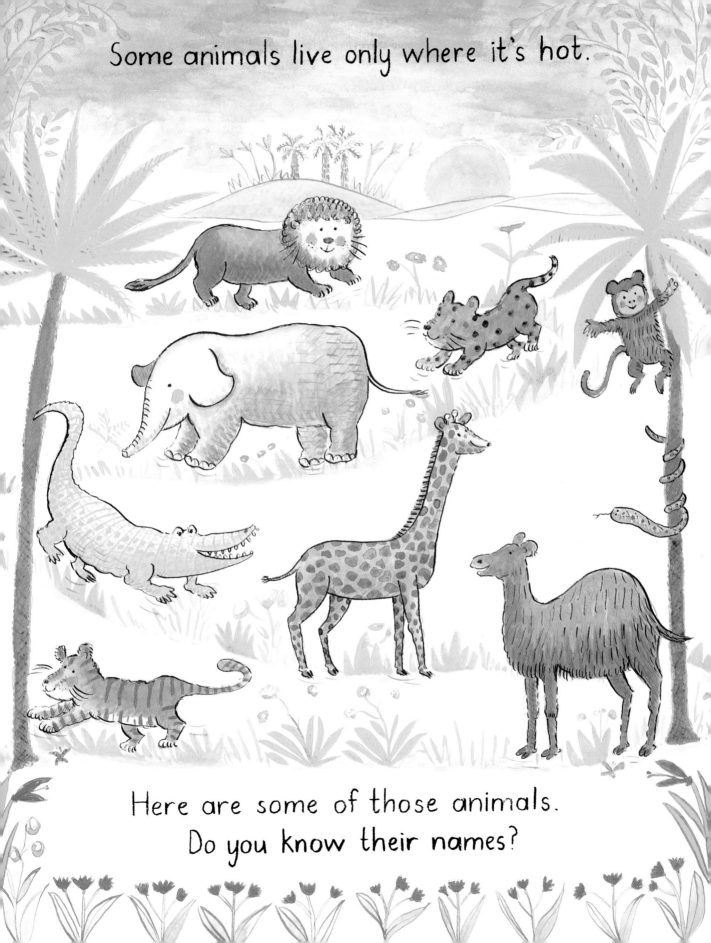

Here are some of those animals.
Do you know their names?

SPRING is the time for...

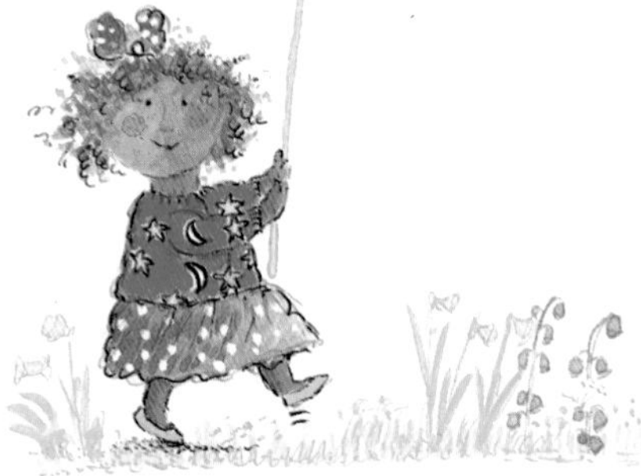

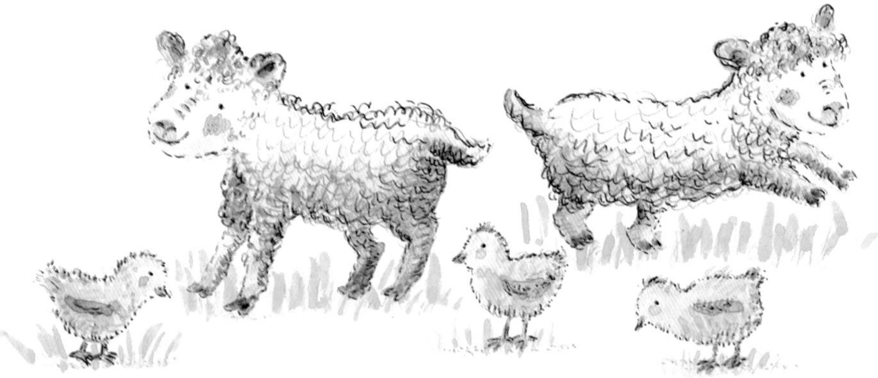

lambs and chicks,

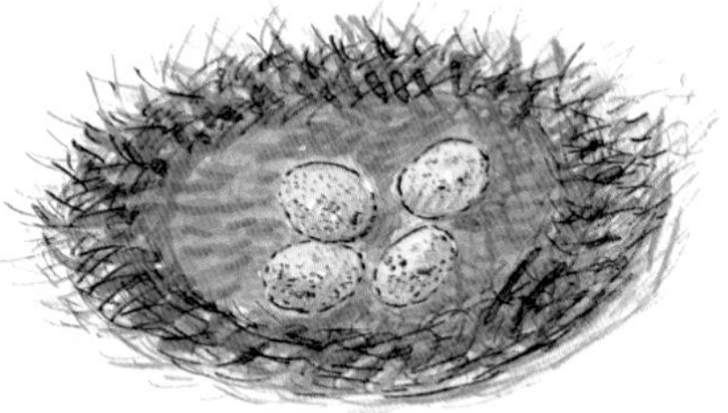

eggs in nests,

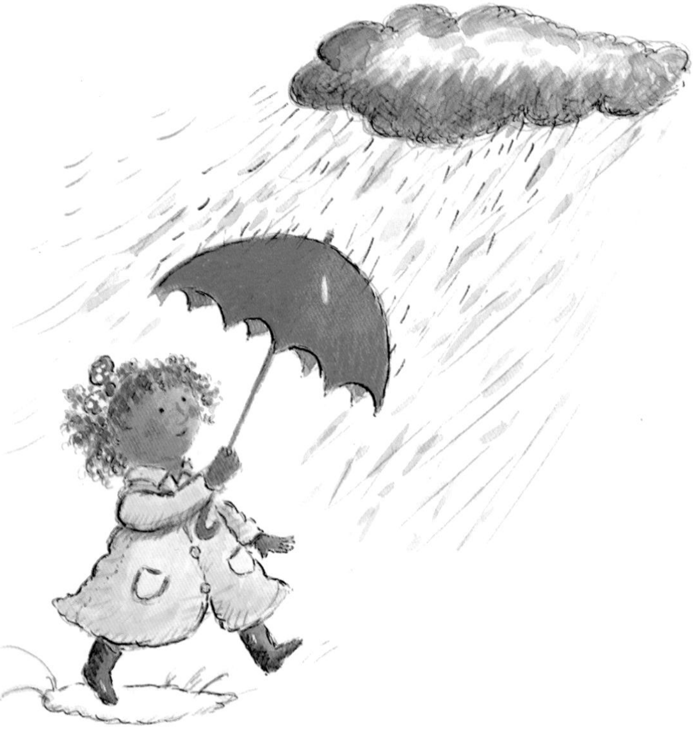

sudden showers,

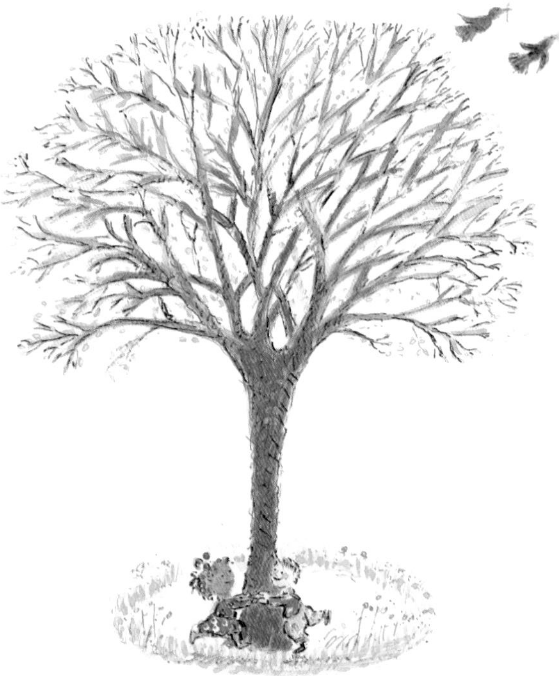

buds on trees.

SUMMER is the time for...

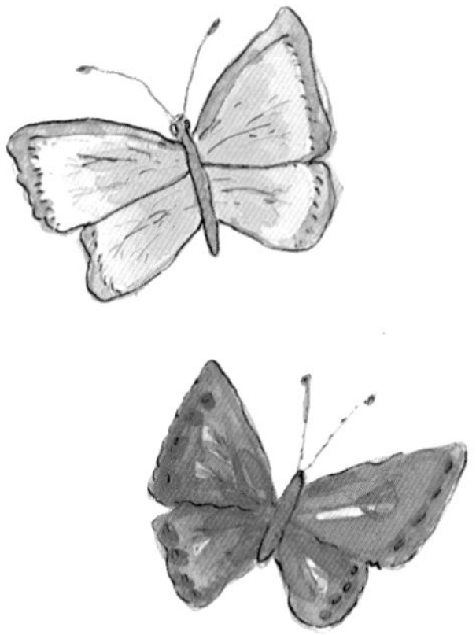

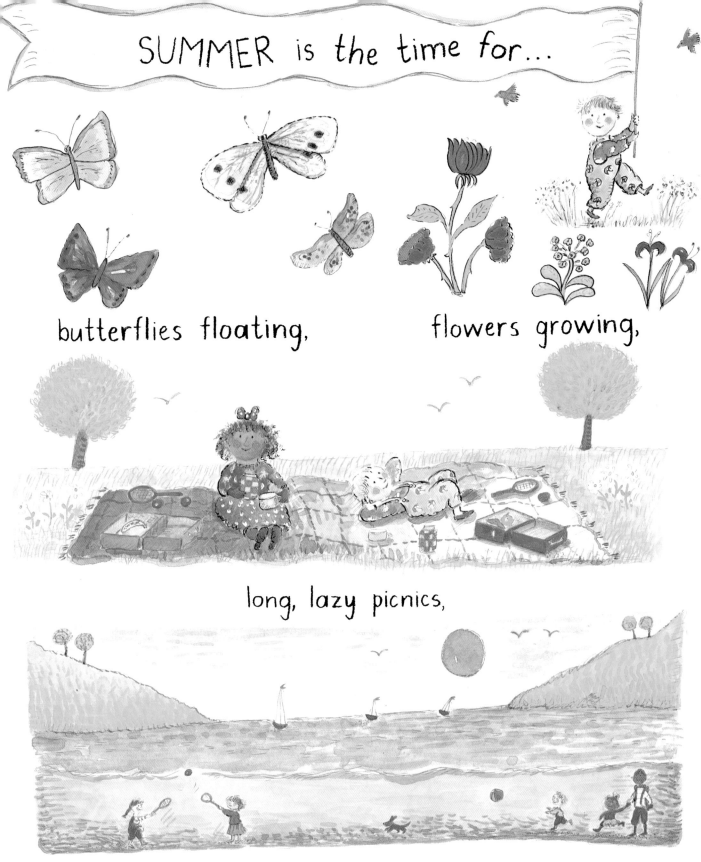

butterflies floating,

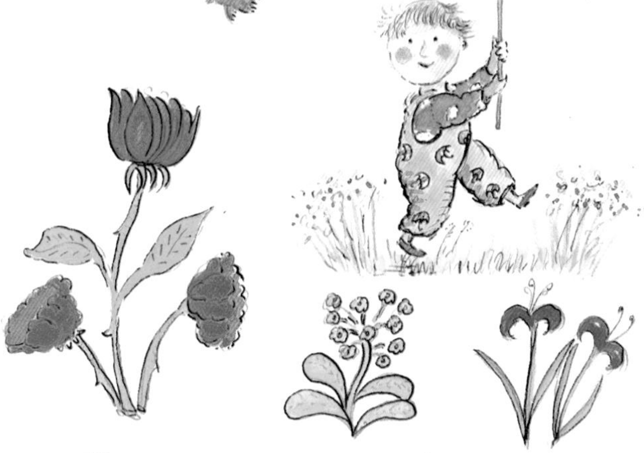

flowers growing,

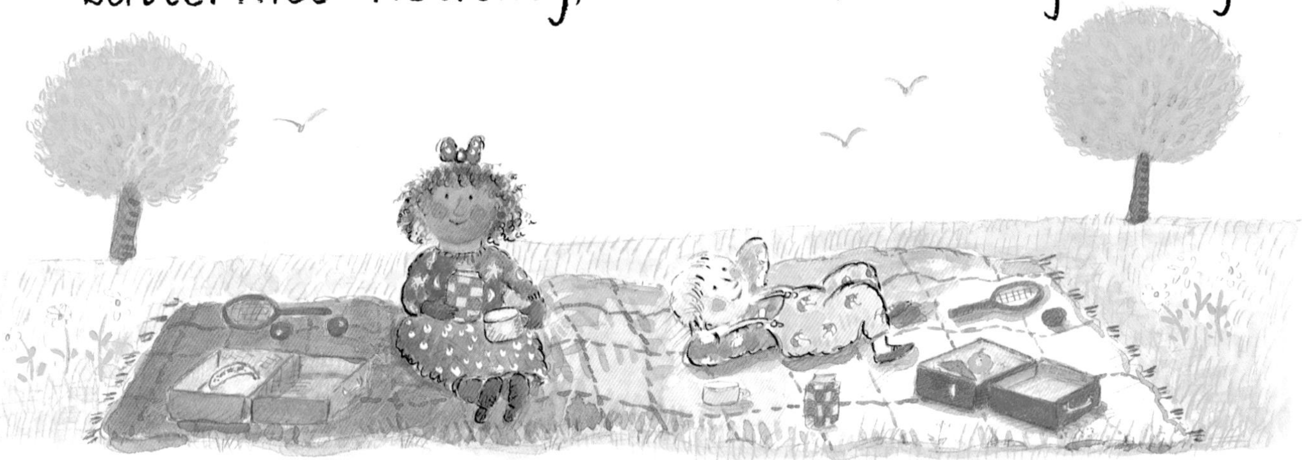

long, lazy picnics,

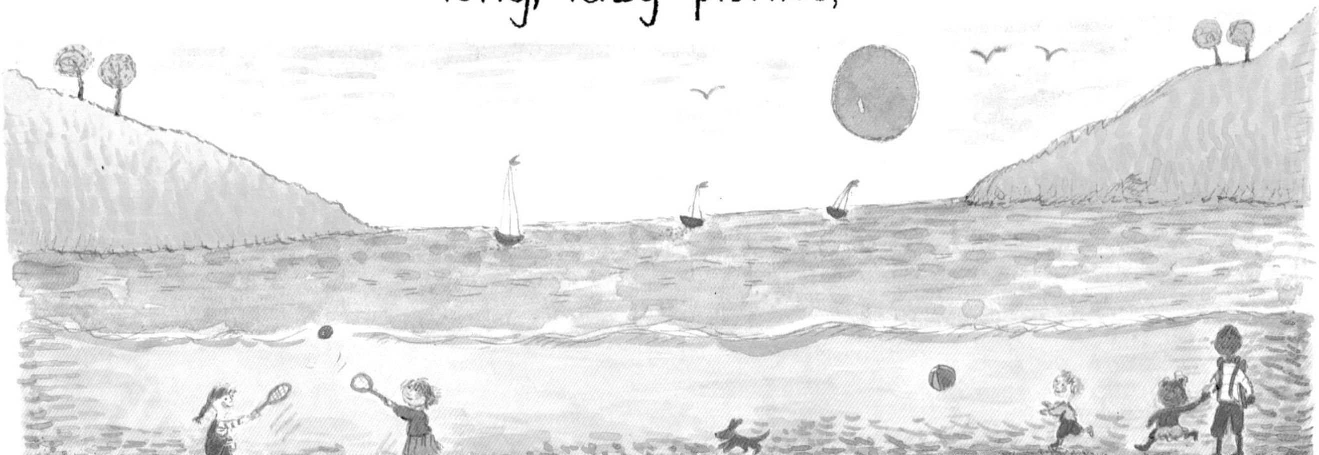

and vacations at the beach.

AUTUMN is the time for…

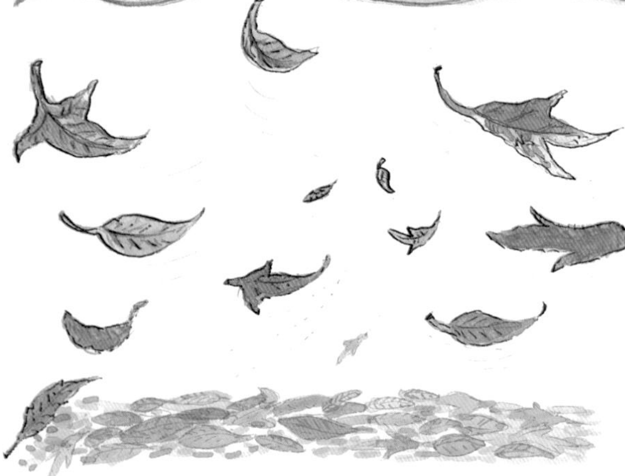

falling leaves,

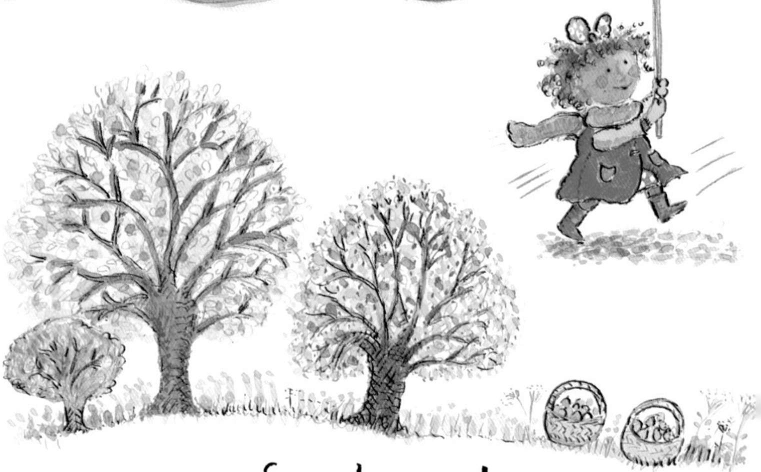

fruit on trees,

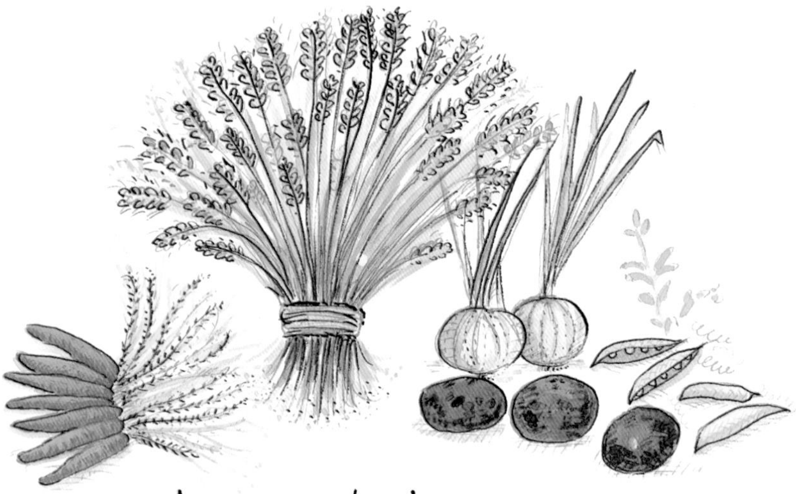

harvest days,

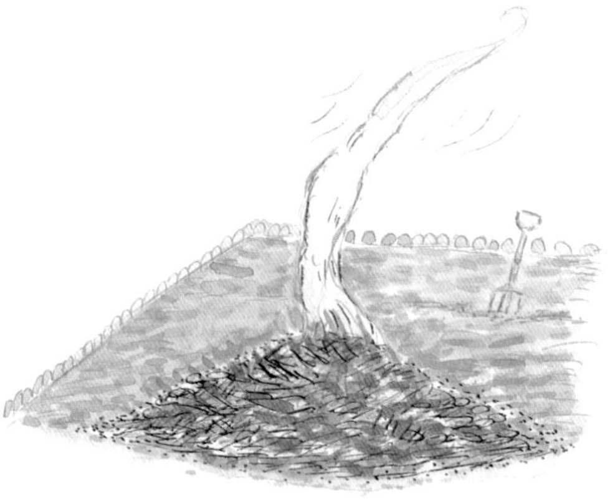

bonfires,

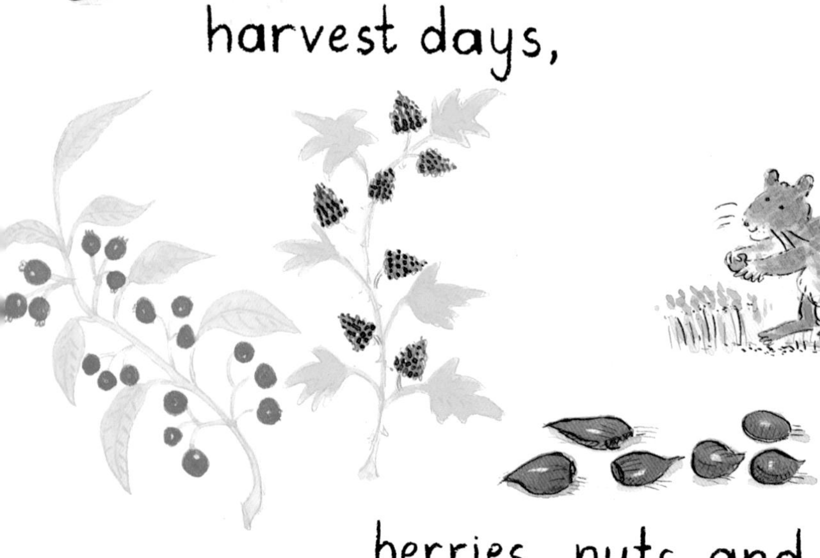

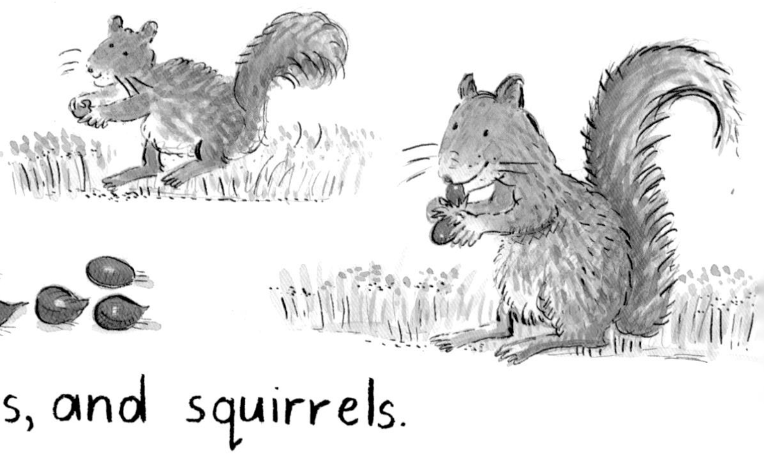

berries, nuts, and squirrels.

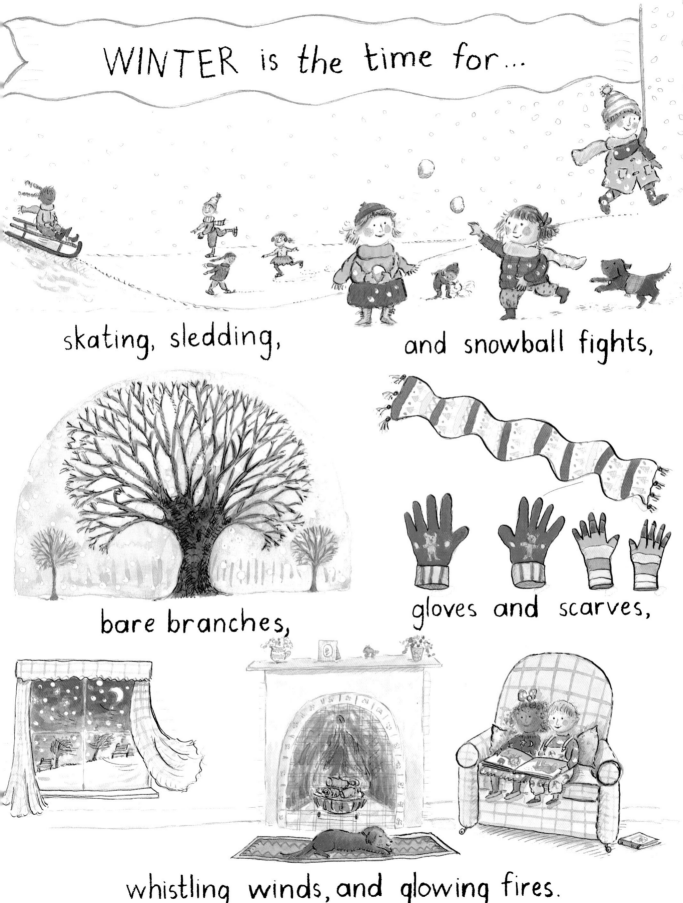

WINTER is the time for...

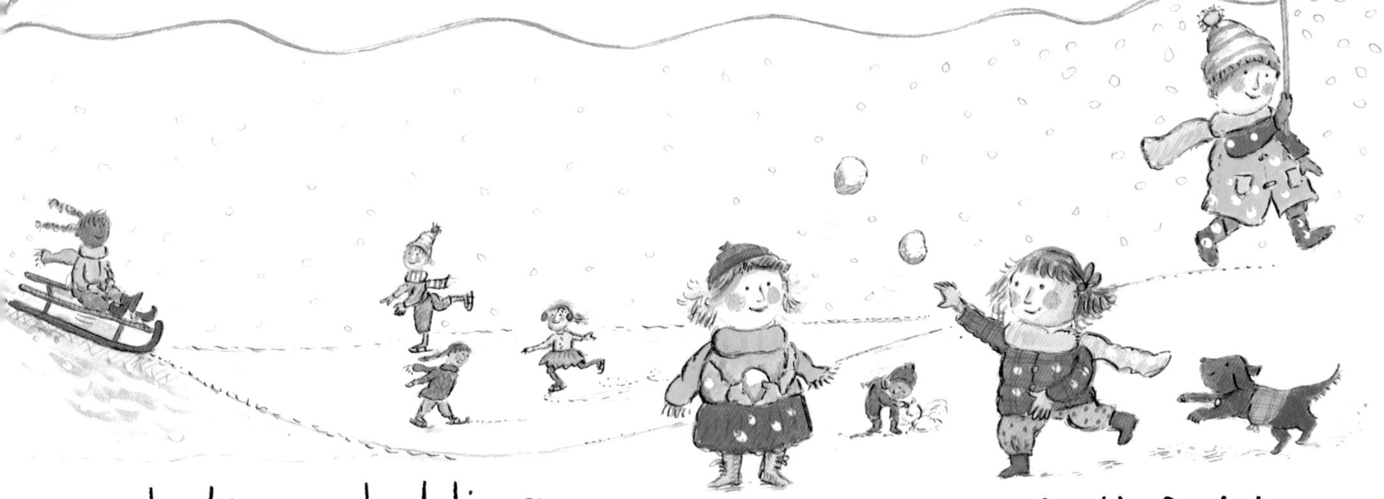

skating, sledding,

and snowball fights,

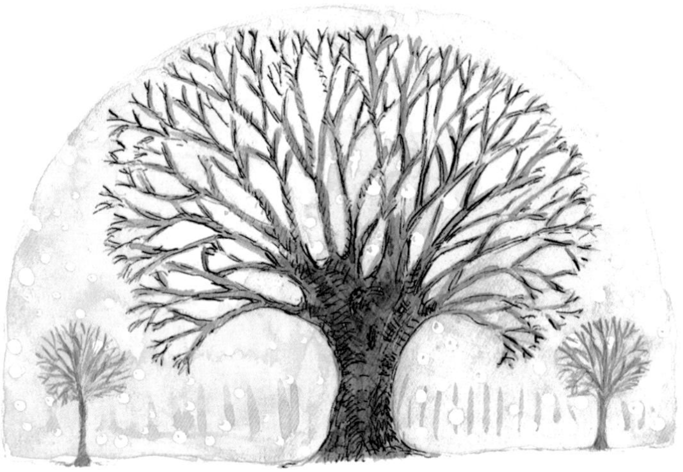

bare branches,

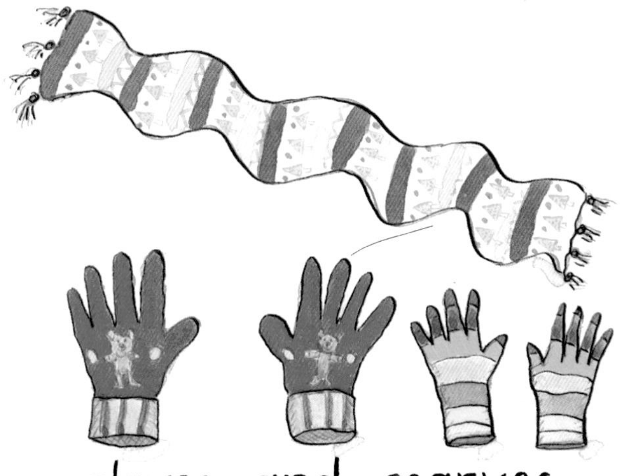

gloves and scarves,

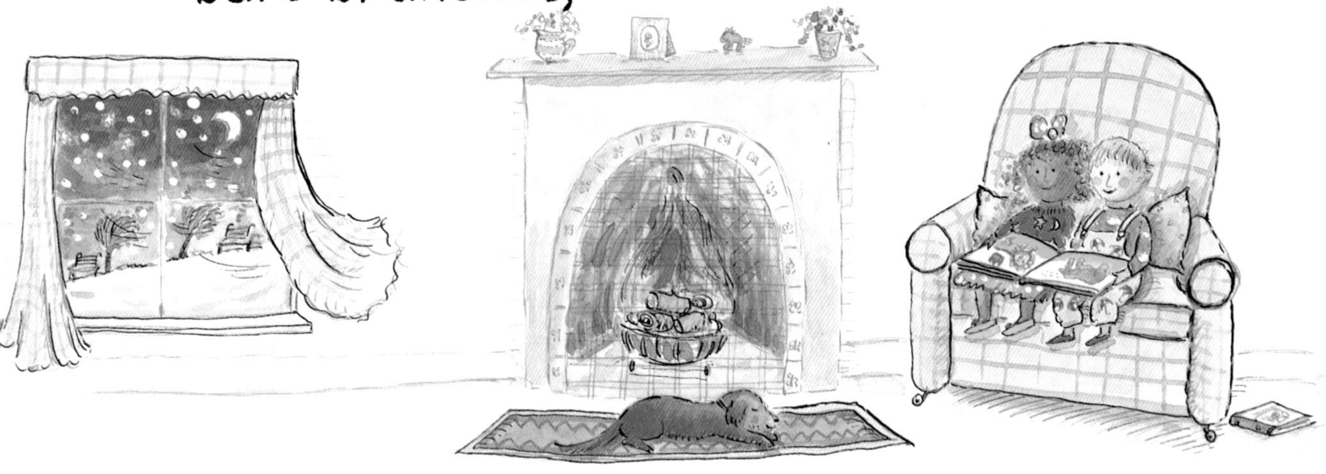

whistling winds, and glowing fires.

People say funny things about the weather.

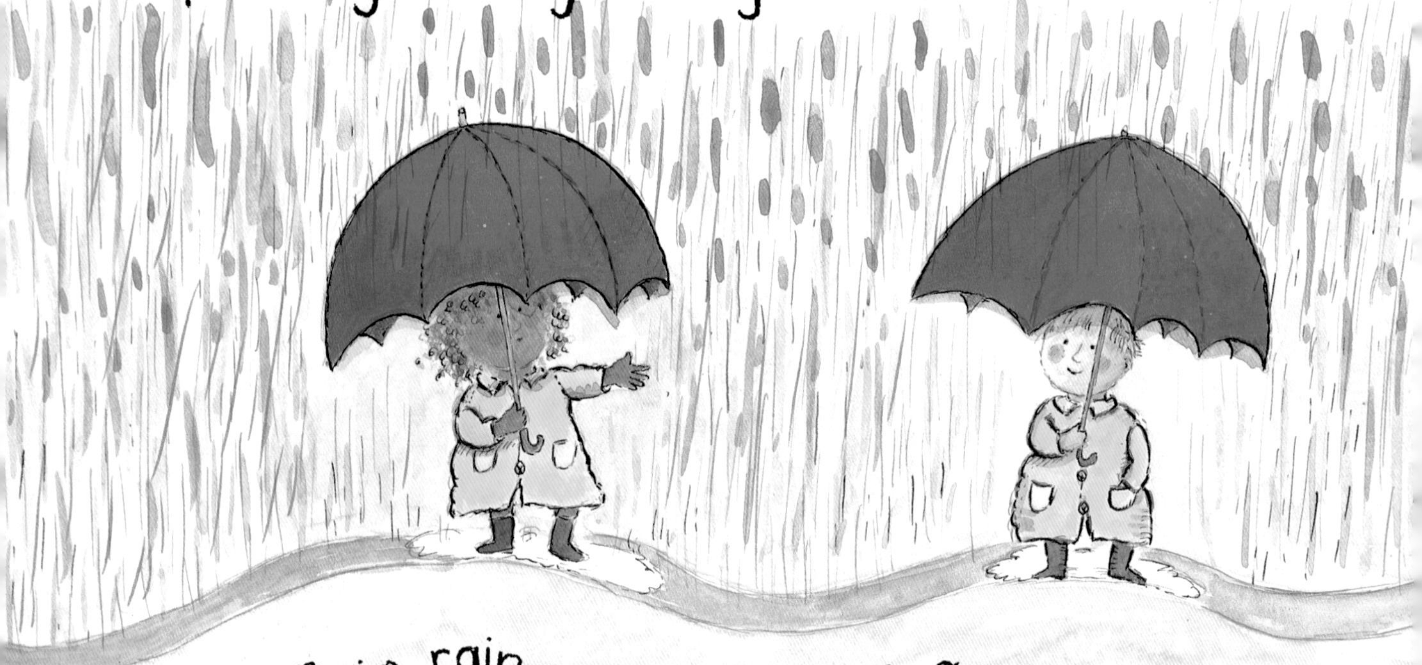

Rain, rain, go away. Come again another day.

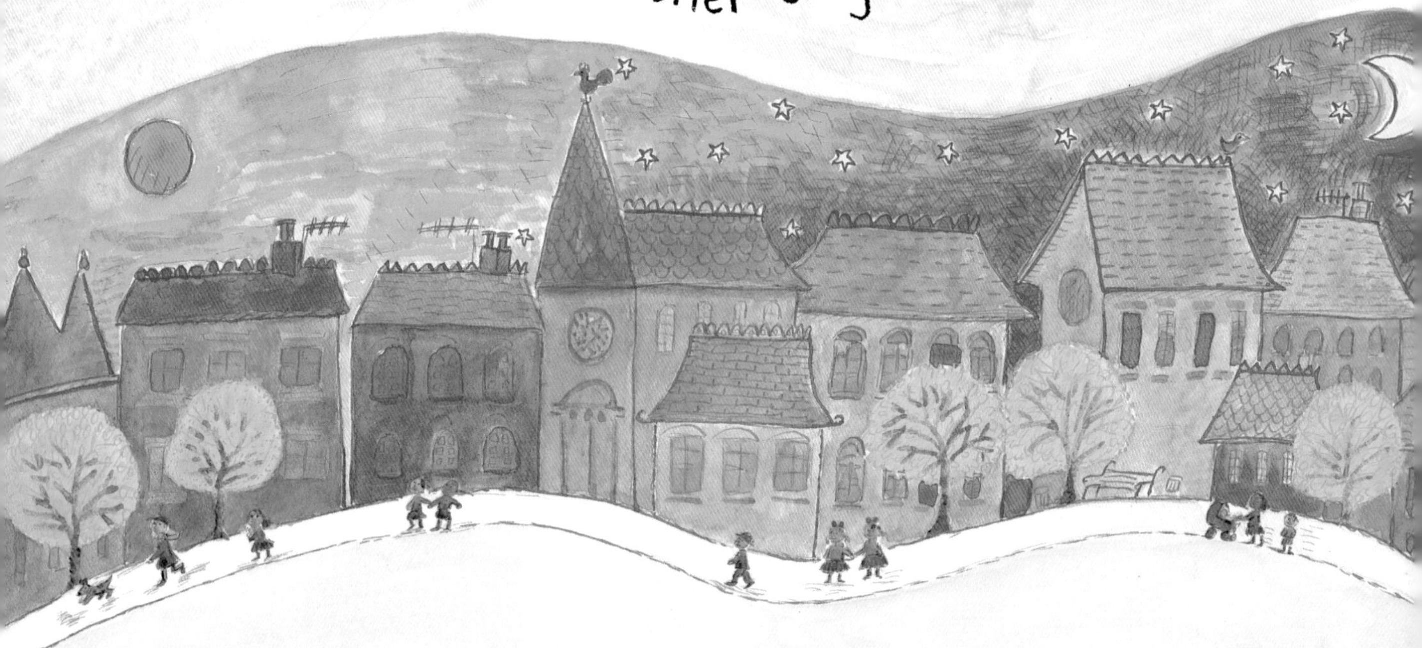

Red sky at night, sailors' delight.
Red sky in the morning, sailors' warning.

If the cows are lying down,
it's going to rain.

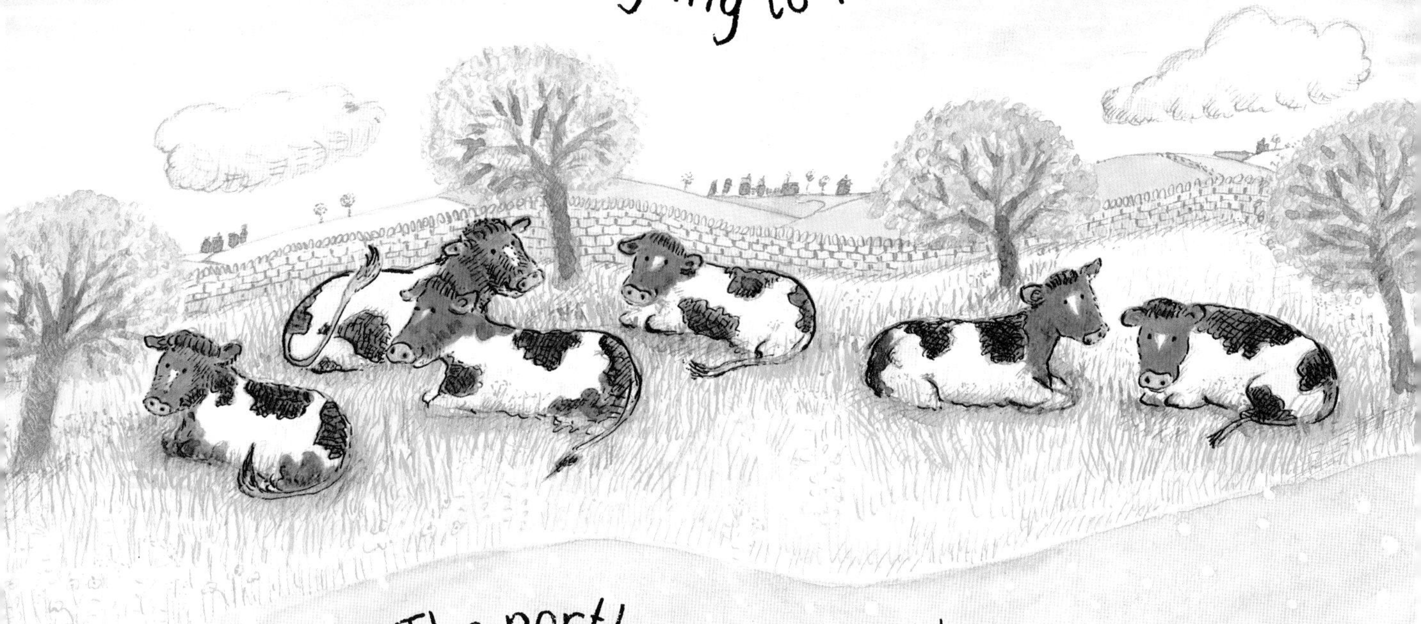

The north wind doth blow,
and we shall have snow.

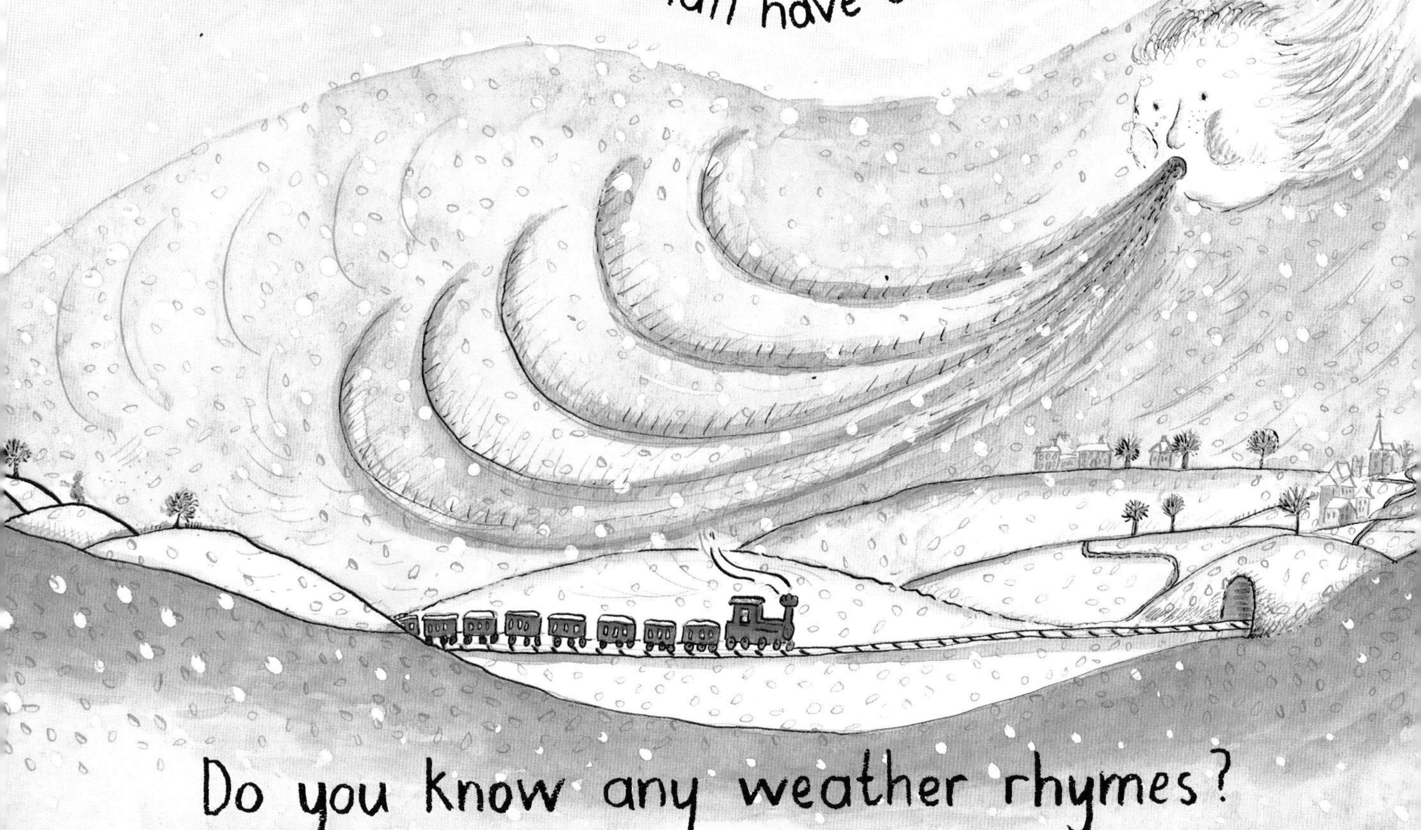

Do you know any weather rhymes?

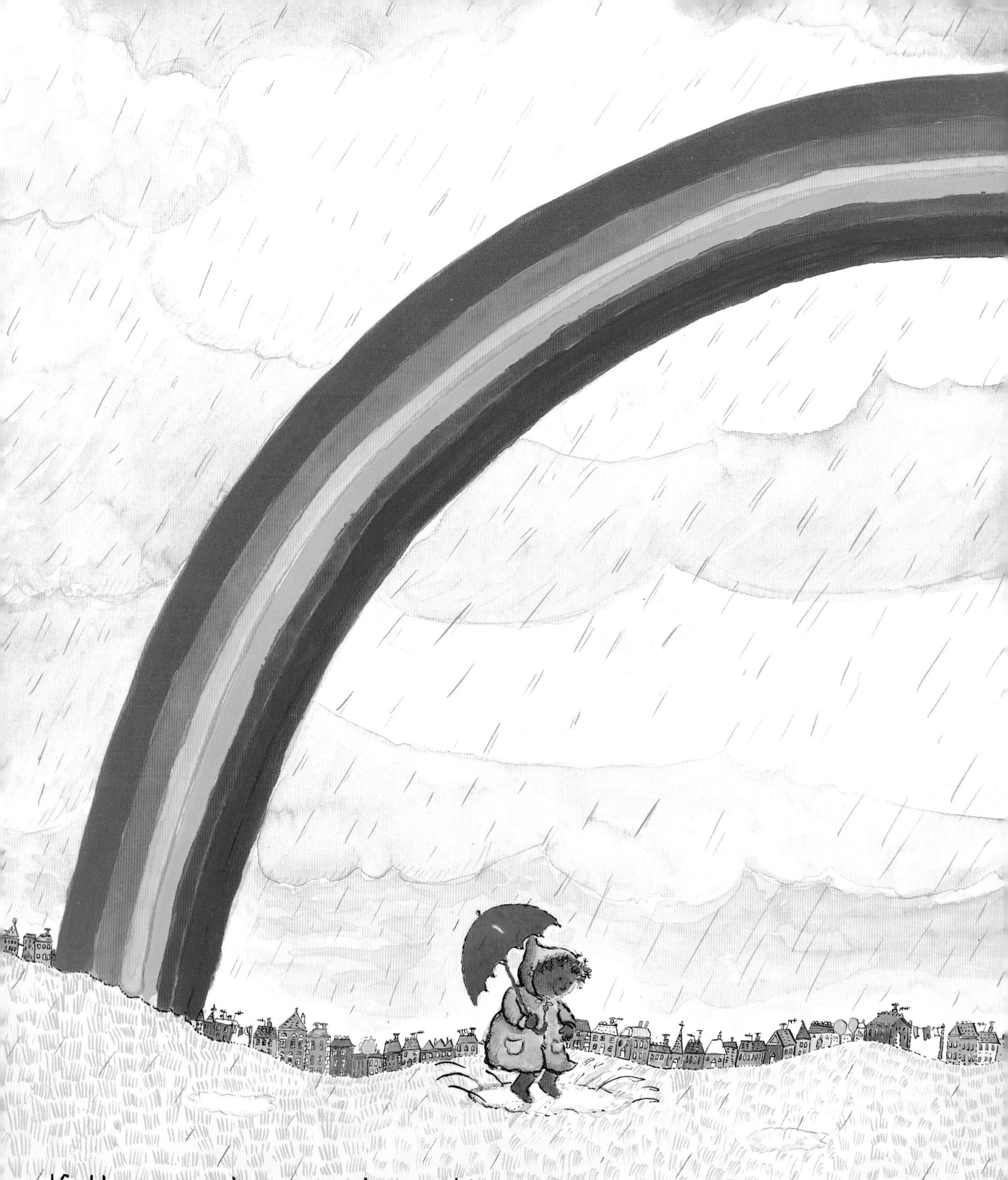

If the sun shines when it's raining, sometimes you can see a rainbow in the sky.

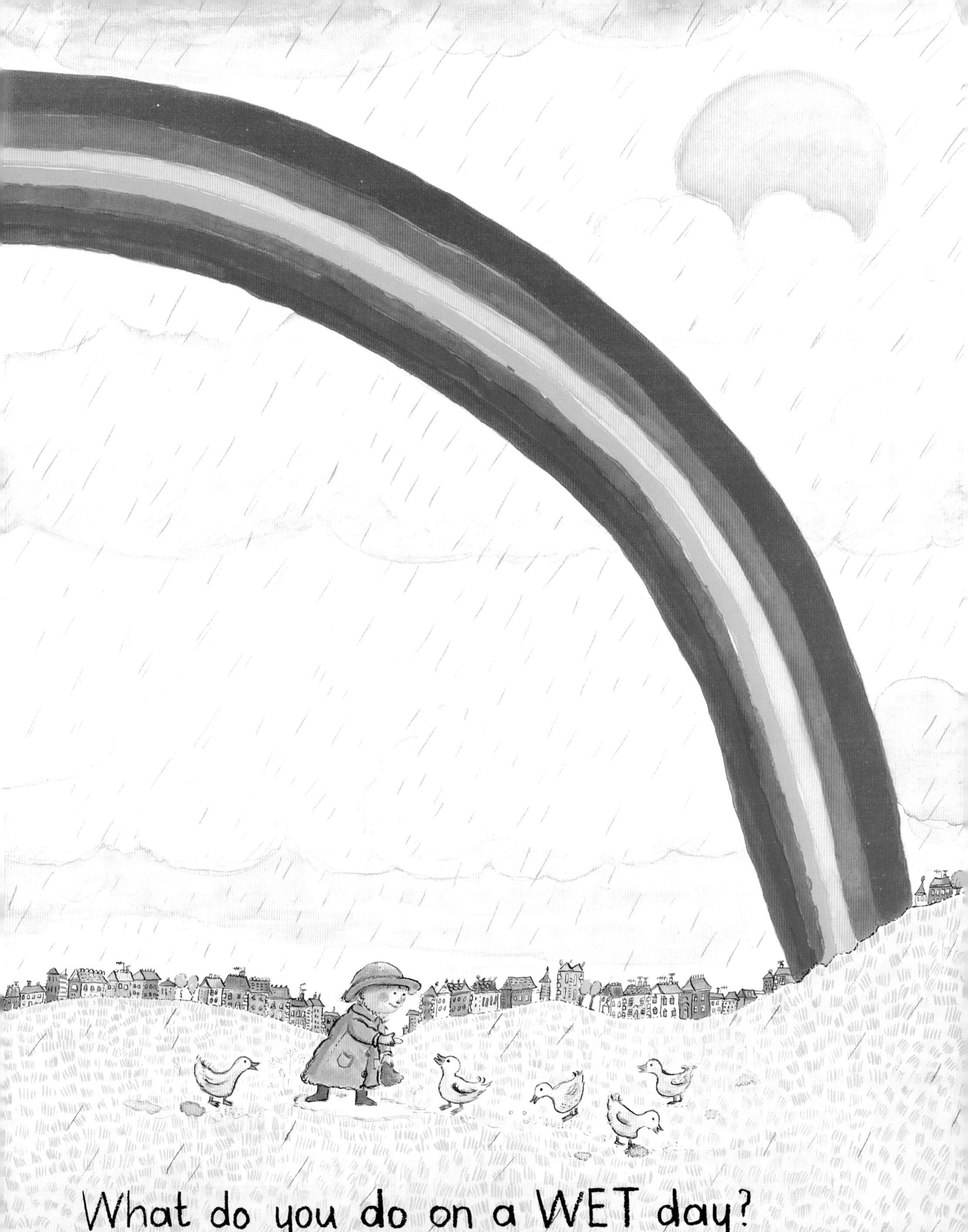

What do you do on a WET day?

It's fun to watch the weather change.
But what happens if there's too much...

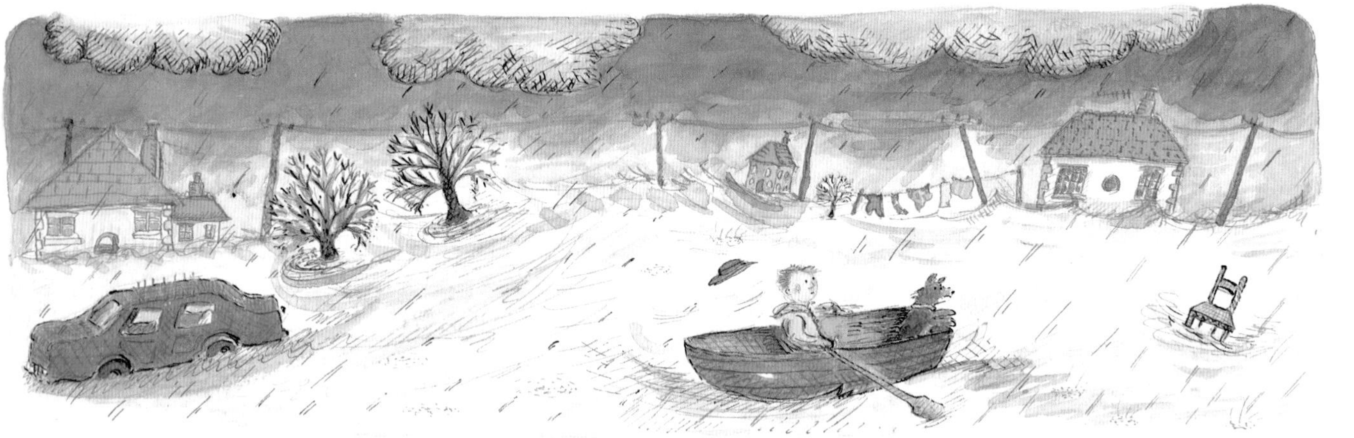

rain,

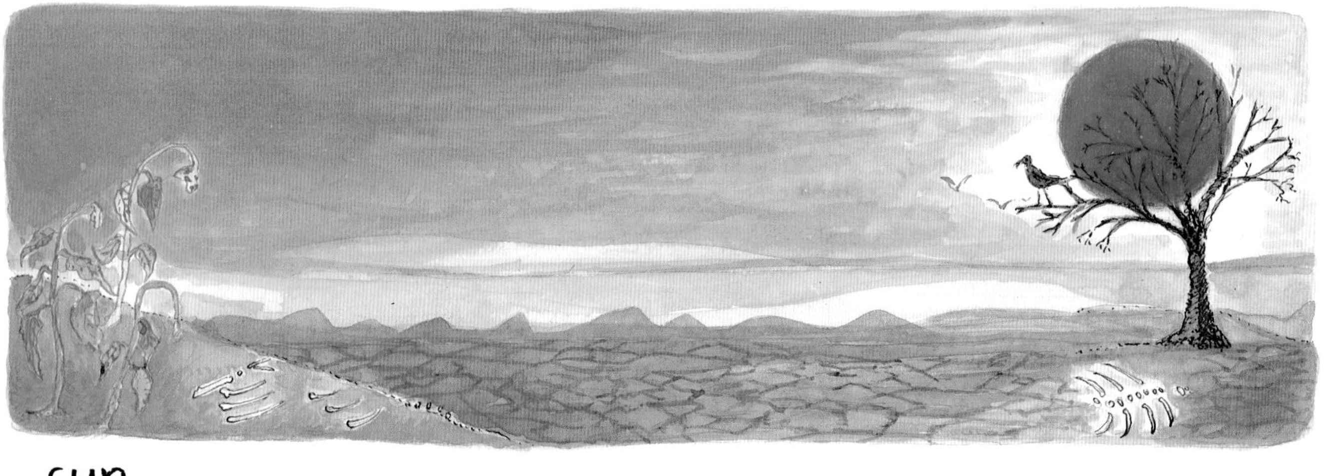

sun,

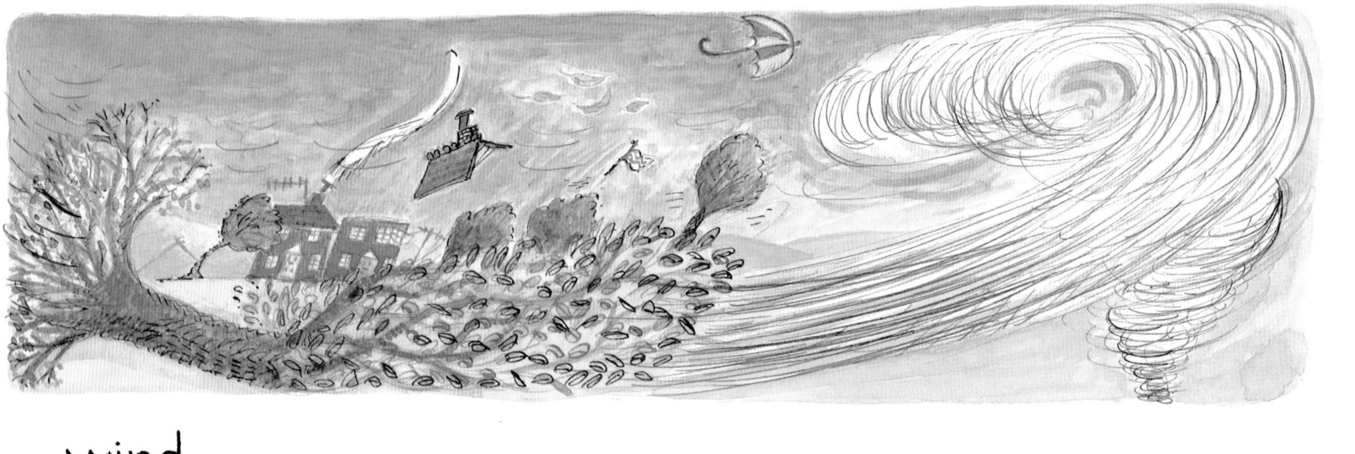

wind,

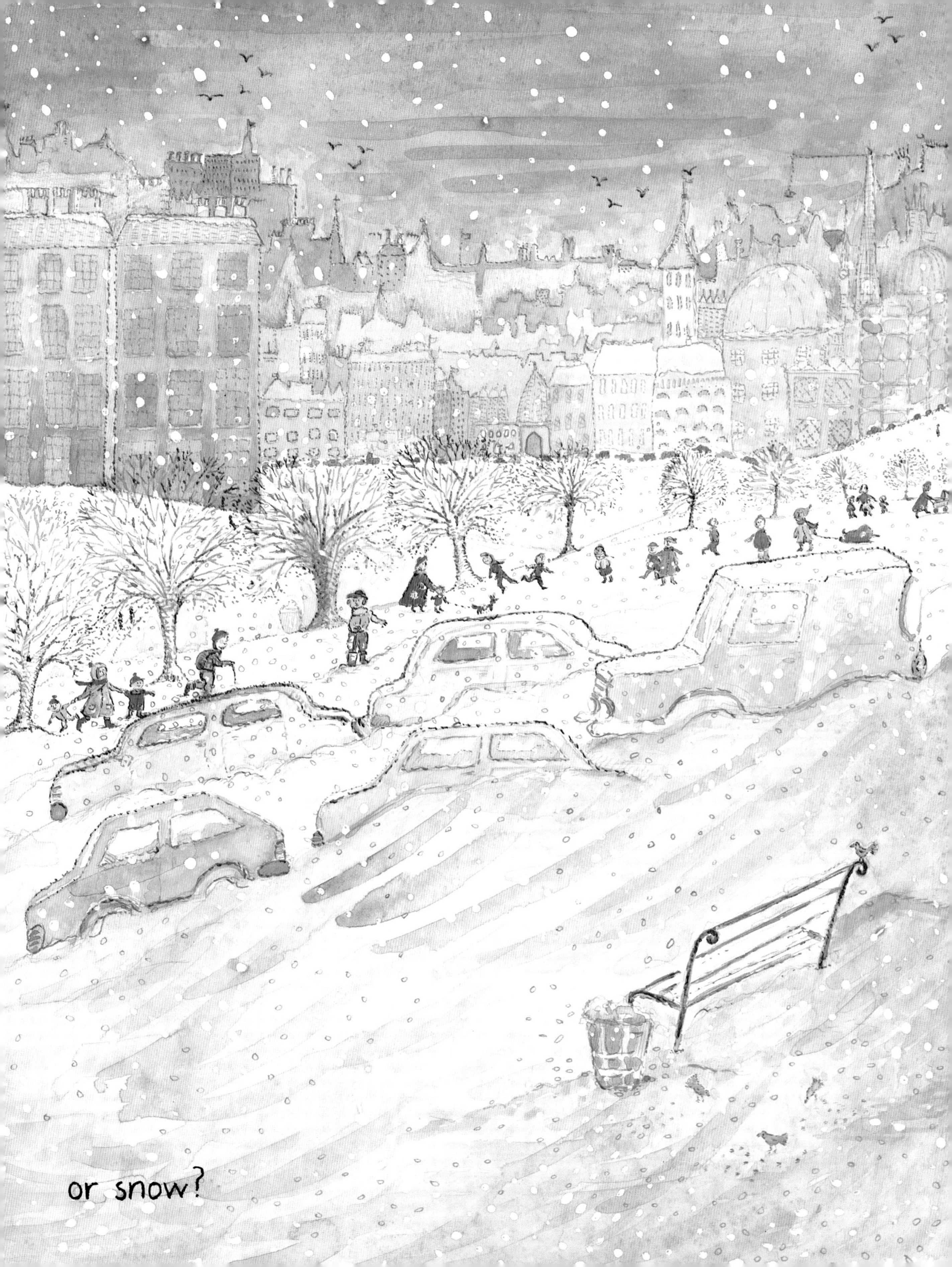

or snow?

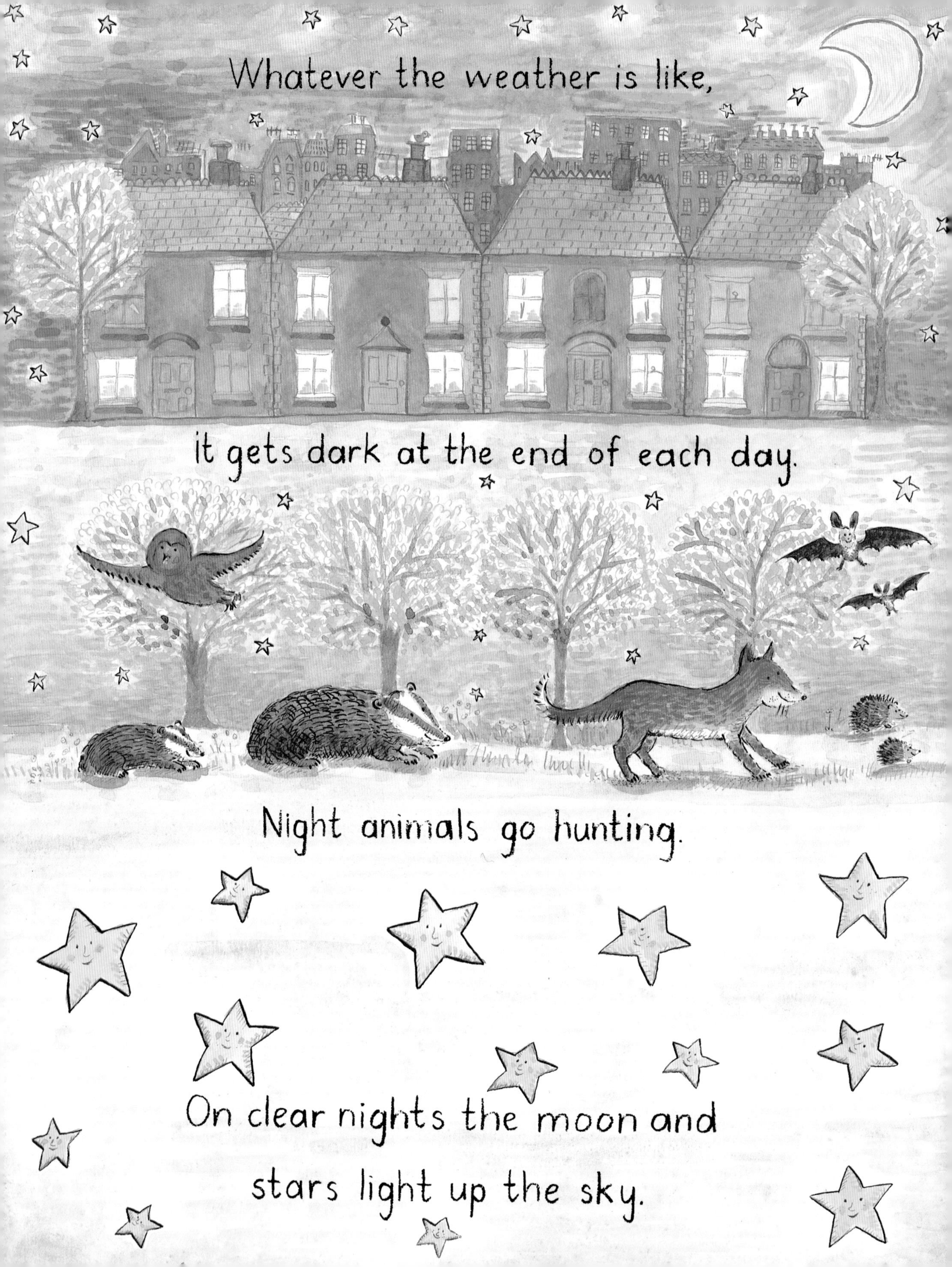

Whatever the weather is like,

it gets dark at the end of each day.

Night animals go hunting.

On clear nights the moon and

stars light up the sky.

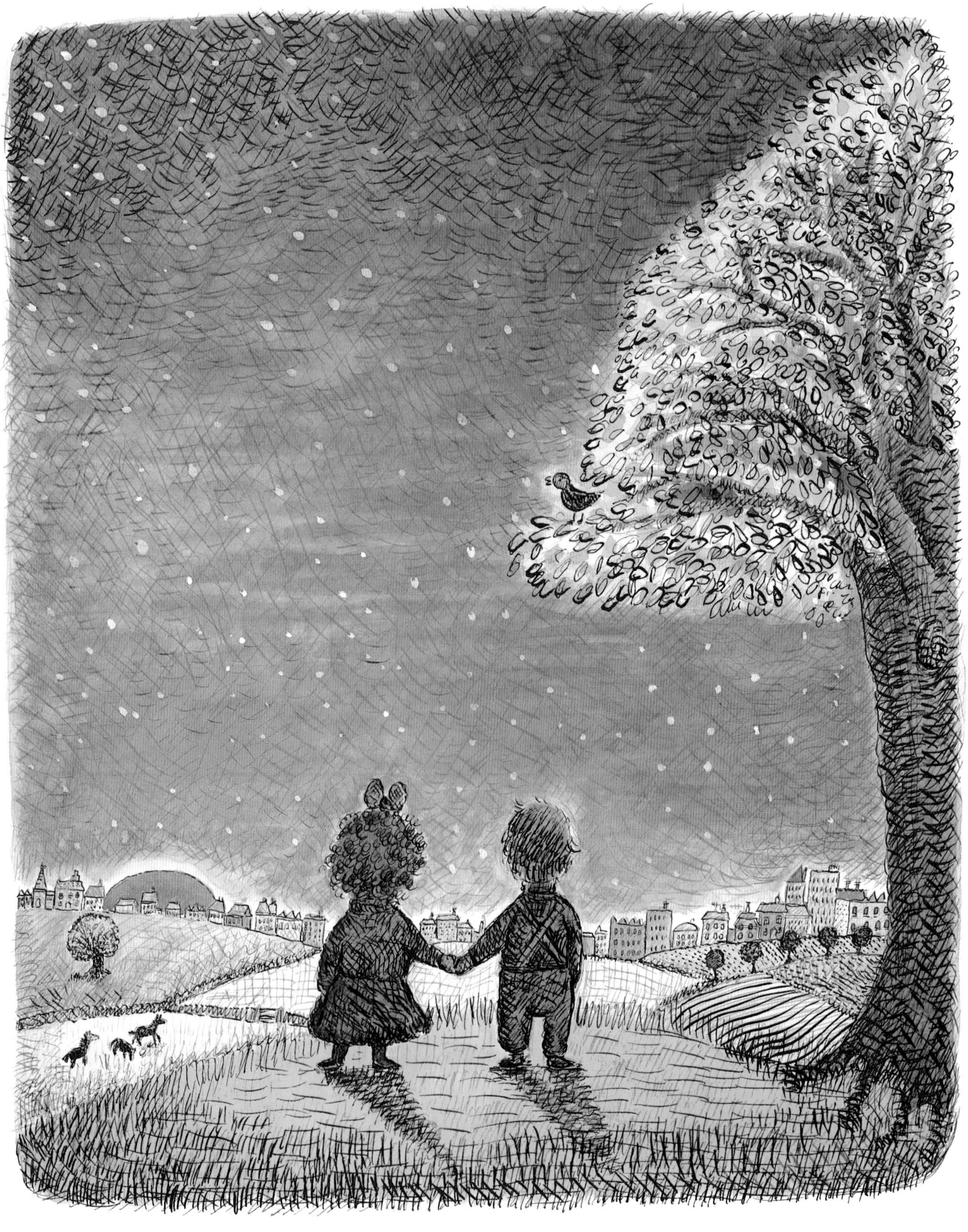

What will the weather be tomorrow?

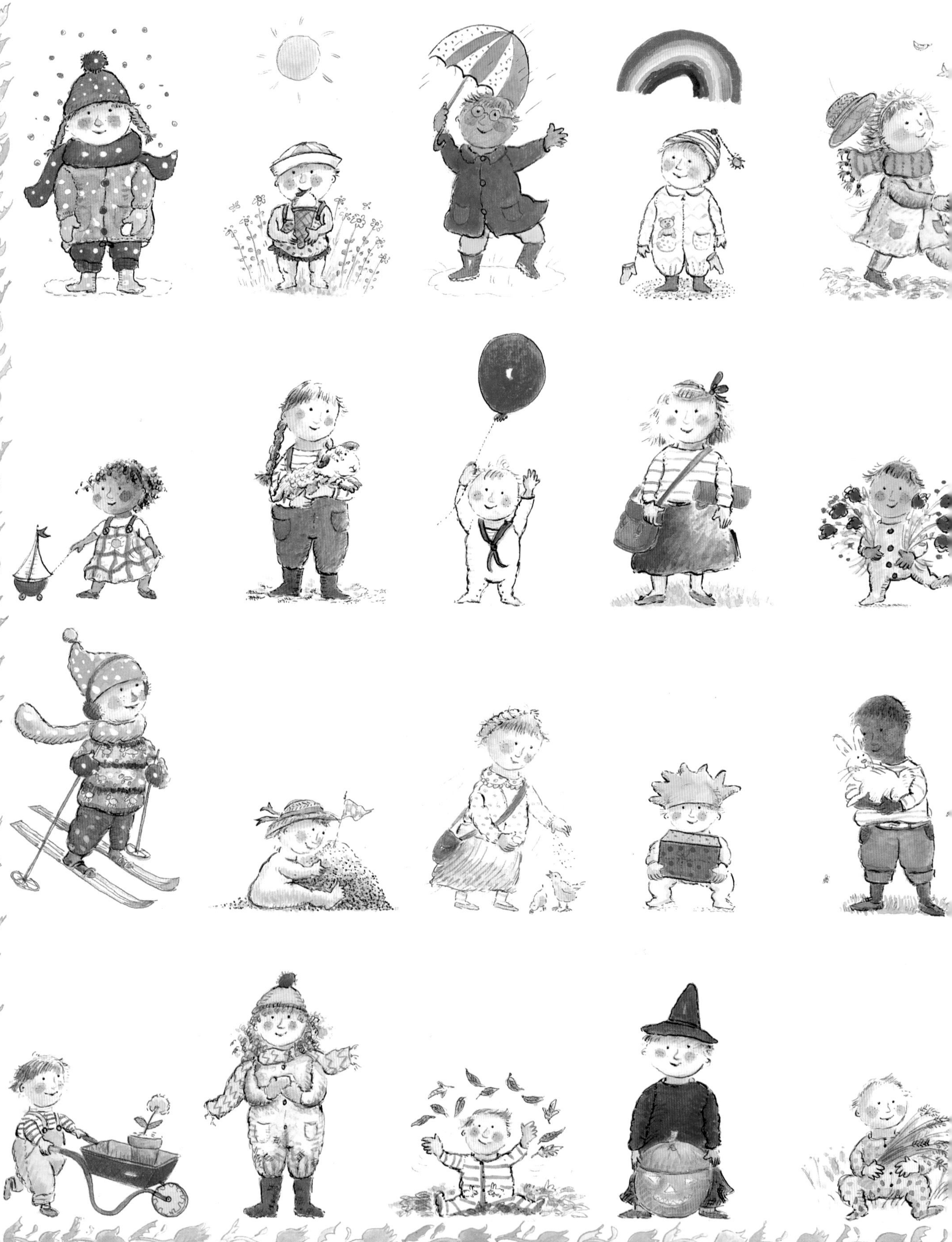